Social Theory in the *Real* World

ONE WEEK LOAN

Social Theory in the *Real* World

Steven Miles

SAGE Publications
London • Thousand Oaks • New Delhi

© Steven Miles 2001

First published 2001
Reprinted 2002

 SAGE Publications Ltd
6 Bonhill Street
London EC2A 4PU

SAGE Publications Inc
2455 Teller Road
Thousand Oaks, California 91320

SAGE Publications India Pvt Ltd
32, M-Block Market
Greater Kailash – I
New Delhi 110 048

British Library Cataloguing in Publication data

A catalogue record for this book is available
from the British Library

ISBN 0 7619 6155 0
ISBN 0 7619 6156 9 (pbk)

Library of Congress Control number available

Typeset by Mayhew Typesetting, Rhayader, Powys
Printed in Great Britain by Biddles Ltd, *www.biddles.co.uk*

CONTENTS

CHAPTER 1

INTRODUCTION

The 'reality' of social theory

Social theory: who needs it? The intention of this book is to illustrate that social theory really can be meaningful, relevant and full of insight, and, as such, can stimulate the theoretical and socio-logical imagination. Social theory can play an invaluable role in unearthing the unexpected and in challenging common-sense con-ceptions of social life. As members or citizens of society we assume that we are well schooled in the underlying dynamics of that society. Because we live in it, we feel that we implicitly understand it. *Social Theory in the 'Real' World* aims to highlight that while this is not necessarily the case, the creative and reflexive use of social theory can really help us come to terms with the ramifications of social change on an everyday basis. The extent to which social theorists are actually able to conceive of a 'real' world is in itself debatable. *Social Theory in the 'Real' World* aims to demonstrate that, at the very least, effective social theory is capable of having a real impact on how we perceive our own individual place in that world and how our own experiences actively reflect broader processes of social change.

There are all sorts of power relationships and structural con-straints of which we are largely unaware and which actively impinge upon the way we behave on a daily basis. We could not possibly fully comprehend or critically digest such pressures as we go about our everyday business. Social life is nothing if not complex. Everything we do is more complicated than it may seem on the surface. So complicated, in fact, that we barely have time to understand or even think about what it all means.

Perhaps the most important question in a world which appears to be changing so rapidly is: do we even have the time to theorize? On the surface social change seems to be so rapid that we as individuals are almost dragged along with it apparently independent of our own free wills. As such, the distance between the nature of social change and the ways in which we try to comprehend that change appear to be becoming ever greater. In short, there is an argument for suggest-ing that social change is more adaptable than the theories which are used to try to make sense of it.

Social theory gets a bad press. The argument here is that this is because it simply is not used in an imaginative or reflexive enough fashion. The real value of social theory lies in relating it to your own experience as a consumer of social life. It is from this origin that the title of this book originates. Many social theorists claim there is no such thing as the 'real' world anymore – that, in effect, there is no reality other than the way we perceive that reality on an individual basis. In this sense I am suggesting that the value of social theory is only real if you as an individual are open to its potential. Social structures and power relationships are manifested in everyday contexts. The theories which attempt to understand that world are relevant to us as consumers of social theory only if they say some-thing of meaning to us; something that sparks off thoughts and feelings in our own minds and social contexts. The 'real' world is the world in which we live both as individuals and as members of groups. If social theory cannot speak to us in this context, then it quite simply isn't doing its job.

The problem with social theory is arguably that many people who study it are simply unable to relate it to the actualities of their everyday lives. Social theory is all too often distant from everyday reality. It often appears to exist on an abstract and remote plane where the ability to theorize appears to be more important than the relevance of the theory itself. As Craib (1992) argues, 'social theory appears to have no practical results. Worse, it takes something we know about already in intimate detail – and makes of it unintelligible nonsense' (p. 4).

Social theorists, then, appear to belong to a club from which the rest of us mere mortals are barred. I myself do not claim to be a social theorist; rather, I am an advocate of the benefits of social theory that is based in grounded contexts and that can help us look at our own lives in new and insightful ways. I am in favour of social theory that operates in the 'real' world. This book is therefore concerned with the way in which broad patterns of social change have actively altered our everyday experiences of social life. Social change is not remote in any sense of the word. It actively impinges on who and what we are. It manifests itself in how we relate to each other as human beings and in how we construct our individual and social identities. Social change is the very stuff of social life. We are indeed the actors in the play of social change. This book will attempt to critically consider some of the themes that social theorists have identified as a means of comprehending the significance of such change. In order to do so, it is thematic in approach. It will not focus on the contributions of specific theorists (although specific theorists will of course be discussed) but will highlight key themes and how they are manifested in the real world.

Why social theory?

So why social theory? How does social theory advance our understanding of social change? Is social theory as irrelevant to real life as it may seem on the surface? This book will attempt to illustrate that the answer to this last question is a resounding no. Social theory provides us with a means of challenging our preconceptions of social life.

> One becomes a social theorist when something is askew in the realm of knowledge, when current explanations are perceived to fail, or when existing theories appear to be inadequate tools in the task of comprehension. Theoretical work is simply an attempt to explain, and thus to assist in understanding, the social world. Sociology's central concern is to view societies at any particular point in their history, in terms of the distinctive structures and processes that shape their character at that moment. (Kivisto, 1998, p. 8)

The above historical dimension is so fundamental to the sociological imagination that it's easy to make the mistake that social theory is simply all about studying classical social theory and applying classical social theory in contemporary contexts. Many undergraduate courses in social theory do, indeed, seem to suggest that there is no theory beyond the sociological 'canon'. In recent decades the hegemony of classical social theory has, however, begun to be challenged. In particular, the legitimacy of the understanding of classical social theory for classical social theory's sake has been increasingly open to question. The philosophy that lies behind this book is that classical theory remains of considerable value, but only where it relates to themes of contemporary social change which are best considered through the discussion of contemporary theoretical themes. This is not a book about classical theory, but it will occasionally highlight aspects of classical theory which are pertinent to the world as we live in it today and the themes that best inform our understanding of that world.

Before we can begin to consider the insights to be provided by particular themes in social theory, it is important to be explicit about what social theory can actually do. In this context, it is worth commenting on what Zygmunt Bauman (1990) says in his discussion of the differences between sociology and common sense. This provides a useful foundation, in turn, upon which we can begin to recognize the value of social theory. Some of the concerns Bauman raises about the legitimacy of sociology are of concern to us here. As Bauman points out, the stuff of which sociological knowledge is made is the experience of ordinary life, which is, in principle, accessible to everybody. But because we are so deeply immersed in our everyday lives we do not stop to think in any great detail about the meaning of what it is we do from day to day. This is the role of the sociologist and indeed of the social theorist. But unlike the scientist, because the sociologist is part of what he or she is studying it is more difficult for him or her to be a detached observer.

> With poorly designed borders whose security is not guaranteed in advance (unlike sciences that explore objects inaccessible to lay experience), the sovereignty of sociology over social knowledge, its right to make authoritative pronouncements on the subject, may always be contested. This is why drawing a boundary between sociological knowledge proper and the common sense that is always full of sociological ideas is such an important matter for the identity of sociology as a cohesive body of knowledge; and why sociologists pay this matter more attention than other scientists. (Bauman, 1990, p. 11)

More specifically, according to Bauman, sociology differs from common sense in four main ways. I want to adapt these principles to a discussion of social theory.

1   Sociology subjects itself to the rigorous rules of responsible speech. In other words, sociologists carefully corroborate any statements through the collection of evidence whatever form that evidence might take. Responsible speech is also reflexive in the sense that a piece of sociological theory will also consider evidence and theories that may appear to provide a conflicting argument. It is the responsibility of the social theorist to provide trustworthy and reliable evidence to back up any proposition.

2   Sociological judgements are based on a different size of field to that of common sense. Common sense is usually confined to the boundaries of our own experience. For the sociologist and the social theorist it is not only quantitative difference that matters here, but also the quality of the field. Any theoretical findings must be based on quality evidence. Just because a theory is theoretical does not mean to say it does not need to be grounded in reality. Indeed, one of the abiding concerns of *Social Theory in the 'Real' World* is that social theory should be grounded or at least relate to people's own personal sense of reality. In order to be successful, my own feeling is that a social theory must somehow shed some light upon the life of the person who is reading it. In this sense some theories will be more useful to you as an individual than others.

3   Sociology also goes about making sense of human reality in a different way to common sense. Rather than basing its findings on the way in which the individual perceives his or her own action

as a means of making sense of all other actions, the sociologist and the social theorist deny the validity of such a personalized viewpoint. He or she is concerned with figurations or networks of dependency rather than individual actions. 'When thinking sociologically, one attempts to make sense of the human condition through analysing the manifold web of human interdependency – that toughest of realities which explains both our motives and the effects of their activation' (Bauman, 1990, p. 14). Social theory may at times seem unnecessarily abstract. But at times it needs to be so, in order to establish some distance from its object of study. However, social theory should not be so distant as to make itself irrelevant.

4   Both the sociologist and the social theorist are very much concerned with defamiliarizing the familiar. People tend to accept the way things are, and because the social world is so familiar to us on a common-sense level it is very difficult to be critical of it. The sociologist scrutinizes the everyday. He or she problematizes social reality. Social theory questions the comfortable familiarity of social life and considers the underlying dimensions of how and why we live in the ways we do (see Bauman, 1990, pp. 12–15).

The above points are important insofar as they provide the grounding upon which sociology and in particular social theory can claim to provide insights that common sense alone cannot. For the purposes of this book, the final of the above four points is especially pertinent. In its attempt to defamiliarize the familiar, social theory has too often failed to engage closely enough with the familiar. Social theory has tended to be remote from real life. By using examples gleaned from real life and by focusing on some of the most apparently mundane aspects of social life, this book will hopefully illustrate the benefits of social theory whilst warning against and criticizing approaches to social theory that are more concerned with theoretical posturing than they are with a grounded analysis of the ramifications of social change.

Social theory, then, is a tool (see Craib, 1997) which can be used to find out what you as an individual already think and to challenge those thoughts. 'To enter fully into thinking about society, we need to understand and in some way come to terms with the truth of other approaches – we need to spend a lot of time *thinking against ourselves* and changing our ideas' (Craib, 1997, p. 10, emphasis in original). I was stirred to write this book precisely because one of the abiding effects of my education, and in particular my theoretical education, is the ability I now have to be critical of the world around me. I feel that social theory has taught me an awful lot above and beyond the particular concerns of particular theorists. It has taught me how to theorize beyond the apparent trivialities of my everyday life, and it has given me the ability to take stock of what is around me. My training in social theory has helped me be critical of all aspects of my own life that I may well otherwise have taken for granted: watching films and television and reading newspapers are now more reflexive pursuits. But more generally I now can also apply a critical eye to the apparent mundanity of everyday life, to the structure of city life, the problem of social exclusion, gender inequalities and race divides amongst other fundamentally important, though not always trans-parent, issues. All of these are areas I think about more than I would have done if I hadn't been exposed to the joys and frustrations of social theory. Social theory is not about rote learning a few ideas cobbled together by long dead men. It is about garnering insights into aspects of life you may well have previously taken for granted. In this sense we are all theorists. Everything we do involves some measure of theory. We might theorize why it is our football team never appears to succeed as much as we may want, regardless of the money invested. We might theorize how we can survive on a student loan, whilst partaking in our fair share of eating, drinking and socializing. Alternatively, we might theorize as to how we might best achieve a first-class degree. As Beeghley (1997) points out, the ability to theorize is an everyday necessity:

> A theory is an abstract explanation of diverse observations. As the puzzle analogy implies, it serves as a frame of reference, a guide to key issues, and a vehicle for non-obvious connections. A theory, in short, provides a way to understand what is going on around us. People develop theories all the time, usually based on their everyday experiences. When your parents say 'you need an education to get ahead in this world,' they have a theory – not a very abstract one, but a theory none the less. Scientists do precisely the same thing, usually based on more systematic observations (or tests) than are available in everyday life. (p. 267)

Social theory is therefore very much concerned with using similar skills to those we call upon in conducting our everyday lives, but it does so as a means of accounting for the changing nature of that everyday life. Most often such change is concerned with a broader historical dimension in terms of the transition from a traditional to a modern and arguably to a post-modern world. These are issues that will crop up again and again throughout this book. At this stage all I want to do is illustrate my contention that social theory can be useful. This is a book about the benefits of social theory in the real world. Here and now. *Social Theory in the 'Real' World* therefore deals with key themes of social theory. But a whole variety of theorists, both classical and contemporary, inform those theories. As a means of illustrating the benefits of a theoretical approach and of how even the most abstract and apparently dated of theories can actively enliven our understanding of the present, I think it would be particularly useful to discuss the work of Georg Simmel (1971), and more specifically his work on fashion.

Simmel and twenty-first-century fashion

Simmel's work was originally published a hundred years ago. And yet the insights and forethought of his work are such that his contribution to theoretical debate is in many respects ahead of its time, to the extent that he raises issues that are of concern to those theorists currently preoccupied with debates over post-modernity. In all but date, Simmel's theories are startlingly contemporary. His contribution to discussions around the meaning of fashion are especially pertinent. Indeed, the insights he provides about nineteenth-century Berlin may just as easily be applied to any British city at the beginning of the twenty-first century. But before I consider the specifics of this particular aspect of Simmel's theory, it is worth briefly thinking about what underlay his general theoretical orientation. Simmel (1971) was very much concerned with the way in which individual behaviour is determined by group membership, but also with the way in which an individual's relationship with modernity is expressed through his or her 'inner' life. In other words, as individuals we react to the extremes of modern life through a general reserve or personal indifference. In this sense Simmel saw social processes as being psychological. Society exists because an individual is conscious that he or she is tied to other individuals. Simmel was therefore concerned with how people actually interact, and in this respect his work can be contrasted with the apparently more macro theories of his contemporaries. In the above context, Simmel (1971) argues that social life is in many senses a battleground in which the individual negotiates the apparently conflicting need to be an individual and to stand out from the crowd with the concomitant tendency to imitate. This reflects his contention that, 'The whole history of society is reflected in the striking conflicts, the compromises, slowly won and quickly lost, between socialistic adaptation to society and individual departure from its demands' (p. 294).

Fashion is important insofar as it provides a cultural resource which helps the individual establish who he or she is in a cultural context. Simmel's work in general was very much concerned with the complex and intense nature of social life, particularly as it was manifested in the city (Simmel, 1950). For Simmel, the modern world is restless and unforgiving. In this context, social life is a battleground 'of which every inch is stubbornly contested' (Simmel, 1971, p. 240). If you bear in mind that Simmel was talking about the world as it was a hundred years ago, you begin to realize how prescient his contribution is in a world that is arguably more restless and more unforgiving than it ever was.

The basic idea that Simmel presents clearly relates to the realities of fashion at the beginning of the twenty-first century. One of my own research interests centres on the relationship between youth consumption and identity. Much of the literature in this area suggests that young people are increasingly having to make their own decisions about their future in a world in which traditional sources of support such as the family, community and religion are being eroded (Furlong and Cartmel, 1997). The risks we therefore associate with the job market and education are met squarely on the individual's shoulders to the extent that he or she is constantly on the look out for a means of escape. Consumption, and more specifically fashion, provides an arena within which young people can express themselves, whilst relieving the tensions they associate with the more structural aspects of their lives. Young people may not feel that they belong to anything in general, but they can use the resources associated with fashion to create an environment in which they are respected; an environment in which they can balance the demands of structure and agency. Thus, as I point out elsewhere, young people use fashion as a sort of mask that protects them from the risks of the outside world (Miles, 1997). The individual cannot take the risk of constructing his or her identity entirely independently but calls upon fashion as an arena in which the way he or she must behave is clearly set out. Simmel regards fashion as helping to ensure that people adapt to the complexities of modern life. As the product of class distinction, fashion not only identifies the individual as being a member of a particular class, but also highlights the fact that he or she is *not* a member of an alternative group. In effect, then, Simmel sees fashion as a product of social demands and how an individual navigates those demands. In this sense, it could often be argued that fashion bears little resemblance to any reasonable aesthetic judgement or individual taste.

> Judging from the ugly and repugnant things that are sometimes in vogue, it would seem that fashion were desirous of exhibiting its power by getting us to adopt the most atrocious things for its own sake. (Simmel, 1971, p. 297)

This argument is no better illustrated than in one aspect of contemporary consumption which also reflects many of the themes developed throughout this book. Retro forms of fashion appear to fulfil many of the functions which Simmel discusses. Shorthand for retrospective or retro-chic, 'retros' are trainers that were originally popular in Britain during the early 1970s (although originating from 1950s America), and though they are beginning to lose their ultra-fashionable edge, they still command a dominant place on sports shop shelves. It is often not the style of this particular product that matters to teenagers, but rather the meanings that product is endowed with by their peers (see Miles et al., 1998b). In effect, it seems that 'retros' identify young consumers with particular youth cultural styles. Perhaps 'retro' trainers give young consumers a feeling that they 'belong' in a culture that very rarely makes them feel that way in other aspects of life: they may not feel that they have much in common with their families; they may feel alienated from their local communities; they may be wary of the confrontational commitment involved in becoming a skinhead or maybe a punk; but by picking and choosing particular aspects of a youth cultural style, aspects that express some form of belonging to a sub-cultural form, teenagers can construct some sort of sense of who they are without committing themselves to a complete youth cultural lifestyle. A definite paradox can therefore be identified here. Although teenagers know that they are buying consumer goods that represent a very popular trend amongst their peers, in effect though they realize that they are following the crowd, they justify this by convincing themselves that they are different to the majority. Such a sense of uniqueness is fostered by the idea that the meanings consumers apply to such goods are individualistic, when in reality those meanings are, to some extent, inevitably communal.

Simmel's insights into fashion as a social realm apply as much today as they did one hundred years ago. Fashion is not simply a reflection of individual taste: it is a complex phenomenon which is intricately bound up with the paradoxes of social life. In this respect, perhaps the best advice this book can give is to relate the theoretical approaches you come across to the actualities of your own life. Only then can you realize the advantages and disadvantages of particular social theories. Yes, social theory can be and often is abstract. This abstract nature, however, should be perceived not as an insurmountable hurdle, but as an invaluable means of making mundane aspects of your everyday existence come to theoretical life. Simmel illustrates the potential social theory has as a means of unlocking the mysteries of social life. Perhaps the biggest mystery of all is the relationship between structure and agency.

Structure and agency

It will become clear throughout the course of this book that one of the most important considerations of virtually any social theory, whether it is referred to explicitly or not, is the more general point to which Simmel (1971) alluded above: that is, the relationship between the individual and society, and more specifically the relationship between structure and agency. In many ways the structure and agency debate underpins contemporary social theory. It could well be argued that the prime concern of the social theorist is whether the actions of individuals or the influence of broader social structures represents the prime influence in the reproduction of social life. This issue has arguably become even more significant in recent decades in a world which many commentators feel is becoming increasingly individualistic. Some years ago the then British Prime Minister, Margaret Thatcher, famously proclaimed that there was no such thing as society, just the individual. Sociologists may not agree with the starkness of this comment, but in recent years they have, at the very least, been forced to recognize that the very fact that it was possible to say such a thing has serious implications for what constitutes social theory. Social theorists are, in turn, forced to contemplate ways in which the relationship between the individual and society may have altered as a direct result of social change.

Regardless of political dimensions of social change, however, Margaret Archer (1995) goes as far as to suggest that the structure and agency problem is the 'acid test' of any general social theory. There is certainly a strong argument for suggesting that the structure and agency question is the central problem of social theory and the guiding 'problematic' (see Fuller, 1998). It is therefore worth recognizing that many contemporary theorists do not take a position at either extreme of the debate. Anthony Giddens (1976), for instance, argues that social structures are both the medium and the outcome of social interaction. In other words, 'social structures are constituted *by* human agency, and yet at the same time are the very *medium* of this constitution' (p. 121 – original emphasis). It is in this sense that all social action involves structure and all structure involves human action. In many ways the social theorist needs to replicate the behaviour of his or her object of study in the sense that human beings reflexively monitor the ongoing flow of activities in which they are involved on an everyday basis, alongside the basic social structures that underlie those activities. These are the very patterns in which the social theorist is interested and which he or she must address in an equally reflexive fashion. The danger, therefore, of viewing social structure as a sort of framework which determines our behaviour is a significant one. Social life is far more complex and interactive than such an approach allows. People are capable of altering the course of their social lives. And above all social life is temporal. It varies from one situation to the next. Giddens argues that social life is constantly being reproduced through the relationship between the individual and society. He therefore argues that structure is effectively internal to actors. In a sense, then, structure is virtual. It is the manifestation of actions on the part of the individual. Constraints on the individual are related to their interpretation of structure and not structure's interpretation of them. In short, as far as Giddens is concerned, structure is both constraining *and* enabling. It is this multi-dimensional aspect of social life which social theorists are currently trying to grapple with.

There is, however, a real problem with the debate over structure and agency, and that is that it is rarely tested at any sort of a practical level. In this context, Layder (1993) identifies Paul Willis's (1977) work *Learning to Labour* as being an especially instructive exception to this rule. Willis, as Layder points out, is basically concerned with why it is that working-class boys end up doing working-class jobs, and the interplay between structure and agency in this context. He studies this issue (although not always directly) by looking in-depth through observations and interviews at the lives of twelve boys. Adopting a Marxist perspective, Willis is concerned with the ways in which the disadvantages experienced by such boys reflect the class structure associated with a capitalist society. However, Willis does not believe that such structures are accepted unreflexively. Rather, he argues that the boys he researched use the structural conditions in which they live to their own ends. They adapt to these conditions and indeed actively choose to operate within them. But in doing so they mould the situation in which they find themselves in their own ways. They actively theorize about their situation in order to maximize its benefits. The boys concerned are therefore more than aware of the structural constraints involved and realize that the system militates against them. But they are actively and visibly defiant of these structures and use certain symbolic expressions of working-class life to reassert their identities in ways they see fit. For instance, they may drink alcohol and smoke cigarettes profusely (Layder, 1993). This therefore symbolizes their reflexive adulthood. The boys may end up structurally determined in one sense: they do not manage to usurp the constraints of the class system in which they find themselves. But, on the other hand, they deal with those constraints reflexively in their own ways. They actively choose how they react to the circumstances they are in, and if this means they continue to be excluded, then so be it (see Layder, 1993).

The benefits and attraction of Willis's work lie in his ability to bring to life people's accounts of their own experiences to the extent that the structural constraints of those lives are not taken for granted. However, as far as social theory in general is concerned, this is not always the case. Social theory can often be extreme in nature, and quite often such extremity takes the form of a world which is perceived to be excessively constraining. For this reason, it is very important to maintain a critical perspective on the themes and approaches discussed in this book. One of the key intentions here is for the reader to consider the theoretical themes considered throughout the book in the context of the structure and agency question. The intention is to encourage the *application* of a theoretical imagination. For this reason, the particular insights provided by a theme on the question of structure are not necessarily referred to explicitly. My intention is to encourage the reader to make his or her own connections and to come to his or her own conclusions in this context. To reiterate, social theory is not about learning particular theorists' work, but about adapting theoretical insights to your own experiences in a critical, reflexive and creative fashion. The point here is that social theory should be as dynamic and reflexive as the social phenomena it attempts to address. In particular, 'social theory ought to take seriously the simple fact that individuals are able to reflect upon their circumstances, and that they might act on that knowledge as they go along' (Baert, 1998, p. 201). However, as Baert notes, the social theorist needs to approach this task with caution. The relationship between the individual and society and structure and agency is undoubtedly important but should not hijack more specific theoretical concerns. In other words, the tendency for social theory to degenerate into a vague and generalized approximation of the structure and agency question should be avoided at all costs. Above all, social theory should be clear and focused (Baert, 1998). If the relationship between structure and agency is in danger of muddying the theoretical waters, then it should be treated with the utmost caution.

The practice of theory

It is easy enough to say that social theory should be reflexive and reflective. Fair enough. But what does that mean in reality? How does a student of social theory know whether or not a piece of social theory is sufficiently reflexive or whether it is indeed 'good' or 'bad'? At one level, there is indeed no such thing as good or bad social theory. Some students would indeed probably suggest that all social theory is, by definition, bad. However, they would probably say so because the language used by social theorists is usually so unfamiliar to them. Social theory, whether contemporary or classical, is, almost without exception, difficult to read. As such, it is very often hard to decide whether or not a theorist has achieved what he or she sets out to achieve because the language deployed is itself so problematic. However, the most important thing to remember in this context is that the student of social theory should not assume that he or she is somehow ignorant or stupid. More often than not, as Beeghley (1997) indicates, such confusion is caused by the fact that the theorist him- or herself is confused. In this context, Beeghley suggests four very useful tips to make the process of reading social theory so much easier:

1   Read the piece of theory concerned more than just once. One read through might be enough to get a general flavour of what is being said, but it won't be enough for you to get to grips with the detail of the text. Do not demand too much of yourself on the first read through. To read social theory effectively, you have to read it patiently. Do not assume the intended meaning is self-evident. It may require some real thought and contemplation on your part. Given such thought, a successful and informative reading of social theory is ever more rewarding.

2   Social theory should not be a solitary exercise. Because of the complex nature of much social theory, interpretations of that theory may vary considerably. You will gain considerable confidence if somebody has the same interpretation as yourself. If alternative interpretations are different to your own, you will learn from that experience and bear in mind what your colleagues may have said during your own second reading. Social theory is not written in stone. It is there to be interpreted and discussed in a critical fashion.

3   Although it is important to use primary sources and read what the theorist concerned has to say, you should not underestimate the benefits of secondary sources. They may help you to consider a specific theorist's contribution to broader debates, whilst summarizing the key points that individual might be making. Secondary sources are never a substitute for original ones, but they might well provide you with that extra bit of confidence in your own ability to read social theory.

4   The best bit of advice of all is to not simply read the piece of social theory concerned, but to take notes. On your first reading, this might involve identifying the three or four key themes identified by the theorist. Your second reading might involve fleshing out those themes. You may identify particular quotations that really get at the crux of what is being said. You should basically be concerned with having a reasonable understanding of the main gist of what a theorist has to say. A critical interpretation of that text may not come until a third or even fourth reading, or at least when you have considered some of the secondary texts. In other words, give yourself the time and the opportunity to understand the theory you are reading as easily as possible. Social theory does not normally come naturally to most people. It is up to you to make social theory as 'natural' as possible (see Beeghley, 1997, p. 271).

Perhaps the best way to approach social theory is, then, not to learn it, as such, but to learn *how to use it* in a reflexive and focused fashion. However, there is an underlying irony to this statement. Social theory is taught in a very instrumental environment. The vast majority of students of social theory are, realistically, not learning social theory because they want to, but because they want to come out at the end of the day with a degree certificate. In this sense we could describe social theory as another example of McDonaldized education (see Chapter 6). There is very little room to use social theory in a creative fashion. The best we can do as consumers of social theory is to use imaginatively the theory we are routinely and rationally exposed to. It is easy to be intimidated by social theorists with big ideas and big reputations. The way to understand those theories is to relate them to your own experience of social life and to do so in a critical fashion. Social theorists do not agree about most things. Indeed, the benefits of social theory reside in its ability to raise and stimulate debate. Students of social theory should approach social theory critically and reflexively as a springboard for discussion and debate. Social theory should act not as a strait-jacket, but as a flexible ally capable of unearthing insights where they hadn't previously been accessible.

Structure of the book

As a means of addressing the above sorts of issue and of looking at the value of social theory in an ever-changing world, *Social Theory in the 'Real' World* will consider what can be regarded as the key themes of contemporary social theory. Each of the themes I critically debate attempts to make some sense of social change, and in doing so they each raise some important issues as to the value and role of social theory at the beginning of the twenty-first century. In Chapter 2 I consider one of the most controversial, and at times alarming, social theories of our time: the body of work associated with the Frankfurt School. I have chosen to begin with a discussion of the Frankfurt School's work on popular or mass culture because it was the first theory I myself read that really made me sit back and think critically about the world in which I live. In particular, this chapter will raise the question as to whether a social theory should be in some sense *political*. It will highlight the fact that even the most taken for granted aspects of our everyday lives are quite possibly ideological in nature, and that, regardless of its limitations, social theory is very probably at its best and its most stimulating when it adopts a critical perspective on the world.

Chapter 3 will focus on a particular issue (and a particular theorist who was responsible for developing that issue) that has been the object of enormous criticism, but that continues to inform debates as to the nature of social change. Daniel Bell's post-industrial society thesis is a remarkable piece of social theory and one which, above all, indicates that the role of social theory is not to provide specific answers to specific questions, but to stimulate debate as to the nature of social change. It may not be appropriate to go as far as to describe contemporary society as 'post-industrial', based on the sorts of trends Bell outlines, but the legacy of Bell's work to social theory in general is an enormous one. Above all, perhaps, Bell illustrates the lengths to which the sociological imagination can go. Whether or not Bell's work actually goes too far is up to you to decide.

In the following chapter I discuss one of the fastest-growing areas of theoretical debate in the social sciences, namely, that of consumption. Do we live in what is first and foremost a consumer society? There is a strong case for suggesting that we take our ability to consume for granted, and because we take it for granted it represents one of the most important expressions – if not *the* most important expression – of the relationship between structure and agency. Chapter 4 considers the suggestion that the ability to consume is not as universal as it may seem, and that the superficial attractions of consumerism as a way of life might well mask more sinister realities.

In Chapter 5 I consider one of the most influential of all theoretical themes or approaches of recent years, which is itself closely bound up with questions of consumption. Love it or hate it, post-modernism has forced social theory to reconsider its role in the 'real' world. It has served to highlight the value of looking at the cultural for its own sake, and it has focused debate on whether or not the apparently fragmented world in which we live amounts to a radical new way of life. Chapter 5 considers whether or not post-modernism is worth the trouble.

The following chapter addresses a theoretical approach that places a particular classical theory, that of Max Weber, in a contemporary context. George Ritzer's theory of McDonaldization is often accused of being overly journalistic and of trivializing social theory. However, in truth the theory of McDonaldization, as discussed in Chapter 6, illustrates the benefits to be had from a theory that applies classical theory in an imaginative and thought-provoking fashion. We may or may not live in a rationalized, dehumanized world, but Ritzer moves this debate away from the domain of abstract classical theory to that of our own everyday lives.

Chapter 7 discusses one of the most recent and influential themes in social theory, that of the risk society. Is the society in which we live as risky as we are led to believe? How can the work of authors such as Beck, Giddens and Douglas inform our understanding of social change? Indeed, is the risk society anything more than a figment of our collective imaginations? This chapter is concerned with what risk tells us about the tendency to perceive social change where, arguably, it does not even exist.

Chapter 8 is concerned with what might be described as *the* buzz-word of contemporary social theory, namely, globalization. The question of globalization illustrates how processes that may appear on the surface to be distant and divorced from our own realities actively impinge on our everyday lives. Social theory is indeed about how broad social change affects the individual in local settings. The notion of globalization has significant social, economic and political implications. This chapter illustrates how these issues are played out in the cultural realm.

In the final chapter, Chapter 9, I bring the above issues together in a broader discussion of what role social theory plays at the beginning of the twenty-first century. What is social change and how can social theorists best account for it? Social theory is undergoing something of an identity crisis in a world in which even the nature of reality is being questioned. How should social theorists respond to such pressures, and what is the status of social theory in the 'real' world?

Social theory is all about learning to be critical about a theorist and the social world which that theorist describes. In many respects, then, a good social theorist and a good student of social theory are prepared to take risks. *Social Theory in the 'Real' World* intends to encourage risk-taking. Above all, its concern is to highlight the fact that social theory cannot or at least should not simply be learned and regurgitated. Social theory should be engaged with and actively criticized. In doing so, the experience of social theory will be less of a means to an end and more of a means in itself. Many theorists of social change describe a world that has been dehumanized and in which the opportunities to actively be creative are few and far between. Only when social theory is perceived positively as an opportunity to be creative will the benefits and insights it provides fulfil their potential. Only then will it be possible to construct a reflexive critical understanding of what social theory can contribute to an everyday understanding of the 'real' world.

Recommended reading

Zygmunt Bauman (1990) *Thinking Sociologically*, Oxford: Blackwell. An illuminating and thankfully understandable introduction to the craft of the sociologist. Provides ideas equally applicable to the skill of social theorizing.

Jon Gubbay and Chris Middleton (eds) (1997) *A Student's Companion to Sociology*, Oxford: Blackwell. An ideal introduction to what it means to be a sociologist and a social theorist both at a conceptual and at a practical level.

Peter Kivisto (1998) *Key Ideas in Sociology*, London: Sage. An engaging introduction to the main components of classic and contemporary social theory.

Derek Layder (1994) *Understanding Social Theory*, London: Sage. An advanced but interesting discussion of the key themes of social theory, and, in particular, the structure and agency debate.

CHAPTER 2

A MASS SOCIETY?

Theories of mass society are élitist and condescending. They portray and betray a world of base instincts in which the population are deluded on a massive scale and in which such delusion is expressed through the consumption of popular culture. From this point of view popular culture is *bad* culture simply because it is popular. How can such a theory possibly inform us about the nature of social change? Hasn't social theory progressed enough over the course of the last fifty years to render such an approach redundant? It has and it hasn't. The continuing appeal of mass society theory and in particular the brand of mass society theory associated with the Frankfurt School is a lucid illustration of how social theory can be so shocking and yet so insightful at one and the same time. The work of the Frankfurt School may not be politically correct; its lack of political correctness may make us positively uncomfortable, but at the same time it is a highly audacious and thought-provoking piece of social theory that may well lead us to question the very basis of the society in which we live. If mass society theory, and indeed any social theory, can achieve this much, then it must surely have an important contribution to make to our understanding of the 'real' world.

By its very nature social theory is critical. Although post-modern social theorists may well disagree (see Chapter 5), there may be a case for arguing that social theory should not solely be about describing or understanding the social world but should represent an active means of addressing why that society went wrong or how it has managed to go right. However misinformed and controversial, the Frankfurt School's approach to social theory manages to do just that: it manages to highlight just how vocal social theory can be. In this chapter I will outline, depending upon your point of view, one of the most controversial social theories that has ever had the misfortune, or good fortune, to have been written. In particular, I will focus on two broad issues. First: how far are human beings actually in control of their social and cultural contexts, and how far could you argue that these contexts actually control them? This issue is therefore very much bound up, as I suggested in Chapter 1, with debates concerning structure and agency. And second: how far is it justified for social theorists to make actual value judgements about the social world in which they operate? Can social theory be objective?

Before I directly address the work of the Frankfurt School I should make two issues absolutely clear. First, the Frankfurt School considered a vast array of sociological issues which are still of interest to social theorists today. Indeed, any attempt to summarize what the Frankfurt School had to say is bound to be problematic because there is not a real sense in which the Frankfurt School presents a uniform position. In this sense, critical theory amounts to a theoretical framework; a framework which incorporates a wide variety of influences, including, most crucially, Marxism and psychoanalysis. For reasons of clarity I do not therefore propose to discuss some of the more recent work of the Frankfurt School, and in particular that of Jürgen Habermas (1984, 1987), who is concerned with the communicative potential of human beings; a complex issue which I cannot do justice to within a broader discussion of mass culture.

Of equal importance is the fact that the Frankfurt School's unique perspective on the above issues, although influential, has undergone considerable and concerted attack (e.g. Swingewood, 1977), while it would certainly be misleading to suggest that its critique of the mass society is entirely representative of the debate. Indeed, as Strinati (1995) points out, there is a long history of commentators who have been concerned with the implications of popular cultural forms and the way in which the processes of industrialization and urbanization somehow serve to control the masses. The work of Dwight MacDonald (1957) is particularly influential in this regard. There are a vast array of approaches to debates over the mass society. But the school of thought that is perhaps most lucid in coming to terms with the ideological dimensions of a mass society is that which we associate with critical theory. It is for this reason that I will concentrate on the work of the Frankfurt School in this chapter. Before I do so I want to discuss briefly the notion of ideology, and in particular the relationship between ideology and popular cultural forms.

Ideology

Authors such as John Storey (1993) and Dominic Strinati (1995) acknowledge that ideology is a key concept in the study of popular culture, and that popular culture amounts to something far more significant than a straightforward discussion of entertainment and leisure. Storey (1993) in particular defines ideology as the way in which certain cultural texts and practices present distorted images of reality. This distortion is seen to benefit the powerful at the expense of the powerless. Ideology, then, fulfils the needs of a particular group who promote a particular set of ideas (at the expense of another set of ideas) which are not actually 'true' in the real sense of the word. Ideologies are constructed for a purpose: to fulfil the aims of a powerful social group, at the expense of a less powerful social group. Some authors have indeed argued that our society is dominated by a patriarchal ideology; that the identities we construct within family contexts appear, on the surface, to reflect a 'natural' state of affairs, but that in fact they are highly ideologically charged. For instance, the family unit and the gender relationships that occur within that unit, and in particular those of the mother and father, who quite often take on the role of 'housewife' and 'breadwinner', respectively, may appear on the surface to be 'natural', but may actively reinforce the ideological requirements of patriarchal capitalism. Patriarchal capitalism entails the male being in charge in both the workplace and the home. From this point of view, the apparent subservience of women props up the capitalist system: women operate as what is, in effect, a reserve army of labour, on hand to produce the future workforce and to provide a supportive home or 'escape' for the current workforce. Herein lies the ideological role of the family (see Mac An Ghaill, 1996; McDowell and Pringle, 1992).

Popular culture may well be said to play a similar ideological role to that of the family. The distorted images which I referred to above may be said from a Marxist point of view to help construct some form of 'false consciousness' (see Storey, 1993, p. 3). In other words, while the powerful do not see themselves as controlling the powerless, the powerless do not perceive themselves to be subordinated; the point being that the capitalist ideology that surrounds them is blinding them to the reality of that subordination and blinding the powerful to the power that they actually have. In this sense, does popular culture amount to an autonomous form of social expression or a powerful means of social control that props up capitalist ideologies?

Many social theorists have pointed out that popular culture is more than simply a time-consuming triviality, and that it actively expresses and reinforces important power relationships (see Storey, 1993; Strinati, 1995). Let us consider *Noel's House Party*, a Saturday night peak-time BBC television programme that ended its run in 1999 after many years. This adopts a set of faintly humourous and formulaic set-pieces, one of which involves a celebrity entering a transparent cage which encloses a wind-machine. The celebrity grabs as many notes (from whichever currency a member of the public may have chosen) as possible in a matter of a few seconds. The studio audience cheer the celebrity on, approvingly. This appears to be a harmless piece of entertainment, but not far below the surface it may be possible to argue that there is a distinct ideological element to this particular part of the programme which tells a lot, in turn, about the sorts of values that underpin our society. We live in what appears to be an acquisitive consumer society (see Miles, 1998a) and *Noel's House Party* is an example of a programme that positively legitimizes this state of affairs. It proclaims that acquisitive individualism is a desirable social trait and it therefore presents an ideological vision of the world that is not natural at all, but which is certainly portrayed as such. The point here is that it is able to do this so effectively because of the medium through which it is being portrayed: popular culture. Precisely because people assume that popular culture is harmless entertainment. As such, it encapsulates and propagates some of the most profound and potentially damaging aspects of dominant power relationships and ideologies.

The subtlety of ideology in the realm of popular culture is well illustrated by John Fiske (1989) when he discusses the apparently extremely straightforward act of wearing jeans. Jeans give us warmth and comfort, but at another level, beyond their functionality, they appear to transcend social categories. Everybody, no matter their social background, gender, age, nationality or education, appears to wear jeans. But the wearing of jeans is clearly just as much a meaningful act as a practical one, in terms of what it says about the individual wearer and wearers in general. Because wearers of jeans are, at least to some extent, bound to the sets of meanings associated with jeans as they are constructed amongst their peers, such garments are ripe for ideological inoculation. Jeans are the cultural norm, and have become so ubiquitous in our culture that they carry meanings beyond those which we invest ourselves. By wearing jeans people actively legitimate capitalist consumer culture, because above all jeans are symbols of capitalism and all the power relations that capitalism entails. Our jeans are an illustration that we accept in a very direct fashion, through our way of dressing, those power relations as being a natural state of affairs. As far as Fiske (1989) is concerned, 'By wearing jeans we adopt the positions of subjects within that ideology, become complicit with it, and therefore give it material expression; we "live" capitalism through its commodities, and, by living it, we validate and invigorate it' (p. 14).

But this process is subtle in nature. The producers and distributors of jeans are not, as Fiske points out, capitalist propagandists, and neither, thankfully, is the TV host Noel Edmonds. Rather the commodities they produce amount to an ideology made material, and as a result, 'Ideology works in the sphere of culture as economics so that it appears to be the only one possible' (p. 14). As Fiske goes on to point out, ideology actually produces false consciousness in two ways: first, it blinds the 'masses' from the conflict of interest that exists between the bourgeoisie and the proletariat, insofar as they become convinced that that relationship is harmonious; and, second, it prevents the development of class consciousness or solidarity. Ideology works in the sphere of culture in order to naturalize the capitalist system, which appears to the consumer of popular culture to be the only system possible. Ideology becomes an essential aspect of social life because we experience it as lived experience. We accept it as entirely natural and operate within the framework that it provides for us.

The apparent 'living out' of ideology is an issue discussed by several authors, including Dick Hebdige (1979) in his book, *Subculture: The Meaning of Style*, in which he describes ideology as lived relation: '. . . ideology by definition thrives *beneath* consciousness. It is here at the level of "normal common sense", that ideological frameworks of reference are most firmly sedimented and most effective, because it is here that their ideological nature is most effectively concealed' (p. 11, emphasis in the original). In this sense ideology is essentially un- or at least sub-conscious. It is the fact that ideology is taken for granted that makes it such a powerful force. Ideology is not merely a speculative theoretical system, but actively shapes desires and wants. It works at the level of the practical consciousness; and it is lived, not merely thought. However, it should not be assumed that ideology completely rules out the possibility of human agency. Human beings are simultaneously the creators and the products of the social world,

> In every testimony to the experience of the dehumanizing pressure of modern industrial society, there is also a testimony to a contrary sense of self, of personal identity, of being human; of what it might be like to be in control of our own lives, to act in and upon the world, to be active human agents. (Dawe, 1978, p. 364)

This proposition forms a basis to a critique of the work of the Frankfurt School, to which I will now turn.

The work of the Frankfurt School

The Frankfurt School is a school of critical theory that, amongst other things, considered some of the cultural implications of the development of capitalism; implications which are encapsulated in the term 'mass society'. The Frankfurt School was set up in 1923 as an Institute for Marxist Studies and studied a variety of topics ranging from the rise of fascism, art and popular culture. The chronology of the work which came out of the Frankfurt School is very much bound up with the impact of Nazism in Europe, which forced the School to move to New York for a period of around sixteen years. The Frankfurt School's analysis of mass society is therefore a unique brew of reflections on Hitler's Germany and the increasingly commercialized culture of the United States. But the key thing about the members of the Frankfurt

School, who include Adorno, Benjamin, Löwenthal, Marcuse, Reich and more recently Habermas, is that their work is concerned with the essence of human freedom and the need to undermine forms of suppression that apparently dominate social life. In this sense, the Frankfurt School was concerned with unwrapping the underlying ideological dimensions of capitalism. From a theoretical point of view the Frankfurt School illustrates an end to dogmatic Marxism and a move towards a more interpretative approach which recognizes that modernity had not fulfilled the promise outlined by the Enlightenment thinkers. As such, Ian MacKenzie (1999) points out that authors such as Horkheimer and Adorno (1972) recognized that the drive towards a rational society was ensnaring human creativity in favour of the efficiency of the social system as a whole. Indeed,

> whereas Weber was sceptical about our ability to free ourselves from the increasingly virulent progress of rationalization, the Frankfurt School theorists still clung, however tentatively, to the Marxist hope of human emancipation. The question they faced was how to criticize the deleterious effects of the Enlightenment's conception of instrumental reason and open the door to the ever present forces of irrationalism. (MacKenzie, 1999, p. 41)

Members of the Frankfurt School therefore owed a debt to both Marx and Weber. They recognized a world of instrumental rationality, described by Weber, in which the needs of human beings were being ignored as part of an 'administered society' in which mass consumer culture systematically integrated and controlled. Meanwhile, the work of Horkheimer and Adorno (1972), in particular, represents a critique of Marxism insofar as they felt that Marx was himself enmeshed in the values underlying the Enlightenment project and was thus simply not critical enough about it. Traditional forms of Marxism were misunderstanding the complex nature of human subjectivity and the way in which people interact with the sorts of conditions that Karl Marx described (see Baert, 1998; Held, 1980). Marxism was in effect complicit in the very ideologies it was attempting to critique, insofar as it naïvely propagated an optimistic view that ultimately human progress and freedom would prevail; a view which simply underestimated the sophistication of capitalism. Capitalism, indeed, as far as the Frankfurt School was concerned was more than capable of reinforcing its dominance through new avenues and perhaps most significantly in the cultural as well as the economic realm. The question that follows, however, is how far the Frankfurt School would actually be capable of undermining this dominance. It is all well and good pointing out that social injustice exists, but how do you actually go about addressing the imbalances of such injustice? Bronner (1994) suggests that 'Critical theory, from the very

first, expressed an explicit interest in the abolition of social injustice.
... The objective was to foster reflexivity, a capacity for fantasy, and a
new basis for praxis in an increasingly alienated world' (p. 3). The
work of the Frankfurt School was self-consciously experimental and
as such was preoccupied by the desire for a better world. In this
sense, it compares, some would say favourably, to a lot of contemporary theory, which, as I will point out later in this chapter and in
Chapter 5, simply concedes that social theory has no such influence or
insight. The Frankfurt School *tried* to make a difference.

Mass society theory and the work of the Frankfurt School therefore
represent an attempt, and a very forthright attempt at that, to place
Marxism in a cultural context and in turn to explore the ideological
sophistication of capitalism, which, far from simply operating at an
economic level, also has a significant cultural dimension. Members of
the Frankfurt School were therefore linked by the concern for the
possibility of human freedom and the ways in which that freedom
had been curtailed, notably through the impact of modern capitalism.
The real appeal of this work, however, is that it is not simply
descriptive, but represents an effort to come to terms with the nature
of social change and, in turn, challenge such change for the sake of
democracy and the basic right of human freedom.

The political dimensions of critical theory, as Held (1980) notes,
are at their most convincing in the work of Marcuse, and, in particular, in his seminal work, *One-Dimensional Man* (1964). Marcuse
argues that advanced industrial society can contain the nature of
qualitative change, and yet forces and tendencies exist which threaten
to break this containment and explode that very same society.
Perhaps most importantly, Marcuse argued that capitalism had
learned how to be effective to the extent that the needs of the public
and private corporations become one and the same thing. In effect,
then, the ideology of the consumer society is historically accepted, to
the extent that any revolutionary intent is simply that of a minority,
and an ineffectual minority at that. The domination of the masses is
not enforced simply through the arbitrary or physical application of
power, but through rational planning. In effect, 'domination is trans-
figured into administration' (Marcuse, 1964, p. 39; see Held, 1980;
Slater, 1997). In particular, docile forms of consumerism reinforced
the status quo and reasserted the powerlessness of the masses.

In the above context, Marcuse identified numerous ways in which
capitalism was able to reproduce itself whilst maintaining the rationality that served to keep the masses at bay. Perhaps the most interesting of those factors from a contemporary point of view is the
creation of affluence and the sense of satisfaction that affluence
apparently brings. The masses begin to see that capitalism actually
has much to offer them, not just a job and enough money to pay for

food and a roof over their heads, but all the added extras that appear to make life worthwhile. The apparent joys of a mass society therefore arguably reached their peak in Ronald Reagan's America and Margaret Thatcher's Britain. The freedoms inherent in consumerism were only partial freedoms, but they were enough to rid the masses of their common identity and to ensure that such an identity could, from then on, only be measured by how much a parent spent on his or her child's Christmas presents. The gradual move towards white-collar work and away from the physicality of the factory and the pit, which characterized this period in Britain at least, did not, for Marcuse, represent any form of genuine liberation, but rather a more subtle means of control. The superficial improvement of working conditions did nothing, from this point of view, to reverse the sickeningly controlling nature of capitalism, which was still as alienating as it had ever been and perhaps more so. All the above 'improvements' reflected an increasingly bureaucratic society which was offered the illusion of freedom but the reality of oppression and the depression of silence. Depoliticization was the name of the game. The superficial gains of a mass consumer society came at a cost and that cost was the concession of political and mental freedom. Work and leisure were now working in harmony to support the capitalist system. For the worker, harmony was something of the past – if it ever even existed in the first place. In Britain, at least, the nearest the masses can apparently come to any sense of joy, even today, is an hour's edition of *Who Wants To Be A Millionaire?* on the ITV network. The question is: does *Who Wants To Be A Millionaire?* represent a genuine means of escape from the alienation apparently inherent in capitalism, or does it simply reinforce the legitimacy of that alienation?

The culture industry

It was probably in the context of their work on the nature of mass culture, hinted at in the above, that the members of the Frankfurt School, and Horkheimer and Adorno in particular, have been most influential. The term 'culture industry' is an especially important one in terms of the intellectual impact of Horkheimer and Adorno's work in the context of mass society and mass culture. As far as ideology is concerned, the point Horkheimer and Adorno were making, in direct contrast to commentators such as Matthew Arnold (1932), author of *Culture and Anarchy*, was that rather than undermining the nature of social authority, culture reinforces such authority in more subtle ways than even Marx could have possibly envisaged. The emergence of a consumer as discussed in Chapter 4 is particularly pertinent here, insofar as consumerism promotes a way of life in which any critique of dominant orders is apparently silenced, amidst the mass seduction promoted by the culture industry. Thus, a key concern was the degree to which the culture industry actively blocked human freedom. The ideological power of the culture industry is a reflection of the fact that capitalist relations of production can never produce freedom, but constantly move towards further integration and domination (see Adorno, 1991).

Adorno's position on the culture industry is most clearly stated in his essay 'The Culture Industry Reconsidered' (1989), in which he points out that in his work with Horkheimer they actually replaced the term 'mass culture' with that of the 'culture industry'. This distinction is important insofar as it reinforces the contention that mass culture does not arise spontaneously from the masses, but is somehow foisted upon them. The culture industry, therefore, 'intentionally integrates its consumers from above'. But the crucial point here is not simply that mass culture is bad, but that the masses are an object of calculation: 'The customer is not king, as the culture industry would like to have us believe, not its subject but its object' (p. 129). Lying at the core of this process is the transfer of the profit motive onto the cultural form. The culture industry prioritizes profit at the expense of quality. Meanwhile, the actualities of culture as we know it are, for Adorno, destroyed by the secondary means of representing that culture. Colour film, for instance, cannot possibly give us something we cannot get from the original object of that film. It can only reduce that object to a standardized interchangeable non-entity. In these circumstances the autonomous, independent, critical individual becomes something of the past. The culture industry despises the masses and obstructs their very emancipation from the productive forces which are themselves becoming ever more ideologically sophisticated. In discussing Adorno's work, Bernstein (1991) sums up the ideological subtleties at work:

> [The culture industry,] which involves the production of works for repro-
> duction and mass consumption, thereby organizing 'free' time, the remnant
> domain of freedom under capital in accordance with the same principles of
> exchange and equivalence that reign in the sphere of production outside
> leisure, presents culture as the realization of the right of all to the grati-
> fication of desire in reality continuing the negative integration of society.
> (p. 3)

But the subtlety of the culture industry and the parallel sophistication of the work of the Frankfurt School in coming to terms with that sophistication is no better expressed than in this well-known quotation, which is more than worth repeating insofar as it highlights the fact that authors such as Horkheimer and Adorno were concerned with the standardizing effects of capitalism, under the guise of technical efficiency:

> The culture industry perpetually cheats its consumers of what it perpetually promises. The promisory note which, with its plots and staging, it draws on pleasure is endlessly prolonged; the promise, which is actually all the spectacle consists of, is illusory: all it actually confirms is that the real point will never be reached, that the diner must be satisfied with the menu. (Horkheimer and Adorno, 1972, p. 139)

What is of particular note here is the fact that the Frankfurt School recognized that the impact of the culture industry and of mass culture in general was psychological as well as sociological. It created a particular kind of mentality: the sort of mentality that rendered human beings helpless in the context of the rising wave of Nazism, but also more presciently in contemporary society, helpless in the context of the rising wave of consumerism. Human beings are not only susceptible to the controlling principles of consumerism, but actively crave such control, because it simply makes life so much easier for them (see Chapter 4). The business imperative and the need for profit can, from this point of view, be said to underlie every aspect of mass culture to the extent that the profit motive is transferred 'naked' onto cultural forms such that art itself is bastardized. 'Movies and radio need no longer pretend to be art. The truth that they are just business is made into an ideology in order to justify the rubbish they deliberately produce' (Horkheimer and Adorno, 1972, p. 31). Any sense of a genuinely creative culture is therefore cast aside in favour of a predictable package of mass culture which is very much dependent upon a very standardized formula. This argument is apparently given credibility when you consider the recent history of mass cultural forms: the popularity of the Hollywood Western and cops and robbers TV shows in the 1970s; the rise of the soap opera in the 1980s; and the apparent dominance on British TV screens of detective drama series, light drama/comedies about the ups and downs of relationships and single life, and, of course, game shows.

   Let's take just one example and subject it to the sort of analysis associated with the Frankfurt School, in this case the hit British game show *The Moment of Truth*, hosted by Cilla Black and broadcast on the ITV network. The programme is formulaic in the extreme in its structure. The premise underlying the programme is that one member of a family is asked to complete a particular task such as recalling a long list of phone numbers or throwing something at a target within a set time limit. Every week the show follows the exact same pattern. The host interviews the family in their home, provides a task, welcomes the family to the TV studio, before encouraging a family member to complete the task, which always takes place after the commercial break in order to maximize tension. Perhaps more importantly, the family play for a bounty chest of prizes. Each family member gets to choose a particular prize. The prizes chosen are highly predictable and will almost always include an expensive family holiday and a family car. *The Moment of Truth* could very well be described as a quintessential piece of mass popular culture in the very guise that Horkheimer and Adorno outline. The programme never strays from a very predictable format to the extent that the host adopts a series of catch-phrases, familiar and suitably dramatic music is consistently played at key moments, whilst those involved appear to follow a carefully planned and reproduced script that never changes from one week to the next. The only unpredictable thing is whether or not the contestants on the show will successfully complete their tasks. But whether they do or not is immaterial; the viewer is always satisfied by the fact that he or she is more than prepared for what's coming next. The programme panders to the desire of the audience for predictability; for only in predictability can they be satisfied that they have received exactly what they were entitled, and exactly what they would expect (see also Chapter 6). The irony of all this is that the whole programme is injected with a consumerist mentality; an ideology which says that consumerism and the 'satisfactions' it can bring is what any 'normal' family should aspire to. *The Moment of Truth* not only depoliticizes its audience; it could well be said to legitimise a world in which mass popular culture can help us to forget all our problems in the name of 'harmless' entertainment.

Mass popular cultural forms may well provide their own evidence to suggest that popular cultural forms are predictable and, in turn, as Adorno might have argued, that mass culture can, at least potentially, have a sort of infantilizing effect. Indeed, the output of the youngest of the available British terrestrial TV channels, Channel 5, whose very *raison d'être* was premised on its predictable schedule and a diet of soaps, chat shows and soft pornography, might well be said to be testament to this fact. The very patterns that members of the Frankfurt School described might well be said to be more prevalent today than they ever have been. The dumbing down of mass culture is arguably reaching new depths, beyond even the collective imaginations of Horkheimer and Adorno.

Music for the masses

The suggestion, or at least implication, that the mass of the population is somehow brainwashed by the immediate offer of gratification that is made available to them through the culture industry is now something I will explore in the particular context of music, which was a particular fascination to Adorno, whilst also informing much of the work he did with Horkheimer. Adorno was concerned that popular music was built on foundations of predictability. In this sense, musical production is not a creative act, but a matter of technique and repetition within which the consumer positively seeks the predictability of the familiar. Adorno (1991) argues that pop music, and films, have degenerated to the extent that they never actually create new ideas, but prefer instead to regurgitate old ones in a safe and predictable fashion:

> As soon as the film begins, it is quite clear how it will end, and who will be rewarded, punished, or forgotten. In light music [popular music], once the trained ear has heard the first notes of the hit song, it can guess what is coming and feel flattered when it does come. (p. 125)

For Horkheimer and Adorno (1972), then, the process of 'pseudo-individualization' is an essential characteristic of popular music consumption. In other words, music is always structured in more or less the same way, with only very minor details of variation. Thus popular music represents a sort of safety blanket for the consumer. He or she will always find such music comfortingly familiar, while the odd snippet that does not conform to this pattern serves to massage the ego of the consumer; convincing him or her of his or her good taste and sophistication. Thus, from this point of view, popular music becomes produced in a uniform fashion as a means of standardizing audience reaction, whilst maximizing economic dividends and ensuring the pliance of the depoliticized consumer, who becomes equally vulnerable to other forms of highly predictable consumption. The standardization of music has a distinct ideological function, as it makes the consumer more pliant; a passive subject for the purpose of programmed consumption. Perhaps more importantly, pop music provides an escape from work but at the same time is moulded into the same psychological state, so it provides the consumer with a perpetual busman's holiday of depoliticized predictability and standardization. The escapism encapsulated in this type of music, its romantic overtones and sexually charged imagery, provide a haven from reality; but a haven that offers no hope of redemption.

Is this portrayal of popular music an accurate one? A straightforward consideration of the sorts of bands which currently populate the charts would indeed suggest that Adorno's diagnosis at least has surface validity. Taking a week at random, the dominance of the boy and girl band phenomenon, perhaps the most extreme example of a standardized formulaic mass musical product, is the most striking pattern. Of the top ten singles of the week beginning Sunday, 14 November 1999, five of those acts represented are either boy or girl bands, former members of boy or girl bands or current members of the Spice Girls exploring a solo project. The key thing about these acts is that they all fulfil the music industry's formula for what constitutes a top-selling band. Style, image and sex appeal are key factors. From a critical perspective original songs and lyrics appear, at times, to be little more than after-thoughts. But Adorno is just as critical of those people who consume popular music as he is of the music itself. This type of music listening is referred to by Adorno as 'regressive'. The consumer of popular music is not happy unless he or she receives the same musical dish time after time, and the irony is that by wallowing in such predictability popular music listeners are able to convince themselves that they are actually in control. Popular music therefore plays an important role in maintaining capitalist power structures. Those people in a reasonably high social position do not need popular music because they do not need to escape from the boredom of their workplace. Such people can listen to classical music, because they are as open to being challenged in their leisure time as they are in their work time. As Strinati (1995) puts it, 'People desire popular music, partly because capitalists "hammer" into their minds and make it appear desirable. But their desire is also fuelled by the symmetry between production and consumption which characterises their lives in a capitalist society' (p. 68). The role of popular music, for Adorno, is at least partly to do with helping people come to terms with the harshness of their own lives. It provides an escape from the real world, but as such is no more than a reprieve from the continued drudgery of the capitalist system. Popular music offsets revolution, a catharsis which ultimately resigns the masses to their fate (see Adorno, 1991; Strinati, 1995).

Criticisms of the Frankfurt School

The extreme nature of the Frankfurt School's position and the political undertones of its members' work have meant that the ideas they present are rarely accepted in their entirety. Above all, and quite understandably, the School is criticized for intellectual snobbery and cultural élitism. Its vision of popular entertainment as being dumbed down to the lowest common denominator and as amounting to little more than debased worthlessness has attracted concerted criticism. A good example of such élitism is Adorno's treatment of the changing nature of art. Adorno sees popular art as being a pale imitation of its classical antecedents. The question is, why should we accept an analysis that seems to think popular culture is resolutely bad and inferior to forms of high culture? Culture should not be a matter for value judgement. If a large proportion of the population (like myself) choose to watch *Who Wants To Be A Millionaire?* and like to listen to Robbie Williams (unlike myself), who has the right to make the judgement that they are wasting their time? There is no reason why mass culture should necessarily be equated with poor quality. Indeed, some of the most fantastic cultural achievements of the twentieth century were extremely popular. The Beatles immediately spring to mind here. And yet members of the Frankfurt School appear to be suggesting that they are entitled to pass judgement on forms of popular culture. The soap opera *EastEnders* might even be said to produce some of the best drama of its day. In a sense Shakespearean theatre was *the* original expression of popular culture!

In short, the members of the Frankfurt School appear to be implying that they have a privileged understanding of the intricacies of popular culture, and that the mass of the population simply do not understand. This position is untenable. Salvador Giner (1976) is not going far wrong when he says that the Frankfurt School is seriously impaired by an 'isolated anti-plebeian aristocratic prejudice'. As Storey (1999) points out, it is almost as if the members of the Frankfurt School know all the answers to any questions about cultural consumption before they have actually been asked. Far from providing a flexible and reflexive body of thought through which contemporary forms of popular culture can be critically evaluated (as might be expected of an adept social theory), their work amounts to what appears to be little more than a theoretical strait-jacket. The problem with that strait-jacket is that it does not really mange to come to terms with the complexity of cultural engagement. If, as Storey notes, you see culture from one of two ends of a spectrum, as something that should simply be celebrated or something that is utterly ideological, then the complex ways in which consumers of popular culture interact with what they consume is inevitably neglected. The Frankfurt School reduces human beings to little more than a template upon which ideology is imposed.

The core criticism of the Frankfurt School and its conception of mass society is therefore the fact that people consume popular culture in a far more reflexive and critical fashion than its members are prepared to admit. For instance, Adorno dismisses popular music because it is popular. But do people really consume Britney Spears or Steps in the same way that they might consume Coldplay or Elvis Costello? The fact is that none of these types of music is consumed in a prescriptive way. They may be produced in such forms, but an analysis which neglects the consumption side of this equation is misleading. Yes, aspects of popular music may be in some sense regressive, but to label all popular music as such is disingenuous. And even if we do accept that, for instance, the boy band is a predictable and standardized formula which placates the consumer, such an explanation is not enough in itself. There may be all sorts of personalized meanings which fans of Westlife invest in their music. The actual music itself may not be particularly original, but that does not mean to say that consumers of that music cannot interpret it in their own original ways. However structured and predictable the music itself, the meanings which individuals might take out and construct from such predictability are virtually limitless. For instance, a very predictable line in a song about a boy loving a girl may be excruciatingly clichéd and utterly predictable, but at the same time it may be unique in the way in which it speaks to one particular individual to whom this particular song resonates at one particular point in time. Even if one such person is moved by that piece of music, then it has fulfilled any creative criterion that could possibly have been expected of it.

The problem with the work of the Frankfurt School, then, is that the forms of popular culture that authors like Horkheimer and Adorno describe are more likely to be subject to an indignant sense of distaste on their part than to a considered, empirically based critique. The attitude of this approach appears to be that popular culture is infantile and regressive. For members of the Frankfurt School, this is self-evidently the case, and as far as they are concerned there is therefore absolutely no need to provide an empirical basis to justify this position. Popular cultural forms should therefore be dismissed out of hand. The suggestion that consumers of popular culture may actually get a lot out of what they are consuming in these contexts is ridiculous, because the members of the Frankfurt School know that popular culture is mass culture and that mass culture is a pale imitation of the real thing. This flagrant snobbishness is characteristic of members of the Frankfurt School's work in general and, more specifically, of the actual style in which they tend to present their work. Their written style is often as inaccessible as the examples of high culture that they appear to be so determined to valorize. It is almost as if they feel that they need to rise above the ill-fitting language of a mass society. Critical theory, like too much of social theory in general, protects itself from the real world through the obscurity of its language, which not only alienates its readers, but simultaneously gives the authors concerned an inflated impression of their own self-importance. Students of social theory should be wary of examples of social theory that seem to wallow in self-adoration. You have to ask yourself the following question: is a social theory actually doing its job if it cannot clearly state a position and be criticized on the basis of that position? Too many social theorists appear to want to divorce their work from reality; to describe and critique reality, but to do so in such a way that it becomes nothing more than their own reality. In these circumstances, social theory tells us more about the needs of the theorist him- or herself than it does about the world he or she is apparently trying to understand. Students of social theory should therefore be courageous enough to criticize social theory for its lack of clarity. A good social theory is a clear social theory that opens your eyes to aspects of social life you had not yet considered. Poor language is the bedfellow of poor social theory. As Strinati (1995) so lucidly puts it in the context of the work of the Frankfurt School,

> Sometimes termed critical theory, the ideas of the Frankfurt School stress that theory is a form of resistance to the commercial impulses of capitalist production and the ideological hold of commodity fetishism. But it can only function in the way that avant-garde music does if it rejects the empiricism which demands that theories be based upon some kind of evidence, and protects itself behind an obscure and inaccessible language. The School's theory and language allow it to stand outside and criticise the 'one-dimensional' world of capitalist thought and culture. However, this stance is only possible if its theory is correct. But is it? (p. 75)

Conclusions

Despite the above criticisms, the members of the Frankfurt School can look back upon a significant legacy and aspects of their body of work continue to inform contemporary theoretical debates. Such a legacy may not be a direct one, inasmuch as such discourses do not necessarily owe their theoretical origins directly or solely to the Frankfurt School, but the indirect influence is considerable, insofar as they pursue very similar themes and concerns, in very different ways. One such example is the way in which post-modern conceptions of popular culture are increasingly likely to acknowledge the significance of popular culture in its own right (see Chapter 5). Popular culture is more than simply a reflection of the more significant realm of work. Both spheres have important things to say about the structure of contemporary social life. Whilst the sorts of ideas discussed by the Frankfurt School may be in some sense élitist, this is not to say they do not reflect the opinion of a significant proportion of the population. They do, and for that reason alone they are worth exploring. In this sense the work of the Frankfurt School may well be less palatable, but more real than some of its critics may be prepared to admit.

In other words, the Frankfurt School has at least left a methodological and philosophical legacy. Indeed, the Frankfurt School played a formative role in illustrating the benefits to be had from looking at aspects of popular culture in their own right and has encouraged many contemporary social theorists to follow in its wake. One such example is Ang's (1985) work on *Watching Dallas*, in which she directly addresses the issue of mass culture. Ang's work contrasts with that of Horkheimer and Adorno in one key way. Ang is concerned with the ways in which viewers actually receive and invest meanings in the consumption of *Dallas* as a popular cultural form, and it is in this context that she builds upon, extends and improves upon the Frankfurt School's legacy. For Ang, popular culture is a two-way process. People's consumption of *Dallas* can actually be positive. Ang's position is that the pleasure which people experience from watching *Dallas* may be somehow false, but it is pleasure and as such should not be dismissed out of hand. The problem with discussions of mass culture, as I pointed out above, is that mass culture automatically carries negative connotations with it. In discussing data collected from a series of letters respondents wrote about their consumption of *Dallas*, Ang suggests that those respondents who hated *Dallas* actually adopted the ideology of mass culture as a guideline for the programme's rejection. In short, the ideology of mass culture amounts to a self-fulfilling philosophy. The label 'mass culture' is gleefully adopted by consumers of culture because of the comfort and reassurance it ensures. It makes them feel that their taste is authentic. As such, 'it makes a search for more detailed and personal explanations superfluous, because it provides a finished explanatory model that convinces, sounds logical and radiates legitimacy' (Ang, 1985, p. 96). There may be no inner logic or accuracy in using notions of mass culture, but they provide a convenient means of dismissing aspects of popular culture without carefully considered analyses of such phenomena. This may indeed be the fundamental problem with mass cultural analyses which presuppose that mass culture is somehow bad. However, Ang goes on to argue that this ideology of mass culture is limited to the discourses people use when talking about culture. Such opinions and rationalizations do not necessarily determine people's cultural practices. Quite often people will deliberately avoid being dictated to by the mass culture ideology, by making sure they find out themselves whether or not popular culture has any real value. This in itself constitutes a subtle ideological process. Indeed,

> The commercial culture industry has understood this well. It employs the populist ideology for its own ends by reinforcing the cultural eclecticism underlying it and propagating the idea that indeed there's no accounting for taste, that in other words no objective aesthetic judgements are possible. It sells its products by propagating the idea that everyone has the right to his or her own taste and has the freedom to enjoy pleasure in his or her own way. (Ang, 1985, pp. 115–16)

It is in this context that Ang makes her most insightful point. Any notion of pleasure is completely removed from the discourse of mass culture, 'Instead it makes things like responsibility, critical distance or aesthetic purity central – moral categories that make pleasure an irrelevant and illegitimate criterion' (p. 115). The routine role mass culture plays in bringing pleasure into people's lives therefore becomes ignored, rendered irrelevant. Mass culture becomes a theoretical issue, and its actual manifestation as an active meaningful aspect of people's everyday life is left in the wastebin of an élitist theory that judges first and analyses second.

Despite the above, it is absolutely essential to remember that human beings do not relate to popular culture in objective ways, but that they do so in a self-consciously subjective (and as such often élitist) fashion. In this respect, the work of the Frankfurt School may indeed be more accurate than its critics are prepared to admit. The above point is illustrated in the work of Kuisel (1993), in which he discusses the Americanization of France and the apparent distate that French cultural commentators and French people in general clearly have for popular American culture. As such, Kuisel presents American popular culture not as a culture as valid and rich as any other but as an affront to more 'genuine' French forms of culture. Kuisel notes that in the post-Second World War era the French took an American path towards the consumer society. More recently, the opening of EuroDisney near Paris in 1992 has refocused critical voices against the apparent evil that is American popular culture. Kuisel therefore quotes Alain Finkelkraut, who, in turn, describes Euro-Disney as 'a terrifying giant step toward world homogenization', whilst French theatre director Ariane Mnouchkine denounces the park as 'a cultural Chernobyl'. Even Jack Lang, then Socialist minister of culture, was worried that EuroDisney might represent the beginnings of an American takeover of the leisure industry in France (Kuisel, 1993). Denying he was hostile to American culture, Lang said that he was one of 'the principal promoters of American culture. I hold dear the America of bold and inventive ideas. The question is different when thinking of standardized culture. . . . This is less a question of American culture than of marketing' (see Kuisel, 1993, p. 22). Kuisel compares the vulgarities and excesses of American mass culture, which he describes as nothing more than a cultural wasteland, and the aesthetic values of civilized French culture. He talks about how France succeeded in 'not succumbing' to Americanization and, indeed, contends that the sense of superiority, difference and universal mission, all of which are bound up in the term *civilisation,* provides an important aspect of the French psyche to the extent that 'The French feel culturally superior and destined to enlighten the globe' (Kuisel, 1993, p. 236).

What this example illustrates is that the sorts of analyses of popular culture in which members of the Frankfurt School indulged are more than simply élitist nonsense that should be dismissed out of hand. Rather, people actually think about popular culture and its effects in these sorts of ways. It may not appeal to our politically correct sensibilities, but it is from this point of view a reflection of real life in which all forms of culture are *not* given equal footing. Human beings are quite likely to have their own opinions of what constitutes a good or bad form of culture. Such judgements are not the preserve of social theory, but represent the very stuff of everyday life. We should not therefore dismiss theory purely on the basis that we are politically uncomfortable with it. Social life itself is politically uncomfortable, and perhaps social theory should reflect this.

Bourdieu's notion of cultural capital is useful in this context. As Bourdieu (1984) points out, people use consumption symbolically as a means of maintaining hierarchical social relationships. Culture is not neutral territory within which we consume in a thoroughly objective fashion. It is a living, fluid context in which people construct different meanings from one situation to another, depending very much on their own particular brand of cultural capital. Education provides an important means of determining where individuals fit in within this hierarchy. 'Cultural capital' allows an individual to make distinctions about the merits of a particular cultural artefact. Different social groups will adopt different measures of what constitutes a 'good' or 'bad' form of culture. This exists in a hierarchy because human beings will always compare one another, and consumption provides one of the most readily available means of doing so. To acknowledge that this is a hierarchical process should be a source not of embarrassment, but of celebration. Perhaps we are simply misunderstanding the complexity of consumption. We do not have to accept that some forms of culture are better than others, but what we do have to accept is that some people think that they are.

The extreme nature of the Frankfurt School's approach to mass culture is remarkable above all for the fact that it continues to encourage debate, whilst genuinely reflecting at least some aspects of popular culture and how we as human beings relate to that culture. Members of the Frankfurt School ask questions that need to be asked. They may have failed to answer those questions, but by raising them in the way they have, they fulfil a need to debate critically what many of us would normally take for granted: the ideological role of popular culture. Perhaps more importantly this chapter has hopefully high-lighted the value of social theory, often regardless of the limitations of its specificities. The appeal of critical theory lies in the fact that it is so clearly critical of mainstream sociology, which members of the Frankfurt School felt was simply too accepting of society. The basis of the critical theorists' perspective was their concern that sociology had rejected any obligation on its part to awaken people to the oppressive nature of their everyday lives. In this respect, the Frankfurt School represents an interesting counter-position to that presented by many post-modern theorists who argue that in this day and age social theorists can no longer legislate or even hope to change the world. The most they can achieve is simply, and rather disappointingly, to describe that world in no more authoritative fashion than anybody else who may have an opinion (see Chapter 5). As far as members of the Frankfurt School were concerned, only by attempting to change things and by constructing a subjective, value-laden sociology could sociology have any real effect on the world it was seeking to understand. In a world in which relativism is apparently increasingly prevalent, social theory appears to be struggling to construct any sense of a coherent identity. Social theorists would do well to remember that although there was a tacit acceptance on the part of members of the Frankfurt School that their work could not transform the world – because the forces that controlled that world were so well entrenched – they did manage to highlight the extent of such forces. This in itself represents a call for change. It is worth taking time out to consider which of these two positions is the more tenable, and it is worth considering, in turn, whether social theory is simply struggling to find an identity, or whether, more worryingly, it is afraid to do just that.

In conclusion, the attraction of the Frankfurt School lies in its ability to address theoretical concerns in practical social and cultural contexts. Like members of the Frankfurt School, human beings react to aspects of social change, not objectively, but as subjective interpreters of their own cultural landscapes. None the less, the Frankfurt School's approach to mass popular culture *is* somewhat one-dimensional, above all in its failure to perceive of social theory as a complex balance between social structures and the socio-cultural interpretation and negotiation of those structures. From this point of view many contemporary theorists have dismissed the credibility of any discussion of mass culture or society.

> . . . the term mass is not a concept. It is a leitmotif of political demagogy, a soft, sticky, lumpenanalytical notion . . . the mass is without attribute, predicate, quality, reference. This is its definition or [rather] its radical lack of definition. It has no sociological reality. (Baudrillard, 1983, p. 22)

Mass culture may not have any sociological reality, but neither does the post-modern conception of a world in which individuals respond to a world of mass-mediated hyper-reality in an equally controlled and yet de-massified state (see Chapter 5). The sign of a good social theory is one that manages to find a balance between these two extremes and, arguably, one which focuses on the following question: can social theorists really do anything to change the world in which they live? Are they too much involved in that world themselves to give an adequate analysis of the ways in which it operates? The great value of critical theory and of assessments of mass society is that they reject the goal of constructing politically neutral knowledge, and by doing so their work questions the very basis of social theory. The Frankfurt School's discussion of critical theory did not change the world, but it did reinforce the fact that social theorists should bear in mind that they are as much part of that world as anybody else.

Recommended reading

Theodor W. Adorno (1991) *The Culture Industry: Selected Essays on Mass Culture*, ed. J.M. Bernstein, London: Routledge. A useful collection of some of Adorno's best work, including his treatment of popular music.

David Held (1980) *Introduction to Critical Theory*, Cambridge: Polity. Remains one of the most authoritative discussions – perhaps *the* most authoritative discussion – of the breadth of the Frankfurt School's theoretical contribution.

Max Horkheimer and Theodor W. Adorno (1972) *Dialectic of Enlightenment*, London: Allen Lane. At times a complex read, but your patience will be rewarded with some of the most thought-provoking social theory you may ever read.

Dominic Strinati (1995) *An Introduction to Theories of Popular Culture*, London: Routledge. A manageable and interesting summary of the Frankfurt School's work and of approaches to mass culture in general.

CHAPTER 3

A POST-INDUSTRIAL SOCIETY?

Of all the social theories under discussion during the course of this book, and along with and as part of debates surrounding post-modernism, post-industrial society is arguably the most disputed. Despite widespread condemnation of its detailed underpinnings, in many respects it also remains one of the most influential of those theories. The emergence of a post-industrial society has fascinated social theorists in recent decades. The theorist *par excellence* of post-industrial society, as Frankel (1987) notes, is undoubtedly Daniel Bell. The sheer ambition and apparent comprehensiveness of Daniel Bell's liberal right-wing vision of a society undergoing massive social and economic change is indeed breathtaking, but what is of more interest here is that despite the overwhelming condemnation of Bell's ideas (which almost constitutes an industry in itself), the critique his work engendered has had a significant influence on the development of social theory since the 1970s. Waters (1996) even goes as far as to suggest that 'Bell's work is a central element in the sociological canon and, like it or not, it infuses the discipline, often guiding the direction of sociological thought and always challenging orthodoxies . . .' (p. 9). This chapter will consider the extent to which the post-industrial society thesis constitutes a worthwhile challenge to the orthodoxies of social theory.

Daniel Bell has a formidable reputation and was undoubtedly one of the most significant sociologists of the twentieth century, but the actual specifics of his theory of the post-industrial society are rarely held in the same esteem (see Waters, 1996). At times criticism of Bell's work and that of his contemporaries is highly venomous: for example, Alex Callinicos (1989) proclaims that 'the idea of postindustrial society is, of course, nonsense' (p. 120). Such a sentiment might make you wonder why this book should even bother considering such a theory if, as it appears, it is so wholeheartedly condemned by the sociological 'community'. But the fact that Bell's work has stimulated such passionate responses actually underlines its value as a piece of macro-social theory; as does the fact that the label 'post-industrial society' continues to be a prominent bone of contention amongst social theorists. Such debate is perhaps most often generated by a misunderstanding of Bell's contribution to social theory, and in particular the neglect of his assertion that it is only the 'social structure' or the techno-economic realm of society that can actually become post-industrial. That, in other words, social structure can become post-industrial no matter what the political regime or cultural context (see Waters, 1996, p. 108). This is a point worth bearing in mind throughout the remainder of this chapter.

Bell developed his ideas about the post-industrial society in the late 1960s and early 1970s, and most influentially in his impressive book *The Coming of Post-Industrial Society: A Venture in Social Forecasting* (1973), which constitutes *the* groundbreaking contribution to the body of work that emerged in the 1970s concerned with the nature of advanced industrial society. Perhaps the greatest attribute of Bell's work is its apparent practicality. It actively addresses aspects of social change and allows the reader to consider the validity of the claims concerned, through observation of the actual manifestation of such change.

Bell's ideas and the work to which they gave rise provide a case study as to the value of social theory, whether right or wrong, in attempting to come to terms with long-term social change. The post-industrial society thesis provides us with a good example of a social theory which actively attempts to relate social change to changes in capitalism and in particular the changing nature of the production process; an issue that represents a key concern of social theory in general. The implication of Bell's work is that social change is undergoing a series of stages from pre-industrial to industrial through to post-industrial society. Bell's contribution to debates surrounding the post-industrial society can, from this point of view, be described as highly modernist. In other words, Bell felt that human beings were capable of taking control of the world around them and of stamping their personality all over it. The post-industrial society is apparently evidence of just this. For that reason it would certainly be fair to say that Bell's work is essentially optimistic in nature and far more optimistic than many of the other classical social theories with which you may be more familiar. For that reason alone Bell's work is a breath of fresh air. It is important to recognize that for a social theory to be critical and insightful it does not necessarily have to be negative or pessimistic.

Bell (1973) is essentially arguing that social change has had a positive impact and that impact resides most fundamentally in the transition from a society based on heavy industry to one characterized by its relationship to the age of information, high technology and the service industries. For Daniel Bell, then, post-industrial society is *after* industrial society. It represents a fundamental shift in the type of society in which human beings have come to live. Bell's theory is in this sense a social forecast 'about a change in the social framework of Western society' (Bell, 1973, p. 32). As Rose (1991) points out, Bell did not argue that the post-industrial society would completely displace the industrial society. Rather, he argued that the social changes emerging were significant enough to warrant the new label 'post-industrial'. Bell presents a highly negative view of industrial capitalism, but a highly positive view of a future when the needs of human beings represent a fundamental priority of the social order. It will come as no surprise, then, that Bell's theories are often criticized for being lofty, over-ambitious and blinkered. Perhaps the cruelest jibe of all is that Bell looks at the world through rose-tinted technologically deterministic glasses. The following discussion will consider how far this is actually the case.

The basis of Bell's post-industrial society

One of the important things to remember about Bell's work is that it is very much concerned with the future, and, indeed, from this point of view might actually be said to be more relevant today than it was when it was originally written back in the 1970s. Bell (1973) argues that the concept of post-industrial society deals primarily with changes in the social structure, 'the way in which the economy is being transformed and the occupational system reworked, and with the new relations between theory and empiricism, particularly science and technology' (p. 13). Bell's claim is not that such changes determine corresponding changes in the political or cultural make-up of society, but that they raise important questions for the nature of social life in general.

In this context, Bell identifies five key dimensions of a post-industrial society:

1) Economic sector: the change from a goods-producing to a service economy;
2) Occupational distribution: the pre-eminence of the professional and technical class;
3) Axial principle: the centrality of theoretical knowledge as the source of innovation and of policy formulation for society;
4) Future orientation: the control of technology and technological assessment;
5) Decision-making: the creation of a new 'intellectual technology'.

(Bell, 1973, p. 14)

Bell describes a radical transformation of society fuelled by economic and social change. Whereas industrial society had been a goods-producing, profit-driven society, a post-industrial society is more about the emergence of a service economy. The contrast with industrial society for Bell is therefore a stark one, epitomized above all, perhaps, by the apparently massive increase of the numbers of people working in service jobs:

> . . . the first and simplest characteristic of a post-industrial society is that the majority of the labor force is no longer engaged in agriculture or manufacturing but in services, which are defined, residually as trade, finance, transport, health, recreation, research, education, and government. (Bell, 1973, p. 15)

But such developments were not solely positive: they also reflected the down-turn in jobs in the manufacturing sector. Despite this, for Bell even this development had its positive implications, namely the corresponding growth in numbers in white-collar workers and the increased autonomy that this meant for the workers concerned. In short, then, Bell portrays a world far away from the alienated discontent of that described by Karl Marx (1990). And in contrast to Max Weber (1992), Bell didn't see the dominant social order as any longer dehumanizing or as bureaucracy stifling human creativity. Rather, the world had emerged triumphant. Modernity appeared, at last, to be fulfilling its promise. And not before time.

As far as occupational distribution is concerned, Bell argued that the professional and technical classes played an increased influential role in the power structures of society. According to Bell, this group becomes the ruling class of the post-industrial society in the sense that those with technical knowledge, such as economic theorists, mathematicians and of course computer technologists, but most pointedly scientists and engineers, come to play important roles in determining the direction of that society. This was in stark contrast to industrial society, in which the contrast between the bourgeoisie and the proletariat played such a prominent role. Bell is essentially arguing that the class basis of industrial society has been undermined by social change.

What the above implies is an increasingly important role of theoretical knowledge in providing the foundations for this post-industrial society. Bell goes as far as to suggest that theoretical knowledge, as opposed to either technology or practical knowledge, amounts to the 'axial principle' of the new society. In other words, in a post-industrial society theoretical knowledge provides the basis on which that society moves forward through policy and social innovation. What characterizes the post-industrial society above all else is that it is 'organized around knowledge for the purpose of social control and the directing of innovation and change' (Bell, 1973, p. 20). A post-industrial society therefore represents the zenith of the scientific mind and of the ideals of scientific progress. As Waters

(1996) notes, a post-industrial society is a planned society in which the control and regulation of the future introduction of technologies becomes a real possibility. In some respects, then, the post-industrial society amounts to a recognition that Enlightenment thinking has, in a sense, been fulfilled. Progress is possible. However, as Smart (1992) argues, it would be misleading to suggest that Bell believed that this scientific culture actually existed in mid-1970s America. Rather, he saw the above, and in particular the move towards a rational organization of society, as *potential* developments. His was a projective theory. It is also worth remembering that in some respects Bell is critical of the developments he describes, and he expresses concern as to the rational aspect of the post-industrial society as potentially losing sight of human need or reason (see Smart, 1992, p. 34).

Bell felt very strongly that the post-industrial society would very much be future- and communally orientated, and this feeling was expressed further in much of his other work and in particular that which specifically deals with the impact of new computer technology and telecommunications technology (see Waters, 1996, for a discussion). Bell (1991) therefore talks about the emergence of a society characterized by the merger between telecommunications and computer-processing, or what he calls 'compunications'. The important thing here, as Waters notes, is that in his more recent work Bell distinguishes the information sector from the other service industries. In this context, Waters (1996) describes Bell as a 'technology freak' (p. 162), which in itself raises questions of technological determinacy which I will return to shortly. Bell (1976) was also concerned with the cultural impact of social change. As such he identified what he described as 'the cultural contradictions of capitalism'. Bell argues that post-industrial capitalism is threatened by a culture of excess which simply cannot sit comfortably with the efficient values of the post-industrial base that underlie it. In effect, Bell's concern is that the hedonism of post-industrial culture saps away at the efficiency of the post-industrial society. In this sense his approach to the future of the post-industrial society is not wholly positive.

Whether or not this post-industrial culture actually exists, and regardless of the role of hedonistic consumerism in this culture (see Chapter 4), it is absolutely crucial to remember that Bell's work amounts to what Waters (1996) describes as a 'speculative construct that identifies emergent features against which future reality can be measured' (p. 120). What is often forgotten about Bell's work is that he never intended it to be a description of the world in which he lived; rather, it was an attempt to forecast the direction in which the world might go 'in the next thirty to fifty years'. On this basis Bell's contribution to the debate remains an enormous one.

Criticisms of Bell's work

Despite, and perhaps because of, the influence of Bell's work, his conception of the post-industrial society has come under considerable scrutiny and no little criticism. Perhaps the most oft-quoted critique of Bell's work is Krishan Kumar's *Prophecy and Progress* (1978), which is worth particular consideration alongside other critiques of Bell's work. Kumar sums up his argument in the following statement:

> . . . many of the changes alleged by Bell and the others are occurring, and are important, [and as such] need not be denied. What needs scrutiny is the central aim that all these changes add up to a movement or a new social order, with a new set of problems, a new social framework within which to resolve them, and new social forces contending. (p. 199)

Kumar is concerned that work like that of Bell over-inflates the importance of the trends he describes. In this respect Kumar is especially critical of Bell's tendency simply to refer to statistics that are used to reinforce his position without recourse to the complexities that underlie those statistics. From this point of view Bell is accused of stating theoretical propositions by, for instance, pointing out that a higher proportion of gross national product is devoted to higher education and research and development in the wealthiest societies. To claim that this illustrates the increasing significance of theoretical knowledge simply serves to construct a complex argument on wafer-thin evidence which has been inappropriately contextualized. Bell's research may be practical in one sense, but in another it is simply not practical or applied *enough*. Kumar takes particular exception to Bell's discussion of the emergence of the service economy. He points out that it is theoretically insignificant to point out alone that service economies have expanded significantly in most Western capitalist societies. What is more important is how this trend relates to longer-term trends, and the crucial point as far as Kumar is concerned is that industrial societies never actually had a majority of their labour force employed in the manufacturing sector. Rises in service sector employment are indicative not of a new departure in the nature of industrial society, but rather of long-term trends characteristic of industrial societies in general. Similarly, research and development is nothing radically new. Industrialists have always invested in the future, and the fact that they are continuing to do so is no surprise. The implication of Kumar's work therefore appears to be that the trends Bell describes are simply a continuation of trends that have already been associated with industrialization. From this point of view the discussion of a post-industrial society arguably becomes little more than a definitional gimmick.

Kumar is equally as critical of the way in which Bell equates the move to a service economy with an exaggerated idea of the role of white-collar work. In other words he tends to generalize about who it is that is a white-collar worker. Not everybody working in a hospital, or a university for that matter, can be described as white-collar. Moreover, Kumar feels that Bell exaggerates the role of professionals. Indeed, Kumar goes as far as to argue that authors like Bell deploy a 'sociological sleight of hand' insofar as they do not investigate the sorts of social currents that underlie the actual redefinition of professional groups upon which they rely. The re-grading of employees may suit the employers of such workers as a means of maintaining good labour relations, but how far does it actually reflect discernible changes in the experience of the workers themselves? In effect, Bell blatantly underestimates the heterogeneity of the service sector and the impact of processes of mechanization on that sector.

Bell can also be said to exaggerate the role of theoretical knowledge in the post-industrial society. In comparison to practical research projects the proportion of gross national product directed towards theoretical knowledge is miniscule, as Swingewood (1984) also points out. You only have to consider the pressures on university academics to produce practicable relevant research to reinforce this point and to undermine Bell's somewhat blinkered interpretation of long-term historical trends. Nor is there any evidence to suggest that those in control of theoretical knowledge constitute a discrete class or wield any real political power. There is no doubt that official definitions of research are notoriously idiosyncratic, with the massive investment in war research illustrating that such research may not always be what it seems. Indeed, the political dimensions of such research may well seriously undermine Bell's contention that a new social order is emerging (Kumar, 1978, p. 225). Bare facts alone are not enough to *prove* such massive social changes. The social and political contexts in which these facts have emerged are more crucial than Daniel Bell may have been prepared to admit.

In the above context, Bell's contestation that the post-industrial society amounts to a social formation in which private property, class interests and class conflict have lost their influence is especially disconcerting. To imply that social change is such that market forces are receding to be replaced by the axial principle of theoretical knowledge is little short of preposterous. Bell saw industrial society as a goods-producing society and the post-industrial society as an information society. The latter does not necessarily preclude the former. You only have to look around you to realize that the market does still play a fundamental role in the construction of social life and perhaps a bigger role than it ever has done before (see Miles, 1998a). Has society really evolved to such an extent that the quality of life as expressed through the provision of health, education, recreation, and so on, has become its number one priority? Is the post-industrial society really an environmentally friendly society, or do the benefits of industrial enterprise continue to outweigh the needs of the planet? Can we really accept the proposition that all this entails the emergence of a new communal society that prioritizes the communal experience and that of the minority rather than that of the individual? Callinicos (1989) expresses this point especially well:

> It is easy enough to pour scorn on such announcements of the death of capitalism, which reflect the circumstances of their initial formulation, during the long economic boom of the 1950s and 1960s. It is indeed hard to take seriously the alleged shift from 'economizing' to 'sociologizing' modes in the wake of the holocaust of manufacturing jobs at the end of the 1970s and the great bull market of the mid-1980s, in the era of concessions and leveraged buyouts, of privatization and greenmail, of Ivan Boesky and Gordon Gecko. (pp. 121–2)

To be fair, as Smart (1992) points out, Bell does discuss the political limitations of such a society. On the other hand, however, he can be criticized for underestimating the broader influence of politics in a post-industrial society. According to Smart, the politics of technological innovation are absolutely essential to the emergence of a post-industrial society. Bell, however, appears to assume that technological innovation has a life of its own. It simply does not.

Perhaps the most vehement criticism of Bell's work is to be found in Callinicos's rather controversial book *Against Postmodernism* (1989), which I have referred to above, and in which he argues that Bell reads social change off technological change. That he is, in effect, a technological determinist who idealizes the beneficial impact that technological innovation can have on society as a whole. Callinicos also suggests that the emergence of a post-industrial society has, in fact, had profoundly negative implications: the fact that wages are on average 40 to 50 per cent lower in the service industries than they are in manufacturing being of particular concern. Callinicos's worry is that it is the entrepreneurs and those with financial assets who benefit from the so-called 'post-industrial' society, and, as such, social change simply reinvigorates the inequalities associated with industrial society. Kumar similarly argues that there is overwhelming evidence to refute the suggestion that the post-industrial society amounts to a radical new social order. Post-industrial society, if it can be said to exist, which is itself doubtful, is from this point of view simply a continuation of industrial society:

> Were Marx or Tocqueville, Weber or Durkheim, to return today what might give them cause for despondency would not be the insufficiency of

their original analysis, but its continuing relevance. The surprise might be that the tendencies they observed had been of such long duration – they had been unduly optimistic about the capacity of industrial society to initiate radically new patterns of social development. (Kumar, 1978, p. 231)

The radical transformation of industrial society is, as far as critics such as Kumar are concerned, an illusion. Indeed, as Rose (1991) points out, it might be argued that, far from highlighting the emergence of a radical new type of society, Bell simply draws attention to an *extension* of industrial society. Ironically, a debate that continues to fascinate those commentators seeking to understand transitions from a modern to a post-modern world also preoccupies those who prefer to think about the 'transformation' from an industrial to a post-industrial society. Could the problem here be that social theorists are simply predisposed to think about *radical* changes in the social world; that, in effect, social theorists are seduced by the melodrama of their subject matter, or will at least look for that melodrama where it does not, in fact, exist?

Far from representing a radical transformation of industrial society, the sorts of changes Bell describes therefore apparently had their origins in the nineteenth century. Rose (1991) goes as far as to suggest that the axial principle of Bell's post-industrial society can be identified in the work of nineteenth-century thinkers such as Babbage and Saint-Simon. Perhaps the post-industrial society thesis does have surface validity – it appears to speak to observable aspects of social and economic change largely associated with globalization (see Chapter 8) – but even the industries in which global tendencies are taking hold are arguably more about continuity than they are about change. The extent to which new technologies fundamentally alter our lives is debatable. How important is the internet, for instance? Who is to say that ultimately it might prove more controlling than it is enabling? Indeed, much of Bell's work on the post-industrial society, notably as regards the spread of scientific rationality, is ironically an extension of trends identified by Weber in his discussion of rationalization (Kumar, 1978, p. 235).

We can thank the post-industrialists for questioning the whole history of industrialization and industrialism. The achievement of theorists such as Bell has been to direct us to the dramatically accelerating tendencies of industrialism, and for that, at least, argues Kumar, we should be grateful. Maybe the oft-touted criticism that the trends Bell describes are simply characteristic of the United States of America at that point in history are more comfortably directed at Bell's critics than him himself. Of course, Bell focuses on the American example, and to dismiss him on that basis is somewhat disingenuous. Bell readily acknowledged that his work was 'a fiction', a necessarily generalized analysis of what could be rather than what actually *is*.

The actual nitty gritty of Daniel Bell's theory of the post-industrial society has had limited staying power. The detail of his work has largely been discredited. The extent to which such ideas really illuminate our understanding of contemporary social life beyond the general insights provided by its technological dimension is questionable. Of all the criticisms of Bell's work, his tendency to generalize without recourse to the social contexts in which the patterns he describes operate is potentially the most damaging. Bell envisaged a world of radical change. Some aspects of that vision were realized, but overall Bell's conception of a highly stable, affluent and communal society was a wildly optimisitc and in many ways naïve one. It is perhaps only in its broadest sense that the notion of the post-industrial society is truly relevant. Indeed, by the 1980s debates as to the nature of post-industrial society appeared to have run their course, not necessarily because the argument was not holding water, but more pointedly as a reflection of a trend towards theoretical approaches that became far more concerned with actually curtailing the excesses of industrial capitalism, than with celebrating them (see Kumar, 1995). In particular, concern about the perishability of the earth began to come to the forefront of theoretical approaches to social change as a mood of crisis replaced the optimism of the 1960s and early 1970s. Bell's legacy to social theory has, however, been a significant one, insofar as it has encouraged further debate along the lines that he had originally intended. I will now go on to outline a number of approaches to social change, all of which have some form of a debt to pay to the debate which was beginning to surround the post-industrial society thesis.

Beyond Daniel Bell

Alain Touraine

There is a tendency to equate post-industrial society theory solely with the work of Daniel Bell. This is a mistake. A variety of authors, including Seymour M. Lipset (1980) and Alain Touraine (1974), have attempted to come to terms with the impact of social change on industrial societies. They may not all have used the same terminology or used the same definitions as Bell, but they were attempting to come to terms with broadly similar aspects of social change. The fact that many of those theorists are of a left-wing persuasion, in contrast to Bell, is of particular interest, and for this reason it might well be worth contrasting Bell's work with that of Alain Touraine who originally published his book *The Post-Industrial Society* in French in 1969 (English edition 1974), and is perhaps the second most prominent of the post-industrial society theorists. Touraine described the post-industrial society as a 'programmed society' in which economic decisions and struggles no longer possess 'either the autonomy or the central importance they had in an earlier society which was defined by the effort to accumulate and anticipate profits from directly productive work' (pp. 4–5). Touraine acknowledged that this represented a paradoxical statement in light of the fact that the society he was mapping was apparently more driven by economic growth than it ever had been before. But the irony as far as Touraine was concerned was that the individualization of private life, the increase in social and geographic mobility, the diffusion of information and propaganda and broadened political participation meant that it was simply no longer possible for economic mechanisms to be at the centre of social life. Like Bell, Touraine identified knowledge as being at the centre of the new society whilst describing 'technocratic power' as dominant. However, in some respects Touraine's analysis is a more overtly and radical political one, insofar as where Bell sees the promise of greater social integration and institutional harmony, Touraine argues that the technocratic society is controlling and inhibiting. As Rose (1991) notes, Touraine's vision of a post-industrial society is a broadly negative one (see also Kumar, 1978).

From Touraine's point of view, the post-industrial society is dominated by bureaucrats and technology. A vision of the emergence of a rational society, Touraine's theory provides an illustration of how social theorists with differing perspectives on the same phenomena can come up with such divergent conclusions. On the other hand, it could be argued that Touraine's work serves to highlight the achievement of Bell's contribution. In this context, Kumar (1978) discusses the manipulative potential of the technocratic society. He also discusses Touraine's conception of the conflict between professionals and students, who uphold the humanist values of a liberal education alongside their ambitious peers controlling the technocratic apparatus in the name of economic advance. Kumar feels that this analysis is essentially flawed and in many ways Touraine's is indeed the less complete of the two theories. Above all, Touraine fails to come to terms with the mechanisms that create this wedge between the educated classes, to the extent that his work almost has the air of a radical interpretation for radicalism's sake. Of equal concern is the fact that the actual term 'post-industrial society' appears only in Touraine's title, as Waters (1996) points out. In the remainder of his book Touraine discusses the emergence of a 'programmed society', thereby inviting the criticism that his title, much like his politics, is itself opportunistic in nature, insofar as it reflects the intellectual climate of the time, as much as the characteristics of the society which he attempts to describe.

Bell and Touraine's work do not acknowledge each other and as such it would be particularly misleading to imply that Bell precipitated a line of thought which Touraine followed, or vice versa. Rather, they were contemporaries following similar lines of inquiry according to the particular character of social change that appeared to be occurring at the time. However, it is also important to note that the extent of the influence of Bell's work in particular stretches far beyond work that was directly concerned with a particular notion of the 'post-industrial society', and certainly well beyond the 1970s.

Jerald Hage and Charles H. Powers

Two authors who appear to have taken on board the intention of Bell's work while avoiding the temptation to assume that Bell was attempting to present a detailed description of all advanced societies are Hage and Powers, who look specifically at the meaning of the post-industrial 'transformation' for work roles and personal relationships. Hage and Powers (1992) admit that the effect of the post-industrial order is somewhat patchy, but argue that the changing nature of knowledge and technology is having a profound impact on the nature of face-to-face relationships, and, perhaps more interestingly, on the nature of the social self. In other words, Hage and Powers argue that the impact of knowledge and technology is most profound in the context of the family and the workplace. Adopting a symbolic interactionist perspective, they see the post-industrial society as having some very positive implications, notably in levelling hierarchical distinctions, the freeing up of roles in the workplace and the increasingly creative and flexible nature of the work experience. Indeed, Hage and Powers suggest we are entering an age of 'complexification', which is characterized, above all, by the creation of increasingly creative occupational specialities. In short, in a post-industrial society, knowledge has transformed the workplace to such an extent that individuals are increasingly fulfilled in an arena of their lives that may well have been highly rationalized and controlled in the past (see also Chapter 6).

The post-industrial family, meanwhile, is far more responsive to the needs of its members to the extent that bringing up children is apparently a more creative task than it may have been in the past, whilst gender roles in the home are less rigid. The contemporary family, from this point of view, is helping to redefine social roles from the ground up. What therefore emerges is what Hage and Powers describe as a 'complex self'. Whereas in industrial society industrial selves feel most comfortable in situations where there is no doubt about who the self is and how he or she relates to others and their feedback, this is in contrast to a post-industrial society in which individuals are more flexible, more likely to be able to look at situations from different points of view, and are therefore more able to deal with circumstances in creative and co-operative ways. A complex self has the capability to switch identities when the need arises and to handle change with confidence.

Hage and Powers (1992) argue that the impact of industrial change is far more subtle than we may have imagined, and that, in turn, this subtlety calls for a new sociological research agenda. The roles we adopt in contemporary society have apparently been fundamentally redefined, and the sociological agenda should reflect this redefinition. Our lives are less routinized than they may have been in the past, our roles are more personalized and diversified than previously, and,

> although we are coming into contact with a greater number of different positions, those positions are generally occupied by fewer people at any given time, so that our relationships develop more personal orientation. Over time role occupants come to be seen less as role automatons and more as unique people. (p. 197)

On the down-side, these developments have resulted in more role conflict because traditional role scripts are simply less tenable than they were in the past. But despite such conflict, Hage and Powers come to the somewhat surprising conclusion that human agency is on the increase. People apparently have more control over the direction of their lives:

> The implication is that the locus of social control has moved closer to the individual. Tradition and authority have less to do with shaping people's lives; they exert less control now than ever before. But anarchy has not resulted, because a new form of social control is taking the place of tradition. This new social control is to be found in interpersonal understanding and commitment. That is why we must consider the ways in which role relationships, and also interaction, are being transformed as we enter the post-industrial era. (p. 199)

Hage and Powers do not expect all this to lead to a trouble-free existence and they do recognize that there are all sorts of challenges facing the post-industrial world. But they do feel that society is being transformed from the ground up. Society, as far as they are concerned, is being reconstituted and will continue to be reconstituted in subtler ways than even Daniel Bell could have imagined in the early

1970s. Broadly speaking, Hage and Powers can therefore be said to have extended some of Bell's original ideas whilst broadening their relevance to the actual playing out of social roles. The degree to which the overt optimism of this work, like that of Bell, is justified remains, however, highly debatable.

Post-Fordism

A further example of the reinterpretation of social change that has occurred in recent years is that which surrounds the so-called emergence of 'post-Fordism' (see Amin, 1994). Although not directly related to the original work of the post-industrialists, post-Fordist theory illustrates the broader influence of Bell and others' approach to social theory. As Hall (1989) points out, post-Fordism is in some senses a broader term than that of post-industrialism. It suggests a whole new epoch, 'distinct from the era of mass production, with its standardised products, concentrations of capital and its "Taylorist" forms of work organisation and discipline' (p. 117). The essence of the debate surrounding post-Fordism, as Murray (1989) points out, is that in recent decades we have witnessed a transition from a Fordist to a post-Fordist economy, that whilst the industrial revolution saw forms of employment move from the farm to the factory, post-Fordism saw the move from the factory to the office and the shop. Clearly then, post-Fordist arguments have a lot in common with those ideas associated with the post-industrial society.

Before it is possible to come to terms with what constitutes post-Fordism, it is important to clarify what we mean by Fordism, a word which is derived from the principles developed by the great American industrialist Henry Ford, who is often credited, through his work with the creation of the car assembly line, with the development of the modern mass production system. Fordism, then, is based on principles of size, uniformity, predictability, but also on the development of maintainable markets. Proponents of post-Fordism, however, argue that all this is in the past and that production and work have been fundamentally reorganized, most markedly in the aftermath of the 1973 oil crisis and the rise of Japanese industry. The shift from Fordism to post-Fordism could arguably be described as a shift from industrial homogeneity to post-industrial heterogeneity. Post-Fordism is apparently constituted by a flexible production process, backed up by an equally flexible workforce, to the extent that the consumer is a far more powerful player in the production process than he or she would have been in the past, precisely because the producer is more able to respond rapidly to his or her requirements. Knowledge plays a key role in this process insofar as the producer needs to respond to the increasingly sophisticated and technical requirements of the consumer. New technology plays a key role in obtaining the information that makes this possible. But for authors like Murray (1989) and Lee (1993) post-Fordism amounts to more than a straightforward change in economic practice,

> Post-Fordism here signals the rise of a new mode of social organisation generally; it marks the maturation of new forms of 'post-industrial' labour (primarily service and white-collar work), whilst marking the beginning of the end for the traditional blue-collar workforce and the older class system to which it was wedded. At the core of these changes lie quite massive technological innovations to the production processes. These not only transform the nature of modern working practices and industrial relations, but also mark the onset of new forms in the construction, surveillance and interpretation of markets and consumption (and all of the social, cultural and aesthetic implications that these changes entail). (Lee, 1993, p. 110)

Post-Fordism is in effect a whole new economic era distinct from mass production and characterized by information technology, flexibility, design, the rise of the multinationals and the globalization of financial markets (see Lee, 1993).

Like 'post-industrial society' before it, the notion of 'post-Fordism' is hotly contested. Callinicos (1989), who can always be relied upon for a critical comment, describes this approach as 'almost caricatured' and as amounting to 'mind-numbing reductionism' (p. 135), due to a tendency to collapse the political and social change into the economic base:

> Nevertheless, analyses of . . . 'post-Fordism' do at least have the merit of seeking to show how systematic changes in the capitalist economy justify us in speaking of a distinctively postmodern era; furthermore, these accounts are supported empirically, at least to the extent that they refer to transformations which have actually occurred. The difficulty is that they grossly exaggerate the extent of the changes involved, and fail to theorize them properly. (Callinicos, 1989, p. 135)

The same might also be said of Piore and Sabel's work, which emerges out of a similar tradition.

Michael Piore, Charles Sabel and the 'second industrial divide'

In describing similar trends, Piore and Sabel (1984) identify an epochal shift in economic organization, brought about by the arrival of what they call 'flexible specialization', which itself can be described as being at the core of post-Fordism (see Lee, 1993, p. 109). They refer to a 'second industrial divide'. That is, they identify the emergence of a smaller multi-skilled flexible workforce who work not on the mass-produced goods of Fordism, but on small-batch production runs. Below them is a periphery workforce who are low-paid, temporary, and often part-time and drawn from socially excluded groups. Piore and Sabel agree that electronic communication and information technology play a crucial role in ensuring a rapidly responsive economic environment. Capitalism has in effect developed new ways to meet the growing demand for more differentiated products. This, then, is a two-way process in which markets appear to be increasingly differentiated, as do the people who consume them. Style and quality appear to supersede uniformity as the consumer's number one priority. In this sense, changes in the nature of the economy have equally significant implications for the nature of people's lifestyles. Economic change might well be said to have given people more control over their own lives. In other words, the economy is less of a top-down process: the consumer apparently has more of a say in what form that economy takes. The economy has become more cultural and more symbolic in nature. The patterns which Piore and Sabel are describing can certainly be said to be broadly in line with some of Daniel Bell's forecasts, although they pay more attention to the cultural and symbolic aspects of the economy than did Bell in his original work.

Scott Lash, John Urry and disorganized capitalism

Authors like Murray (1989) and Piore and Sabel (1984) have indeed been criticized for coming to some of the same misleading conclusions as the post-industrialists, particularly as far as exaggerating the expansion of the service class is concerned (see Lee, 1993, p. 116). Having said that, the fact that many authors have turned to discussions of post-Fordism and flexible specialization should not imply that the notion of post-industrialism has itself died a death. In their book *Economies of Signs and Space* (1994), Lash and Urry go as far as to argue that knowledge does play a key role in the production process and that in this context 'flexible production is always necessarily reflexive production, [and] . . . post-Fordism must always be post-industrialism' (p. 112). In this their second book together, Lash and Urry build upon their previous work (1987), which charted the transition from the concentrated regulated national markets of organized capitalism, with their highly bureaucratic and hierarchical social system, to disorganized capitalism, which is characterized by the globalization of markets and by centralized bureaucracy and power:

> The world of a 'disorganized capitalism' is one in which the 'fixed, fast-frozen relations' of organized capitalist relations have been swept away. Societies are being transformed from above, from below, and from within. All that is solid about organized capitalism, class, industry, cities, collectivity, nation-state, even the world, melts into air. (Lash and Urry, 1987, pp. 312–13)

In this context, Lash and Urry appear to be identifying a new phase of capitalist development; a systematic process of restructuring in the face of a new set of economic circumstances and a new type of economic actor who appears to mirror the actor Hage and Powers (1992) identified above. Disorganized capitalism disorganizes everything; nothing is fixed, given and certain, while everything rests upon greater knowledge and information, on institutionalized reflexivity. In effect, people are increasingly knowledgeable about how very little they actually know about the capitalist structures that surround them. All this amounts to a complex, dare we say it, 'post-industrial' society which is characterized by ever-new forms of information, knowledge and aesthetic taste.

Devoting a chapter to 'post-industrial spaces', Lash and Urry (1994) argue that the economy is increasingly based upon the delivery of the provision of services to both individuals and organizations, and most importantly that these services are increasingly design-intensive and/or semiotic. What is more, they are geographically specific. Post-industrialism therefore has significant implications for the nature of social space. According to Lash and Urry, some localities are indeed dominated by service industries: the tourism industry being a particularly important example. Meanwhile, Lash and Urry consider Sassen's (1991) efforts in discussing the relationship between Bell's concept of a hierarchy in the growth of services and an improved quality of life. More specifically, Sassen's concern is the apparent move towards services at the top of the hierarchy such as psychotherapy, windsurfing lessons and exotic restaurants, all of which have an increased symbolic content. Changes in tourism away from 'sun, sea and sex' towards a model of cultural diversity and contrast best illustrate such a change (Lash and Urry, 1994, p. 221). In this context, Lash and Urry (1994) appear to be agreeing with some of the broader aspects of post-industrialism, notably insofar as they actively intervene in class-derived aspects of space

> We thus live in increasingly individuated and symbol-saturated societies, in which the advanced-services middle class plays an increasing role in the

accumulation process. This class assumes a critical mass in the present restructuration: as symbol-producing producers and as consumers of processed symbols working and living in certain towns and cities. To talk of services is to talk of information and symbol and of the increasing importance of both within many diverse kinds of industrial space. (p. 222)

In short, although Lash and Urry far from unconditionally accept that we live in a post-industrial society, they do accept that there are examples, however geographically patchy, of post-industrial spaces. The role of symbolic forms of consumption is particularly significant in this process, as I will argue in Chapter 4, and could well be said to represent a key development in sociological conceptions of the post-industrial.

Conclusions

In considering the above theories, you could well argue that the sorts of projections made by the post-industrialists, and by Daniel Bell in particular, have been realized, but simply not in as fundamental or complete a form as may have been anticipated. Ultimately, as Lee (1993) argues, the idea that the mass production/mass consumption economy, which dominated the post-war years, up until its rapid decline at the end of the twentieth century, has disappeared completely does not stand up to empirical scrutiny. Nor, indeed, does the suggestion that social life has equally radically been transformed. Approaches to socio-economic changes are often, and at least to some extent, technologically determinist. Their proponents are apparently all too easily seduced by the appeal of technological transformation, at the expense of a grounded analysis of the social and cultural ways in which such changes alter the reality of everyday life. More recent approaches have been more concerned with the manifestation of industrial change in a cultural context. In short, there may be evidence of 'post-industrial' change, but that change is at best erratic and at worst peripheral. But the main point to remember here is that the diverse group of authors discussed above, although disagreeing about the detail of their analyses, do agree that the society in which we live is undergoing considerable social and economic change. The real debate surrounds how radical that change is and whether or not it constitutes a whole new kind of society. Daniel Bell played his not insignificant part in ensuring that this debate remained on the sociological agenda.

In one sense, any social theory is successful if it provokes discussion and debate. As far as the post-industrial society thesis is concerned, there is no doubt that contemporary theory has taken on

Bell's legacy. Perhaps this legacy is most clearly in evidence in the context of current theoretical debates such as those discussed above, but perhaps most presciently in the context of surrounding post-modernity (see Chapter 5). Many authors have pointed out the links between the post-industrial society thesis and broader and less technologically deterministic debates over post-modernism. Wagner (1994) even suggests that the sociology of post-modernity is

> the legitimate heir to the sociology of post-industrial society – so much so that one could see the promoters of the former as the children revolting against the realism and complacency of their parents, the promoters of the latter. In many respects, postmodernists endorse the theorems of postindustrialists and radicalize them. (p. 149)

The link between post-industrialism and post-modernism is undoubtedly a real one. Commenting on the above, Kumar (1995) goes as far as to describe post-modernism as 'the culture of post-industrial society', while authors such as Hollinger (1994) have discussed the link between the work of the post-industrialists and that of Jean-François Lyotard (1984), who discusses the emergence of a post-industrial age and the 'computerization of society' alongside that of a post-modern culture (Best and Kellner, 1991). Perhaps the crucial point about Lyotard's analysis is that although he recognizes the significance of scientific knowledge, he also recognizes that scientific knowledge is only really of value if it is economically viable. In this respect Lyotard gives Bell's contribution a realistic edge, falling short of claiming that the world which he describes is somehow 'post-capitalist'. This latter point is an important one. Bell's work represents a brave effort to come to terms with and predict the nature of social change. The problem may be that social change is *un*predictable and that any attempt to predict social change is quite possibly doomed. Social change is problematic, and, as such so is the post-industrial thesis. This argument is given some credence by Lee (1993):

> . . . it may be difficult to assemble any clear or coherent picture of the nature of the changes taking place to capitalism as we approach the end of the century. When seen in their totality, the sum of recent developments to labour and protection often seem unconnected and, in many instances, even contradictory. They are far from logical pieces in a smooth, unproblematical process of economic transition. (p. 117)

The danger is that social theorists often appear to be tempted into making rather crass generalizations about nothing more than macro-symptoms of economic change that may not have as fundamental social and cultural implications as they might hope. Indeed, although 'there has certainly been a sea-change in the surface appearance of capitalism since 1973 . . . the underlying logic of capitalist accumulation and its crisis tendencies remain the same' (Harvey, 1989, p. 189). But this does not mean that we should dispense with social forecasting or with social theory in general, because through the ambitions of social theory we can begin to come to terms with the complexity of the social world. Social theory cannot provide all the answers and is quite often manifestly misleading, but it also raises important questions and debates that social theorists need actively to address.

In assessing the contribution that post-industrial society has made to social theory it may well therefore be reasonable to suggest that Alex Callinicos is at least partially correct. The detail associated with the post-industrial society is indeed a nonsense. Only as a general facilitative concept is the notion of post-industrial society of any real use, as the following definition provided by Block (1990) implies:

> 'Post-industrial society' is the historical period that begins when the concept of industrial society ceases to provide an adequate account of actual social development. This definition is meant to locate the key change as occurring at the level of ideas and understanding – that is, our loss of a persuasive master concept for making sense of our own society. (p. 11)

We should certainly be wary of accepting the proposition that the society in which we live represents such a radical break with industrial society that it amounts to some form of an epochal shift. On the other hand, to dismiss completely what is intended as a piece of social forecasting on the basis that Bell's vision never completely matched the eventual reality is entirely unfair. It is equivalent to blaming the weather forecaster for the fact that the weather is not quite as sunny as he or she had predicted. Bell's vision may not have been an accurate one, but it encourages the reader to challenge his or her own perceptions of contemporary society. Bell's work illustrates the unpredictability of social change and, perhaps above all, the fact that we do live in what is an eminently rational society that may not always serve the needs of the human beings who constitute it. In effect, then, the real benefit of post-industrial society theory is the way in which it leads us to ask: 'If we do not live in a post-industrial society, then what do we live in?' Daniel Bell cannot answer that question, but at least he forces us, as social theorists, to consider and address it. Many students forget that social theory is not written on tablets of stone. Social theorists, believe it or not, are human beings and their theories are not always entirely accurate. This is not such a bad thing. If Daniel Bell's ideas and those ideas associated with the post-industrial society in general had been 'proven' to be correct, then perhaps his work would not have been as stimulating or as challenging as it has actually proven to be. Bell *is* a great social theorist and a great social forecaster; the implications of globalization, for instance, represented an important theme of his work long before it was parachuted into the theoretical mainstream (see Chapter 8). But his lasting achievement and the real legacy of the post-industrial society thesis is that, however misguided its detail, it had a key influence on the development of social theory throughout the remainder of the twentieth century.

Recommended reading

Daniel Bell (1973) *The Coming of Post-Industrial Society: A Venture in Social Forecasting*, New York: Basic Books. A classic, if flawed, treatise on the ongoing transition to a post-industrial society.

Krishan Kumar (1978) *Prophecy and Progress: The Sociology of Industrial and Post-Industrial Society*, London: Allen Lane. The most comprehensive and insightful critique of Bell's work on post-industrial society. A fine illustration of how social theory creates debates far more than it resolves them. And rightly so.

Scott Lash and John Urry (1987) *The End of Organized Capitalism*, Cambridge: Polity. A complex discussion of contemporary changes in capitalism which will help to contextualize how debates concerning the post-industrial society have developed since Bell's original contribution.

Malcolm Waters (1996) *Daniel Bell*, London: Routledge. A useful and revealing discussion of Bell's life work which illustrates the extent of his contribution to the breadth of social theory and sociological knowledge in general.

CHAPTER 4

A CONSUMER SOCIETY?*

Consumption clearly plays an important role in the everyday construction of social life. The recent and rapid growth of consumption as an arena of considerable concern to social theorists is testament to that fact. Traditionally consumption has not been a central concern of social theorists. In recent decades this situation has markedly changed to the extent that consumption appears to be one of the fastest expanding areas of theoretical advance and discussion. This trend is of particular interest when you consider the political changes that accompany the social change for which theorists are attempting to account. Indeed, the changes we associate with a consumer society quite clearly have a massive impact on the 'real' world. It could indeed be argued that if the society in which we live is anything it is a *consumer* society.

A good place to begin in understanding the significance of the above point would be to consider what we actually mean when we talk about consumption. There is a considerable danger that we assume we know what we are talking about precisely because consumption is part and parcel of our everyday lives. We take the consumer society for granted. As I have noted elsewhere (Miles, 1998a), it is therefore especially important that we avoid confusing the notions of 'consumption' and 'consumerism'. Campbell (1995) describes consumption as 'the selection, purchase, use, maintenance, repair and disposal of any product or service' (p. 102), but what is of more significance from a sociological point of view, as Campbell points out (see also Lee, 1993), is how, historically, consumption came to take on some form of a 'magical' quality. How is it that consumption came to be such an important aspect of our everyday lives? In this sense consumption is a thoroughly cultural phenomenon. Consumer goods are 'key instruments for the reproduction, representation, and manipulation of their culture' (McCracken, 1990, p. xi). Social theorists are therefore concerned about more than the simple act of purchase involved in consumption, also the sorts of influences, experiences and social relationships that surround that process. The notion of consumerism is arguably concerned with the hidden properties of consumption, and, in particular, the ideological dimensions of a consumer society. The study of consumerism is therefore focused, or at least should be focused, on the way in which 'the ubiquitous nature of consumption is reconstructed on a day-to-day basis' (Miles, 1998a, p. 4). A useful way of summarizing the perspectives sociologists have begun to take on consumption in recent decades is perhaps through the following quotation:

> Consumption embodies the basic social and cultural processes that characterize the transition, in some countries, from an industrial to a service economy. Consumption abstracts cultural and financial value from material production; it plays an integral role in the internationalization of investments and production, and it represents a significant shift in the derivation of social meaning from the public world of production to a more private world of buying, using and imagining – rather than making – goods. (Zukin, 1990, p. 53)

Consumption is part of the fabric of everyday life. It is for this very reason that it is so important. In Chapter 2, I discussed the work of the Frankfurt School, which criticized the cultural industries as providing the arena, in the form of popular culture, in which capitalism could extend its control over the masses. The question of consumption raises similar issues and it does so because at one and the same time it appears liberating and yet constraining. It is in this sense that consumption is so important to the social theorist. It represents a key arena of social life in which the tensions of structure and agency are played out on an everyday basis.

It might well be argued that we live in a society of opportunity: in a post-modern world where the ability to consume appears to be everything. There certainly appears to be more and more choice available to the consumer. The world of consumption appears to be growing every day. But the question remains: does consumption really provide the consumer what he or she wants, or is it, in actual fact, a socially divisive force that simply serves to keep consumers in their place?

Consumption in classical social theory

Before I consider the above issues I want to outline briefly the role which consumption has traditionally played within the realm of social theory. This should help us come to terms with the degree of social change that appears to have occurred in recent years and how social theorists have had to respond to such changes. Until recent decades social theorists actually paid very little attention to the question of consumption and more often than not simply saw consumption as a by-product of production, which itself was seen to have a far more fundamental influence on the character of social life.

The way in which social theory has tended to treat consumption is perhaps best illustrated in the work of Karl Marx (1990). Clearly, Marx, above all, prioritizes the impact of production and the relationship with the means of production as the key determinant of social structures and relationships. However, this is not to say that consumption, and more specifically the commodity, doesn't play an important role in his work. The main thing to remember is that Marx approached consumption from a somewhat different perspective to a contemporary social theorist. In other words, he saw the commodity, first and foremost, as something to be sold and exchanged on the marketplace. It therefore had a role in determining your social position, but that position was not, from Marx's point of view, determined by how you actively engaged with consumer goods. Marx did argue, however, that the commodity symbolized the power of capitalism, because the power structures that lay behind the commodity underpinned capitalism as a whole. The commodity therefore plays a fundamental role in relating the individual to the capitalist system. It promotes a sense of false consciousness that camouflages the realities of alienation. Commodification, the process by which everything is valued according to its value in the system of exchange, creates a world in which a person's priorities become subject to the requirements of the market. Marx therefore bemoans a situation in which the worker is alienated by the fact he or she no longer has ownership of the commodity he or she helps to produce. The worker is a bit-part player who no longer uses the products of his or her own labour. He or she is, in effect, dehumanized. Marx (2000) therefore describes the fetishism of the commodity. By this, Marx means that the commodity has a mystical quality: to the extent that objects become external to the self, and are therefore ascribed a significance beyond their use-value. The commodity is treated with an awe and reverence previously reserved for religion. But even in this analysis, for Marx, the fetishism of the commodity is only a by-product of independent labour:

> The fetishism of the world of commodities arises from the peculiar social character of the labour which produces them. . . . Objects of utility become commodities only because they are the products of labour of private individuals who work independently of each other. . . . Since the producers do not come into social contact until they exchange the products of their labour, the specific social characteristics of their private labours appear only within this exchange. (Marx, 2000, pp. 11–12)

Marx was certainly accurate insofar as there can be no doubt that the process of commodification has reached new extremes. Culture has been commodified, if anything, to a greater degree than he could ever have envisaged. Let's briefly consider an example of a particular realm of sociology within which this can certainly be said to be the case.

Consuming sport

I have argued elsewhere that sport is perhaps the single area of social life to have been most profoundly altered in recent years by the everyday impact of consumption (Miles, 1998a). In the last fifty years football, in particular, has been completely transformed as a spectator sport. More recently the last ten years or so have seen a massive injection of money into the game. The war over television rights to Premiership games has been especially important in this regard. The impact of the European Champions League on the way in which football is consumed has also been profound. The end product of all this is that the game is top-heavy with money and that only very few top clubs can afford to buy the top players. Meanwhile, those clubs lower down the leagues are less and less likely to be able to compete in such a competitive market. Any young players in which they invest are more than likely to be poached by the bigger clubs who can afford to pay higher wages, whilst offering a big stage on which the player concerned can perform. Meanwhile, those big clubs having to pay thousands of pounds per week to attract the best players may well become increasingly distanced from the grass-roots supporter. In February 2000, for instance, a group of Newcastle United season ticket holders were taking the club to the High Court after the club decided it would force the fans to move from their preferred seats in order that the club could build corporate facilities. Despite a 15,000-strong waiting list for Newcastle United season tickets, the club's priorities appear to lie elsewhere (Chaudhary, 2000). The supporters lost their case and were left with the prospect of having to raise £10,000 to fund an appeal.

The above trends reflect an ongoing process where sport as a participatory experience becomes superseded by sport as a spectator event. Nowadays, people's experience of sport is increasingly third-hand, through the media in general and television in particular. Clubs are sponsored to the tune of millions of pounds while top manufacturers compete for the honour of producing replica football kits. From a Marxist point of view, then, the commodification of sport might not always work in the interests of the consumer. Hunter Davies' (1995) feelings about the state of football are especially pertinent in this respect:

> Football should not be run like a supermarket, or Alton Towers, a Take That concert or a raincoat factory. Football is not about profit and loss. It is

about glory and excitement, about loyalty and legends, about local identity and family history, about skills and talents, none of which can be computed on balance sheets. Football doesn't have a product. Every year United fans have their ashes scattered on the turf at Old Trafford. How often do you see that happening at Tesco's? (p. 2)

Looking at what Davies says from a more Marxist perspective, the above trends promote a situation in which modern consumers of sport are generally more and more physically *passive*. They watch sport, often from the comfort of their own living rooms, but rarely participate in it. They are, in effect, mentally active, yet physically *passive*. In this sense, it could be argued that sport plays an active role in camouflaging the excesses of consumer culture by providing a form of escape from the everyday tensions of capitalist exploitation whilst reinforcing the very excesses that this exploitation propagates. In other words, consumer capitalism promotes accumulation and in the process simultaneously legitimizes itself. Sport appears to have become nothing more than a vehicle for profit; a vehicle symbolized most graphically in the shape of the global money-making machine which is Manchester United, a club who, in the 1999–2000 season, pulled out of the FA Cup due, apparently, to two primary factors: (a) the commercial opportunities involved in partaking in the World Club Championship; and (b) the financial benefits to be reaped from promoting England's case to host the 2006 World Cup (and the pressure put on Manchester United from the Football Association in this respect). But in this equation the desire of the actual fan always appears to be forgotten. The key point here, as noted by Alex Flynn, is that 'There is a difference between a fan and a customer. A fan cannot take his business elsewhere' (quoted in Connett and Tomas, 1996, p. 10). In the spring of 2000, Manchester United's stock market value reached a staggering £1 billion. As I write they are one of the richest sporting clubs in the entire world. But the question remains: who come first? Their share-holders or their fans? It could well be too much of a simplification to describe the commodification of sport as a process that imparts 'false consciousness' on the masses. Consumers are indeed at least partly aware of the ideological parameters within which sport operates. But ultimately commodification may well be more in the interests of those who control sport than those who watch and consume it. Sport clearly provides a useful example of how culture itself is becoming increasingly commodified. In short, virtually nothing is free from the economic imperative of exchange. If anything, as a product of his own time Marx may well have under-estimated the impact of commodification and the extent to which it would spread. You may even go as far as to argue that com-modification is so well entrenched and appears to offer consumers so much that there appears little chance of an alternative, and least of all a revolution.

The emergence of a consumer society

The evidence seems to suggest that, as time went by, the sorts of issues that Marx raised were actually becoming increasingly pertinent to the underlying nature of social change. But Marx was not the only classical theorist who paid at least some attention, however indirect, to questions of consumption. The work of Thorsten Veblen, *The Theory of the Leisure Class* (1899), for instance, although originally written around the turn of the twentieth century, is a remarkably biting analysis of aspirational forms of consumption that at times seems as relevant today as it was just over a hundred years ago. If anything, the lack of any sustained sociology of consumption, at least until the 1980s, illustrates the value of Veblen's contribution. His work starts from the premise that the value of goods springs not from their inherent material qualities but from their role as symbols which actively serve to mediate social relationships. He was therefore specifically concerned with the consumption patterns of the *nouveaux riches* of the late nineteenth century. In this context, Veblen described the emergence of a 'new leisure class' who were conscious that their money was indeed new and that they needed to take advantage of any means possible to accrue the status that the money they had had to work for had not been able to give them. Consumption therefore provided the canvas upon which the new lesiure class could reaffirm their social pretensions:

> The means of communication and the mobility of the population now expose the individual to the observation of many other persons who have no other means of judging of his reputability than the display of goods (and perhaps of breeding) which he is able to make while he is under their direct observation. (Veblen, 1899, pp. 53–4)

Veblen therefore highlighted the way in which social status appeared to be delineated by conspicuous forms of consumption. This, then, is a trickle-down theory of consumption within which the lessons of fashion are taught by those higher up the social hierarchy and in which those lower down that hierarchy are constantly catching up. But the important point here then is that consumption clearly is not simply about exchange on the market. It has an important social and cultural role as well as an economic one. People use consumption as a language in its own right, as a means of establishing social markers. Consumption is not simply about fulfilling some form of an intrinsic need; it's about traversing social wants and desires. This is not to say that Veblen saw consumption as inherently liberating. Far from it. Conspicuous consumption actively encouraged competition and social isolation. But it also actively encouraged more consumption. And herein lies the real preoccupation for the social theorist: the way in which the process of consumption appears to balance the needs and wants of the individual against the needs and wants of the social system of which he or she is a part. Veblen was concerned with the wasteful nature of consumption and the way in which it undermined the efficiency of production and, in turn, the work ethic.

Veblen's work has been much criticized, most notably for constituting an overly rigid status-driven analysis of consumption which underestimates its symbolic complexities (Campbell, 1995). In particular, Campbell is concerned that individuals do not take all cues about appropriate forms of behaviour from one group and that, historically at least, consumers have come to adopt a wider variety of influences on what and why they consume from day to day. Consumption is therefore at least potentially innovative at all points in the social hierarchy and not necessarily just at the top. This argument has recently preoccupied many theorists concerned with charting the emergence of the consumer society.

Veblen realized that consumption was not simply an inconsequential by-product of production. However, you could say that his contribution to debates over consumption did not really come into its own until eighty years after he originally published *The Theory of the Leisure Class*. It wasn't until around this time that a sociology of consumption emerged in its own right, as a response to radical social and political change, perhaps symbolized above all by Margaret Thatcher's government's policy of selling off council houses which was symbolic of the empowering potential of a consumer-driven lifestyle. A world seemed to be emerging in which people were just as likely to be identified by their relationship to consumption as they were to the means of production. By the 1970s sociologists were beginning to realize that there was more to people's lives than their relationship with the workplace.

One author whose work was particularly important in putting consumption on the sociological agenda is Peter Saunders (1981), who is perhaps best known as an urban sociologist. Saunders illustrated the benefits to be had from turning attention away from the class conflicts centred on the means of production, towards a concern with differentials in access to consumption. Writing in the 1980s and from a free market liberal perspective, Saunders recognized that privatized forms of consumption were creating their own kinds of social divide. But Saunders' conception of such divides was largely a positive one. Although he saw a divide between those who could afford to operate according to the machinations of the free market and those who were subject to the constraints and controls of the welfare state, he basically saw the market as an opportunity rather than a divisive social force. In this context, Saunders is particularly concerned with the consumption of housing. Home ownership gives the individual a crucial degree of control over a significant realm of his or her life. As far as Saunders (1984) is concerned, housing provides 'An expression of personal identity and a source of ontological security' (p. 203). Private ownership is empowering from this point of view. It gives the consumer control that wouldn't otherwise be available. If a consumer has access to a car, for instance, he or she is not constrained by the pre-set routes and rigid timetables of the public transport system.

Saunders' perspective tends to put the market on a theoretical pedestal. Although he talks about the fact that a significant proportion of the population are potentially excluded from the freedoms he propagates, he tends to imply that this is a price worth paying. At times, he appears to be shouting from the rooftops about the benefits of the free market in contrast to the wieldy cumbersome efforts of the state. There does seem to be an underlying political message here: that power should be directed away from the state and towards the individual. Critics such as Warde (1992) have admonished Saunders for adopting an overly rigid conception of consumption which creates too harsh a distinction between the market and the state and which thereby underestimates the complex relationships that consumers have with consumer goods and services.

It could well be said that Saunders' ideas about consumption were still bound up with economic perceptions of the market. It wasn't until theorists of the post-modern became so preoccupied with consumption that consumer culture became recognized as significant in its own right. A key aspect of this transformation was that commentators were beginning to recognize that consumption wasn't simply an act of exchange which propped up the system of production, but that it was significant in its own right. Two authors who have played a significant role in this respect are Pierre Bourdieu (1984), who is perhaps the single most important contemporary theorist of consumption, and Colin Campbell (1987), who discusses the imaginative pleasure-seeking aspects of the consuming experience.

Pierre Bourdieu and *Distinction*

Pierre Bourdieu is arguably the theorist most responsible for putting consumption back on the theoretical agenda. The reason for this, ironically, is that Bourdieu's work is most remarkable for its empirical basis, a basis which gives his theoretical work so much credibility. Written in French in 1979 (English edition 1984), Bourdieu's seminal work, *Distinction* was primarily based on surveys conducted with over one thousand respondents in the late 1960s. Bourdieu's analysis is similar in some respects to that of Veblen (1899), but is more sophisticated insofar as he presents a less restrictive conception of hierarchies of consumption. Bourdieu is concerned with how consumption is used to create social boundaries through systems of taste. In other words, consumption is so important to the nature of the social fabric that nowadays it actually reflects and reproduces social stratification (Bourdieu, 1984). This is more than simply a process controlled by the upper classes, as Veblen tends to imply. Rather, what is important is access to the 'cultural capital of consumption'. From this point of view, education plays a key role in providing the necessary resources upon which people can actively partake in social life. Cultural capital allows them to behave appropriately in the appropriate context. For example, as a lecturer, I may be expected to appreciate or partake in certain forms of culture. It may not be appropriate for me to admit, for instance, that I am a regular viewer of the soap opera *Hollyoaks* or that I am partial to the occasional edition of *Who Wants To Be A Millionaire?* I have chosen to interpret my cultural capital in such a fashion, but by doing so am in danger of undermining my own class position. Bourdieu is not so concerned with such class discretions, but prefers to argue that, in effect, a consumer's taste will reflect his or her education and class. It is not the actual material possession of a good that is significant here, but the cultural capital associated with such goods.

A particularly significant theoretical aspect of Bourdieu's work in the above context is the habitus: the cognitive framework the individual carries around in his or her head as a means of interpreting the cultural situations he or she encounters. The habitus therefore provides some structure according to which a person can compose his or her behaviour. The habitus provides an internalized form of class condition 'and of the conditioning it entails' (Bourdieu, 1984, p. 101). Such conditioning indicates to the individual how he or she should behave and therefore provides a context in which the appropriate cultural strategies can be adopted. This approach has significant implications for sociology and social theory in general. In particular, if we give suitable attention to the question of consumption, this raises some important issues as regards how we define class in the first place. In other words, a class is not solely defined by its relationship with the means of production:

> Taste classifies, and it classifies the classifier. Social subjects, classified by their classifications, distinguish themselves by the distinctions they make, between the beautiful and the ugly, the distinguished and the vulgar, in

which their position in the objective classifications is expressed or betrayed. (Bourdieu, 1984, p. 6)

Social change is such that consumption is indeed having an increasingly fundamental influence on the structure of social life, to the extent that even those phenomena that seem so clearly to be rooted in dimensions of work, in this case, class, are arguably influenced by the ways in which people consume. Bourdieu's work represents an enormous achievement in realizing this, and in providing theories of consumption with a more empirical basis than had previously been the case.

Colin Campbell, the romantic ethic and the spirit of modern consumerism

One contemporary theorist of consumption who has managed to put the historical underpinnings of consumer society readily in focus is Colin Campbell (1987). The appeal of Campbell's work lies in the fact that he illustrates that consumption is important on more than simply a materialistic level. Thus, in critiquing the work of Max Weber, Campbell describes how the late eighteenth and early nineteenth centuries, although a period that fostered the puritanical values of reinvestment that were so important to the longevity of capitalism, also witnessed the emergence of the romantic ethic, an increasingly emotionalist way of life in which people became more and more aware of their own pleasures and desires. Campbell's core argument is therefore that

> the spirit of modern consumerism is anything but materialistic. The idea that contemporary consumers have an insatiable desire to consume objects represents a serious misunderstanding of the mechanism which impels people to want goods. Their basic motivation is the desire to experience in reality the pleasurable dramas which they have already enjoyed in imagination, and each 'new' product is seen as offering a possibility of realizing this ambition. (Campbell, 1987, pp. 89–90)

Campbell's work is important because, as Dant (1999) points out, he recognizes that consumerism emerges as a social force as much at the level of knowledge and ideas as it does at the economic level. In particular, in our everyday lives we may tend towards the opinion that somehow consumption is 'natural' and that as human beings we are predisposed to 'display insatiable wanting' (Campbell, 1987, p. 39). Campbell doubts this. He prefers to discuss the way in which the individual seeks pleasure, which is an issue very different to the need to seek satisfaction. The hedonistic world in which we have come to live is underlied, according to Campbell (1987), by a shift of emphasis from sensations to emotions:

> . . . modern hedonism tends to be covert and self-illusory; that is to say, individuals employ their imaginative and creative powers to construct mental images which they consume for the intrinsic pleasure they provide, a practice best described as day-dreaming or fantasizing. (p. 77)

Consumerism therefore becomes a state of mind as much as the fulfilment of a need or a want. This perhaps is the crucial point that underlies any understanding of what constitutes a consumer society:

> The central insight required is the realization that individuals do not so much seek satisfaction from products, as pleasure from the self-illusory experiences which they construct from their associated meanings. The essential activity of consumption is thus not the actual selection, purchase or use of products, but the imaginative pleasure-seeking to which the product image lends itself, 'real' consumption being largely a resultant of 'mentalistic' hedonism. (p. 89)

For Campbell, then, consumer society is all about the dissatisfactions of reality. Consumption gives us the belief that we can fulfil our fantasies. But the actual pleasures afforded by consumption always fall short of that to which we aspire. We are dissatisfied with reality and therefore seize any pleasures consumption can offer us. By doing so we sustain a constant sense of longing, and unfulfilled longing at that. We consume as an aid to the construction of our day-dreams rather than for the fulfilment of a physical need. The consumer society leaves us constantly frustrated.

Structures of consumption

Consumption is clearly not simply about fulfilling an actual need and is therefore not entirely liberatory in nature, as some commentators of a right-wing political persuasion might infer. For this reason some theorists have argued that consumption lies at the core of what is perhaps the fundamental concern of social theory: the relationship between structure and agency. In other words, we play out a lot of the frustrations of contemporary social life through consumption, which gives some sort of control and certainty to our lives, alongside the concomitant feeling that through consumption we can be ourselves. To paraphrase Anthony Giddens, consumption is both constraining and enabling (see Miles, 2000).

It is important to recognize in the above regard that consumption does indeed have an important ideological dimension. We may not accept a Marxist approach to consumption in its entirety, but none the less neither should we accept a consumer society uncritically. Some authors have therefore recognized that culture, and, in particular, consumer culture, no longer provides a means of disguising the economic activities of capitalism, but is itself an economic activity (Jameson, 1984; Miles, 1998a). It is in this sense that consumerism has emerged as the dominant mode of cultural reproduction in the West over the course of modernity (Slater, 1997). Consumption is no trivial matter in the sense that 'The ideological dimensions of consumerism are, in effect, shielded from consumers by their ability to consume' (Miles, 1998a, p. 152). It is precisely because of Campbell's point that consumers are never entirely satisfied that consumerism manages to maintain its powerful ideological element. But ideology should not necessarily be assumed to operate as a one-way street. Consumers are at least partially aware of the sorts of power dimensions that underlie what it is we consume (and in particular the power of massive multi-national companies such as Microsoft, Coca-Cola and Nike). Consumers are perfectly capable of endowing their own meanings in their Microsoft software or their Nike training shoes. Regardless of how commodified a particular football club may or may not be, the emotional investment an individual places in that club ensures that such consumption is, at least in one sense, personal in nature. The irony of all this, of course, is the fact that we feel such consumption is personal makes it utterly impersonal, in the sense that the ideological impact of consumerism is inevitably intensified as a result.

Various authors have attempted to come to terms with the para-doxical dimensions of consumerism. I myself have used the notion of the 'consuming paradox'. That is, the degree to which consumerism, on the one hand, appears to offer all sorts of opportunities and pre-viously unexplored experiences, and yet, on the other, we appear to be directed down certain predetermined routes of consumption which ensure the constraining dimensions of consumerism as a way of life (Miles, 1998a). It is this paradox which serves to create a situation in which consumerist ideology is actively lived. As Lee (1993) notes, consumer goods therefore live a double life as agents of social control and active sources for the construction of culture. Con-sumers are not simply dupes of the capitalist system, as a member of the Frankfurt School might argue. If they were, capitalism would not be able to extend its boundaries so easily. Capitalism depends upon a degree of freedom and individuality to ensure its own longevity:

> Consumer capitalism actively wants consumers to experience what might be described as 'pseudo-sovereignty'. The individual's experience of

consumerism is therefore a balancing act between structure and agency. . . .
The consumer is offered a veneer of sovereignty and maximizes his or her
personal freedom within the veneer provided, despite a tacit acceptance
that consumerism is a more powerful beast than any one individual at any
one time. (Miles, 1998a, p. 156)

The changing face of gendered consumption

As a means of illustrating the above issues, I want to consider one
specific example of the way in which consumer capitalism manages to
find new avenues of exploration. One of the fastest growth areas of
consumption in recent decades has been the men's market. The
traditional view has always been that women were actually the
'natural' consumers and that if men consumed at all, they did so
reluctantly. It might indeed be argued that gender consumption roles
are somehow symbolic of gender relations in society in general. But
what is of more concern to us here is how consumer capitalism
appears to have recognized that men remain, or at least remained,
one of the great unexplored market niches. The argument I want to
put forward here then is that capitalism is essentially chameleon-like,
and is forever seeking new avenues in which it can expand, whilst
maintaining its ideological pull.

As Bocock (1993) points out, consumption has always been
associated with women, notably in its earliest incarnations as a means
of personal adornment and luxury. The traditional gender divide
therefore operated between the public and the private. Men were
perceived to be public providers, usefully contributing to society
whilst acting as the breadwinner of the household. Women, meanwhile, engaged in more 'trivial' activities such as rearing children and
consuming. As Lee (1993) notes, the family no longer merely played
the role of a domestic space of self-sufficiency, but acted as a modern
consumption unit which efficiently managed consumer demand. It
was in this context that consumption became associated with femin-
inity (Bocock, 1993). The stereotypical woman would therefore spend
her hard-working man's money as though there were no tomorrow.
Consumption had no social value and simply served to reinforce
gender inequalities. Bowlby (1987) therefore argues that the fact that
women were becoming or being made to become willing consumers
reflected an ideological paradigm whereby women were being
seduced by men. Women were yielding objects answerable only to
men, who told them what their desires should and shouldn't be. This
issue is discussed further by Firat (1994), who points out that
consumption came to be perceived as a sensual and emotional (and
therefore feminine) act rather than a rational masculine one.

However, it is important to note here that, regardless of the gender imbalances involved, the relationship consumers had with consumer goods was not simply a material one, but also symbolic. In this sense, women are able to use consumer goods in their own ways, endowing their own meanings as they do so. But the danger, as authors such as Susan Willis (1990) have illustrated, is that, regardless of such meanings, consumption may actively reassert gender divides. Willis discusses the consumption of fitness, which she suggests is liberating in one sense, insofar as it entails very positive images of independent, successful and self-assured women, but oppressive in another. She therefore describes the workout as a highly evolved commodity form which in fact creates a situation in which women define themselves through their bodies. Because men are more powerful than women, they have no need to assert themselves in this way. But ironically, women actively define themselves as gendered objects, thereby intensifying the core of their very oppression. In this sense, despite offering some degree of freedom, consumption can potentially and simultaneously reassert gender subordination.

But what about men? How do they fit into all of this? In recent decades, there is a strong suggestion that men have struggled to maintain a strong sense of their own masculinity with the breakdown of manufacturing industry and the lack of a long-term military conflict. This arguably came to a head in the 1980s, by which time men were being forced to question their social roles (Mort, 1996). In discussing recent developments in gendered consumption, Firat (1994) debates whether or not consumption has emerged as such a fundamental aspect of the disjointed and fragmented post-modern world that it has effectively risen above and beyond gender differentiations. For instance, the commodification of the body is no longer simply about women. The advertising industry regularly uses the male form to sell products. There is a long way to go in this respect (indeed, probably *too* far to go), but there may be evidence that things are changing. The suggestion is that consumption has become a legitimate male activity. The rapid growth of the men's fashion industry is testament to this fact, as is the growth of the men's magazine market. Men's magazines have become vehicles for masculine forms of consumption. By encouraging men that they can make themselves objects of the female (and male) gaze, consumer capitalism is able to explore and exploit new, as yet untapped, markets. In this sense gender roles are becoming more flexible than they were in the past.

Several authors have focused in particular on recent developments in the men's fashion market. For instance, Nixon (1996) points out that capitalist economies have undergone many significant structural changes since the 1970s and 1980s. Above all, the production process has become increasingly flexible. Basically, a technologically advanced economy is emerging which can respond more readily to the changing needs of the market. The production system has therefore arguably been transformed from an economy of scale to an economy of scope. Standardization is, in this context, a thing of the past. What is more important now is what the consumer actually *wants* to consume. The economy is far more responsive to the needs of the market than it would have been in the past. These changes have provided the foundations on which the men's fashion market has developed. In these circumstances, producers were able to make considered calculations about shifts in the nature of masculine culture outside the immediate realm of consumption (Nixon, 1996, p. 197). Marketers were therefore able to exploit imagery associated with the 'new man' in order to construct a more focused and segmented market that had previously remained unexplored. This 'new man' imagery, according to Nixon, sanctioned a new form of masculinity based on staged narcissism through dress and grooming. This had particular implications for the loosening of gender identities and especially the rigid differentiations that existed between gay and straight men. The fashion industry, as Mort (1996) points out, saw these uncertainties as an opportunity. Consumer culture became the key focus for debates as to what it actually meant to be a man:

> In the 1980s the debate over men's changing roles was concretised in a wide variety of settings. But it was in one area that the issue was given its most extended hearing. This was in the sphere of consumer culture. In all the exchanges, commercial debates over the identities and consumption patterns of younger men loomed large. Such discussions were urgent and energetic, and they competed for attention with the more sententious claims of sexual politics. For during the decade the dynamics of the marketplace occupied a privileged place in shaping young men's wants and needs. (Mort, 1996, pp. 17–18)

In this context Edwards (1997) argues that the recent interest in men and fashion does not constitute an élitist and designer-driven cultural practice, but is more about the increasing role that consumption and consumer lifestyles play in the construction of identities (see Chapter 5). Underlying all this, according to Edwards, is a democratic ideal which implies that any man can partake in consumption-orientated activities and enjoy the benefits of fashion regardless of his background. Of course, he cannot. Yes, masculinity was increasingly commodified and marketed in the 1980s, and men's magazines, in particular, were used to stimulate demand in what was and is a growth sector. But the problem with all this, and an issue I want to go on to consider, is that although consumer society may bring with it all sorts of pleasures, there will always be a price to pay, as Edwards (1997) illustrates in his discussion of men's style:

> These are pleasures indeed: deeply sensual, sexual and auto-erotic indulgences where consuming new costumes, their colours, details and sensations, as well as their looks and poses, is as delicious as eating expensive ice cream. But those without the luck, the looks or the time have never had it so bad, and are consigned to looking and longing, or even exclusion and castigation for not playing the game. In this sense fashion is fascism: conform in the mirror of judgements or else take the consequences. (p. 134)

Edwards' point here is that masculinity may well be in crisis not as a result of the ups and downs of sexual politics, but due to the pressures placed upon men by the market. This brief example therefore illustrates the fact that consumer capitalism is intent on finding new market niches to exploit. It does so relentlessly. But it is not always aware of or willing to act upon the social consequences of such explorations. Consumer capitalism is ideological in the sense that it naturalizes consumerism as a way of life. But the implications of that ideology cut far deeper than many social theorists have been prepared to admit.

The disenfranchised 'consumer'

Discourses concerning consumption tend to imply that all of us have the opportunity to consume: that consumption is a God-given right. To be a consumer is to be a citizen of contemporary society (see Urry, 1990). But sadly things aren't that simple. The key debate here centres on whether consumption offers freedom of choice or whether that choice is illusory: the implication being that consumerism divides as much as it provides. One author who considers this issue is Mica Nava (1991), who argues that consumerism potentially represents a significant source of power. The all too prevalent assumption that consumers are easily duped by advertisers and politically pacified by 'the buying of useless objects' (p. 162) is therefore criticized by Nava, who argues that commentators tend to underestimate the political subtleties of consumerism. In this context, she points out that

> twentieth-century Western consumerism . . . has already generated new grass-roots constituencies – constituencies of the market-place – and has enfranchised modern citizens in new ways, making possible a new and

quite different economic, political and personal and creative participation in society. The full scale of its power is yet to be imagined. (Nava, 1991, p. 173)

The above is all well and good, but there could well be a corollary argument that the true power of consumerism lies in the degree to which it excludes. There is an inherent danger in the rhetoric we associate with consumerism which masks from us the realities of everyday life. The reality, as Gabriel and Lang (1995) point out, is if you do not have the necessary resources, you cannot be a fully fledged citizen of consumer culture:

> The key barrier to consumer choice is money. The message? If you want choice, and who doesn't, you have to get out there and get going. Money gives choice. Choice gives freedom. Whatever the area of consumption, from crime protection to clothes, from health to education, from cultural industries to cars, money is the final arbiter. (p. 32)

Money is indeed the final arbiter. But it is also worth pointing out that the consumer society may be as significant to those who do not have access to resources as to those who do. In short, as Campbell suggests, the social significance of consumption is as much about the longing for consumption as it is about the actual consuming itself. This point may also be worth considering on a global scale. But before I do so I want to consider briefly one of the most important theoretical contributions to this debate, that of Zygmunt Bauman (1988). Bauman accepts that choice, and most pointedly consumer choice, represents the foundation of a new concept of freedom in contemporary society. Underlying this shift, according to Bauman, is the move from inter-individual rivalry based on wealth and power to a new form of rivalry based on the display of symbols:

> Far from suppressing the potential for individual expansion, capitalism brought about a kind of society in which the life-pattern of free choice and self-assertion can be practised on a scale unheard of before. . . . with consumption firmly established as a focus and the playground for individual freedom, the future of capitalism looks more secure than ever. Social control becomes an easier task. . . . Reproduction of the capitalist system is therefore achieved through individual freedom and not through its suppression. (pp. 60–1)

The attractions of consumerism lie in the fact that it offers freedoms to people who feel constrained in other aspects of their lives. In this context, the individual can be free and secure at one and the same time. But the problem here is that those people who are excluded from such choice are instantly oppressed and ultimately disenfranchized. Bauman therefore distinguishes between what he describes as the 'seduced' and the 'oppressed'. A proportion of people are therefore able to exploit the freedoms provided for them by the market. It provides them with a means of self-expression which they clearly welcome. However, a significant proportion of people are excluded from such freedoms and are forced to depend upon the state, which, in effect, determines the parameters within which they consume. The price to pay for consumer freedom is therefore a significant one. Consumerism only offers consumers a partial freedom and some members of the social world receive that freedom at the expense of others. Consumerism and the process of commodification shield the realities of such divisions. Consumerism appears to give us freedoms, but those freedoms are socially divisive. The problem is that consumerism manages to shield those who can consume from those who cannot. And even those who cannot are seduced by the fantasy that they can.

Bauman (1998b) extends this idea in his more recent work, in which he argues that the emergence of a consumer society has fundamentally altered what it actually means to be poor. Being poor is no longer about being unemployed, according to Bauman, but is more about the plight of the flawed consumer. In these circumstances, far from being liberated by social change, the poor can no longer fall back on their social role as a reserve army of labour, and as such no longer have any useful social function. Poor people are simply 'inadequate consumers', and this inadequacy is the main source of the unemployed's shame and stigma, precisely because we live in a consumer society (as opposed to a producer society) in a world where symbols of consumption are constantly raising the ante. Ironically, as Bauman points out, the poor get poorer while the rich get richer, and so the symbols of consumption to which the poor aspire are more and more out of their reach. Their 'subjective sense of insufficiency' is therefore intensified.

Global consumption

The above problems are paralleled on a global scale. Consumption divides the world as much as it divides the classes. The work of Serge Latouche (1993), who addresses the global inequalities of ideologies of consumption, is particularly important in this respect. Latouche argues that on a global scale a process of Westernization is taking place which is accompanied by a preoccupation with material standards of living. The problem, for Latouche, lies in the fact that both the mass media and politicians are constantly exalting ideologies which promote the idea that success lies in material improvement. In this environment the belief is perpetuated that everyone can be a winner in a consumer society. Nature therefore becomes the victim because the consensus appears to be that if everybody works together in exploiting the resources that surround them (and despite the move towards consuming individualistically), everybody can share in a general prosperity. Latouche therefore discusses the emergence of a sort of social contract in which individual gain is the end product of a form of social teamwork.

The idea that everybody can win in a consumer society is, as far as Latouche is concerned, an illusory nonsense. Of course, people in all parts of the social hierarchy can acquire tokens of consumerism. But in real terms, the truth is that while some win a great deal in terms of the world-wide impact of consumption, a great many more win very little. None the less, wealth is lauded as the true path to happiness. This becomes a global ideology which increases the divide between the developed and developing worlds. Latouche therefore points out that developing countries are in this context forced to compete uncompetitively in the global marketplace, dealing in goods that may sell, but which may not represent the best means of economic salvation. The developing world therefore becomes economically dependent upon the consumption habits of the developed world, but any opportunity to partake in the same level of consumption is a distant reality. In a sense, then, it is actually in the interests of the first world to keep the third world underdeveloped. The third world is locked in a constant cycle of global debt. Latouche therefore argues that the rise in per capita standards of living that we associate with consumer societies has been achieved at the cost of a deeper malaise: the emergence of what is essentially an immoral and spiritually degrading society; a society in which ultimately everybody is attempting to exploit everybody else. The key principle here then is 'maximine', maximum results and enjoyment through minimum cost and effort (Latouche, 1993). Ultimately a consumer society is intent on ensuring individual happiness, regardless of the degree of unhappiness this will inevitably result in for the majority:

> The happiness of persons, if this is taken as an objective of a society, cannot be a simple addition of states of pleasure of all its members separately obtained, each to the detriment of others. Even if happiness is no more than the mere symbolic enjoyment felt by the subjects as a consequence of that of a ruler, it still possesses an irreducible personal aspect. A society cannot be said to be perfectly happy if one of its members is in misery. (Latouche, 1993, p. 241)

Conclusions

The suggestion here is that the consumer society is far more complex than it may appear to be on the surface. As de Certeau (1984) points out, consumption is far more than an economic by-product of production. It plays an active role in maintaining the conflictual nature of everyday life. The meanings with which consumers endow consumer goods and services and the ideological contexts in which they do so are therefore of primary interest to the social theorist.

The social theorist therefore plays a key role in undercutting common-sense notions of consumerism. A key concern is the extent to which the consumer society is a democratic society, and the degree to which it really can offer the freedoms which it claims it can offer continues to be a matter for heated debate. So how do we best conceptualize the contemporary consumer? One suggestion is that consumers are essentially 'unmanageable'. Gabriel and Lang (1995) therefore argue that theorists have failed to come to terms with the complex nature of the consuming experience. In other words, consumer researchers have used a variety of discourses to understand the consumer and as such have constructed a series of parallel discourses which include the consumer as a citizen, an identity-seeker or a hedonist. None of these parallel discourses is sufficient alone. The experience of consumption is in its very essence unpredictable, and as consumers we behave in an unpredictable fashion. Comparisons between the impact of consumption on the developing and developed worlds illustrate how consumption and our experience of it have become increasingly fragmented:

> Given such social chasms, it is difficult to talk about all consumption and all consumers as coming under the same ethos or constraints, that is, as being uniform entities or acting as a uniform force. . . . economic conditions have become fraught, the social inequalities have once again widened, insecurity is experienced across social classes, poverty and homelessness have resurfaced on a massive scale. Cultural fatigue threatens to overcome even the well-off. The brashness has been knocked off the consumer society. (Gabriel and Lang, 1995, pp. 189–90)

This may be the case, but it does not necessarily follow that consumerism is any less theoretically interesting as a result. For, as Gabriel and Lang (1995) note, it is in this sense that consumers are unmanageable and it is in this sense that social theory needs to be especially careful in managing consumption in a more reflexive fashion. We cannot assume that all-encompassing theoretical propositions can adequately account for the complexity of the consumer experience.

So what next for theorists concerned with the impact of the so-called consumer society? The big problem here, as authors such as Gabriel and Lang (1995) and Warde (1998) argue, is the fact that the study of consumption is so diverse in nature and yet there is so little evidence of inter-disciplinary overlap. Realistically, it is unlikely that this trend is about to change overnight. A cross-disciplinary synthesis of theory and research is a long way off. Perhaps the best we can hope for, as Warde (1998) suggests, is 'much more internal theoretical clarity' (p. 302). Warde goes on to suggest that there exists a considerable tension between approaches to the consumer society which come from a cultural studies tradition and those adopting a political economy perspective. The suggestion, then, is that the chasm between the two needs to be bridged. Most pointedly, the everyday relationship which consumers have with consumption needs to become more of a priority. At the moment theoretical discussions of consumption might well be criticized for existing in a theoretical vacuum, a vacuum most clearly associated with post-modernism (see Chapter 5).

In recent decades, theoretical advances in the realm of consumption have been enormous, but those advances need to go one stage further: they need to be applied in actual contexts in which they are of benefit to the consumer him- or herself. It is all well and good to outline the theoretical connotations of a society divided along lines of consumption. But how will such insights be applied? The evidence that somehow a consumer society is 'natural' and that indicators of economic prosperity have to be a good thing for everybody is overwhelming, indeed seducing (see Bauman, 1998b). The actual detailed impact of a prosperous society at all levels is uncertain and will remain uncertain until the ideological dimensions of consumerism are fully realized and acted upon. Having said that, it is important that discussions concerning consumer culture are sober in nature. Many commentators have argued that with the emergence of a post-modern world our identities are less and less determined by pre-defined social roles and more and more the product of the ways in which we consume from one minute to the next (see Chapter 5). All I want to say here is that discussions over the role of consumption in the construction of identity have tended to water down the practical benefits of theories of consumption. The danger is that we exaggerate the impact of consumption and underestimate other aspects of identity that may be far more important in constructing who it is we are.

Consumption plays an important role in constructing people's lives, but it may only actually provide a resource through which aspects of gender, sexuality, race, class and community are played out. Theories of consumption therefore need to address the way in which consumption relates to other important aspects of social life, and in particular how consumption affects the relationship between structure and agency.

Ultimately, the role of the social theorist is to highlight the above issues and encourage policy makers to act upon them. As I point out in Chapters 5 and 9, the degree to which the social theorist can actually change the world is a matter for debate. The society in which we live may appear to be economically efficient, but we achieve such efficiency at a human cost. From a sociological perspective there would be a similar cost to pay if social theorists were not prepared to rise above the efficient and the predictable in order to discover the richness which consumers actively endow in their consumer life-styles. The main priority is to avoid the tendency to see consumers as mindless dupes and to devise theoretical and research-based strategies which address the active ways in which consumers engage with the consumer society.

Recommended reading

Robert Bocock (1993) *Consumption*, London: Routledge. An accessible introduction to the area which is especially informative in terms of the historical emergence of the consumer society.

Pierre Bourdieu (1984) *Distinction: A Social Critique of the Judgement of Taste*, London: Routledge and Kegan Paul. An impressive piece of sociology which applies the theoretical in empirical contexts. A testament to the potential insights to be provided by social theory.

Yiannis Gabriel and Tim Lang (1998) *The Unmanageable Consumer: Contemporary Consumption and Its Fragmentation*, London: Sage. A comprehensive and wide-ranging discussion of the different facets of consumption. Includes an especially useful section on the consumer as identity-seeker.

Steven Miles (1998) *Consumerism as a Way of Life*, London: Sage. A user-friendly discussion of the key aspects of 'consumerism' which introduces the reader to a series of case studies of areas of life in which the ideological power of consumerism takes effect.

CHAPTER 5

A POST-MODERN 'SOCIETY'?

Many years ago I attended a course on the subject of 'postmodernity' which was taught by one of the leading and most respected contributors to the field of contemporary social theory. The end result of this particular course was that by its conclusion I felt I knew less about the subject matter concerned than I had done to begin with! This was less the fault of that particular lecturer and more a testament to the problematic and quite often mystifying nature of debates which stubbornly continue to surround post-modernity. The core of the problem, as Kellner (1990) points out, is that post-modern theory is not unified in any real sense, but constitutes a sort of 'unholy' marriage which joins together a variety of theories and positions (see also Ritzer, 1992). In this chapter I want to suggest that post-modernity represents one of the most important foci of debate in contemporary social theory, but that, in addition, simply by being so influential, it actively, and in some senses usefully, undermines the foundations of social theory in general. In short, post-modernity problematizes the role of the social theorist in a changing world, and, as such, provides a fascinating means of addressing the changing role of the social world *and* the social theorist at the beginning of the twenty-first century.

Post-modernity has given social theory a much needed injection of imagination, whilst precipitating an extensive and often overwhelming level of debate. This level of debate is signified by the very fact that I prefer to refer to post-modernity rather than postmodernity. The hyphen hints at the disputed nature of the term itself (see also Rosenau, 1992). As such, it raises some genuine doubts as to whether or not social theory can actually continue to serve any real purpose at all, and, perhaps more importantly, whether or not social theorists and social scientists in general can actually claim to be studying any such thing as the 'real' world. Alternatively, it could be argued that the recent focus on post-modernity actually represents an extremely damaging trend for social theory. You might even go as far as to say that it amounts to a theoretical bandwagon upon which social theorists have jumped. Unfortunately, many of them have fallen off the other side. Defenders of post-modernism might well argue that the informal vitriol and the strength of feeling of those concerned with rebuffing post-modernism simply reflect an inability or unwillingness to come to terms with its complexities. From this point of view, people who dismiss post-modernism out of hand simply do not understand it. Either way, if you dismiss post-modernism entirely you are simply adding further fuel to the post-modern fire.

This chapter will attempt to answer the following question: do debates concerned with post-modernity amount to little more than a theoretical blind alley, or do they have a significant contribution to make to our understanding of the social world at the beginning of the twenty-first century? Before we answer this question, there cannot be any doubt that at least at one level the trends we associate with post-modernism pervade our everyday lives. We only have to switch on our television sets to hear about the influence of post-modern art, film, philosophy and literature. In many ways we *live* the post-modern. Like other aspects of social life discussed elsewhere in this book, we therefore take it for granted. It is worth noting in this context that in many ways social theorists are more concerned with theorising about post-modernity than they are with post-modernism; that is, with the underlying aspects and characteristics of social change which conspire to create post-modernism in all its various guises. Post-modernism and post-modernity remain highly contested terms, and this is partly their attraction. The debates they engender are never resolved. As Bryman argues in his book *Disney and His Worlds* (1995), 'summarizing this genre is no easy matter and can be compared to trying to grab hold of jelly with a clamp – it changes shape and consistency and then fragments' (p. 161). Post-modernism is a highly influential intellectual movement, and an abstract and disconcerting movement at that, but it also actively impinges upon our everyday lives. By discussing how this might be the case, it might be possible to develop a deeper understanding of whether or not we do actually live in a post-modern world and whether or not that world is 'real'.

An epochal shift?

The debate over post-modernity is concerned with the nature of social change and the extent of that change. It therefore reflects an ongoing preoccupation of social theorists, who are concerned with explaining or at least describing social changes that appear to exert influence on how we as individuals conduct our everyday lives in individual settings. As I have already said, the range of approaches that broadly fit under the umbrella of post-modernism is absolutely enormous. In order, therefore, to try to comprehend the essence of the debates concerning post-modernism, I will attempt to simplify things at this stage by focusing on what is perhaps the core matter for dispute: whether or not the social changes that have occurred over the last thirty to forty years actually constitute an epochal shift. In other words, do we live in an entirely 'new' society, or is that society simply an extension of modernity?

Perhaps what characterized or characterizes modernity above all is its quest for human freedom and autonomy. Debates over post-modernity suggest that the problem with modernity was that it could never fulfil its promise. Ultimately, modernity was undone by the requirements of instrumental reason and the suggestion that the ends and the needs of the social system in general were more important than the needs of those human beings propping up that system. In effect, progress seemed to create more problems for human beings than it actually solved. Alienation, anomie and bureaucracy were all aspects of modern life that appeared actively to go against what it means to be a human being. The system controlled people. Far from liberating them, it created a world in which they had very little say. This set of circumstances could not be maintained indefinitely, and post-modernity is arguably the end result or reaction to this process. It amounts to a period of uncertainty and dislocation in which the secure foundations and stabilities of modern life have been radically undermined. The question is, however, how far does such dislocation amount to a whole new way of life? In order to address this question I want to consider the contribution of two key theorists of the post-modern, Fredric Jameson and Jean Baudrillard, who have been chosen not necessarily because they are the most important theorists of the post-modern, but because their work highlights some of the concerns of the broader debate. Perhaps the main thing to take from this brief discussion is that although broadly speaking the theorists concerned are talking about the same trends, they do so from somewhat different perspectives and disagree as to how far these trends constitute a radical break with modernity.

Fredric Jameson

Fredric Jameson is the author of one of the single most important essays on the question of post-modernism: 'Postmodernism, or, the Cultural Logic of Late Capitalism' (1984). As this title suggests, Jameson argues that post-modernism does not constitute a radical shift in the nature of social life at all. Rather the sorts of social changes we experience are simply part of the logical and ongoing cultural development of capitalism. Jameson's work is very refreshing in the sense that he does not discuss post-modernism from an abstract distance, but actively relates it to broader social processes. For Jameson, to describe post-modernism as a rupture in history is extremely misleading and underestimates the continuities that characterize capitalism in general. Borrowing from the work of Ernest Mandel (1978), Jameson therefore identifies three periods in the development of capitalism:

(a) market capitalism, whereby markets where highly integrated and the character of capitalism was very much dependent upon the confines of the nation-state;
(b) imperial/monopoly capitalism, which saw capitalism extending its markets, notably through the colonies, which provided new opportunities for expansion;
(c) multinational or consumer capitalism, which saw the increasingly sophisticated tentacles of capitalism exploring new areas and exploiting individual forms of acquisitiveness to the benefit of the market on a global scale.

Jameson is keen to point out, therefore, that post-modernism is very much bound up with the global progression of capitalism and the expanison of a global culture which this incorporates. These processes have resulted in the individual being taken out of his or her immediate locality in some form, to be engulfed by a global culture. Although this amounts to an apparently significant change in the nature of social life, it should not be assumed that it constitutes an epochal shift. The factors underlying such changes are the same factors that have been underlying social change for over a century. But what *is* different is *how* capitalism operates. It has become more and more sophisticated and subtle in nature, and, as such, we tend to *feel* we are experiencing an epochal shift: 'What has happened is that aesthetic production today has become integrated into commodity production generally: the frantic economic urgency of producing fresh waves of turnover, now assigns an increasingly essential structural function and position to aesthetic innovation and experimentation' (Jameson, 1984, p. 56).

For Jameson, post-modernism is a hopelessly commercial culture. And perhaps the most significant point he makes in this respect is that culture is no longer ideological. Its role is not to disguise economic activity. It has, in itself, become an economic activity, and in a post-modern world it is perhaps more an important economic activity than any other. Jameson therefore describes a depthless culture of surfaces and pastiche in which the past is used to sustain the present. He sees post-modernism as a 'culture of quotations'. But ironically, and despite this suggestion, he does not criticize the label directly. Rather, he extends Marx's discussion of capitalism as being both constraining and yet potentially liberating at the same time. In this sense, his criticism of other post-modern approaches to social change might well be that they are not sufficiently grounded in the economic conditions that provide the foundations for such change.

This is a point equally well made by another Marxist commentator, David Harvey (1989), who argues that there are serious weaknesses with a post-modern perspective. In particular, post-modernists neglect the material conditions in which contemporary societies operate. More seriously, Harvey criticizes post-modernists for simply describing the problems inherent in a post-modern world rather than actually doing something about them. He is concerned with the apathetic tendencies of post-modernism: 'The rhetoric of postmodernism is dangerous for it avoids confronting the realities of political economy and the circumstances of global power' (p. 117). From this point of view, what postmodernism doesn't do yet should do is to confront the political and economic conditions in which the depthless culture Jameson (1984) describes has emerged.

Jean Baudrillard

Jean Baudrillard (1983) is often described as the 'high priest' of post-modernism, and there is no doubt that his controversial and at times somewhat perplexing work has played an influential role in the construction of a post-modern agenda. As Ritzer (1992) notes, Jean Baudrillard's work has had a profound impact on post-modern social theory despite the fact that he himself has expressed dissatisfaction with the label 'post-modern'. Indeed, there is an argument voiced both by Ritzer and by Gane (1991) that Baudrillard is actually _against_ post-modernism. From this point of view it is actually very difficult to pigeon-hole Baudrillard. But the same could equally be said of post-modernists in general. The important thing is that Baudrillard's work continues to be among the most influential contributions to the debates in question.

The key which unlocks Baudrillard's work is the suggestion that we have come to a point in history when the social has ended. The social has imploded into the mass to the extent that we can no longer usefully use the concept at all. Baudrillard therefore describes a world dominated by the image, and in particular those images generated by the mass media. These images are so dominant that we can no longer genuinely identify anything that can be described as 'real':

> . . . our world has become truly infinite, or rather exponential by means of images. It is caught up in a mad pursuit of images, and an even greater fascination which is only accentuated by video and digital images. We have thus come to the paradox that these images describe the equal impossibility of the real and the imaginary. . . . In the absence of rules of the game, things

become caught up in their own game; images become more real than real; cinema itself becomes more cinema than cinema, in a kind of vertigo in which it does no more than resemble itself and escape in its own logic, in the very perfection of its own model. (Baudrillard, 1993, pp. 194–5)

In the post-modern world, if that's what you want to call it, everyday experience is radically different from what it may have been in the past. The essence of this change lies in the collapse of meaning and reality and the dominance of the image or signifier. These images therefore become more real than reality. This is what Baudrillard calls 'hyper-simulation'. Historical boundaries are blurred by the constant borrowing and rehashing of cultural artefacts. The mixture of historical contexts creates a heady cocktail that seems to be contemporary, but is simply about reproducing the past in 'new' ways.

Reality is actively defined by the mass media. As such, Baudrillard (1995) (in)famously claimed that the Gulf War never actually happened, but was a product of a mass media age. In discussing this proposition, Dunn (1998) uses the example of mass-mediated sporting events. The top American stadia will now almost always deploy video technology so that important incidents are repeated instantaneously, whilst advertisements are played even when the action is actually taking place in the stadium. The same can be said of major rock concerts, which have become orgies of imagery in which the basic talents of the actual performers are dwarfed by the screens and videos that surround them. Indeed, 'While in such examples the media do not literally replace reality, they are endowed by spectators with a power to verify and sanction it and a visual pleasure that makes reality subservient to its representation' (Dunn, 1998, p. 101). The process of commodification is central to everything Baudrillard describes. Along with technological advance, commodification has created a world of superficiality and simulation. To give another example of the dominance of the image. The Nike Swoosh, a sign recognizable on a global scale, constructs a particular image and vision of what the world is all about. But at the same time it hides the reality that lies behind that image, such as the thousands of workers employed as cheap labour to bring Nike goods to the marketplace. The social has, in effect, been taken out of social life. The meanings lying behind the commodified culture we consume become camouflaged by the surfaces that constrain those meanings. Because such images dominate how we perceive our social world (if we can indeed describe it as such), that world becomes a mere mass, and our humanity is based on nothing more than our ability to consume spectacular simulations of reality. The epochal nature of social change is such that we can no longer even identify any such thing as the social. In short, as McGuigan (1999) points out, Baudrillard recognizes a sharp break between prevailing forms of sociality and representation. And herein, arguably, lies Baudrillard's greatest fault. Authors such as McGuigan (1999) and Kellner (1994) have pointed out that Baudrillard exaggerates any perceived break with the past. Baudrillard's insights are incisive, but cannot be accepted in their entirety. His ironic, playful style is one thing, but style alone is ironically not enough.

Post-modern fragmentation and popular culture

Perhaps the best way to come to terms with the complexity of debates over modernity and post-modernity is to focus, to begin with, on the question of fragmentation. Many theorists argue that social life has become less predictable and more fragmented than it was in the past. The old certainties and securities that left us entirely sure as to our role in the social world have apparently broken down. Contemporary societies therefore feel increasingly directionless in nature. We seem to live in what is more and more of an individualistic world in which class cultures, and in particular working-class culture, are less unified than they have been in the past and in which there are fewer and fewer reference points or sources of stability upon which we can depend. The suggestion here then is that whereas in the past our identities may have been based on our relationship to work, our class position, or our family role, in the contemporary world our social experience is far more tenuous and we are increasingly subject to momentary actions and transitory feelings. The question of fragmentation is taken up especially effectively in the work of Zygmunt Bauman (1995), who argues that modernity is characterized by pilgrims who actively seek predefined goals while post-modernity in contrast is characterized by a diverse range of 'strollers', 'players', 'tourists' and 'vagabonds'. All of these groups are forced to deal with the transient inconsequential uncertainties of everyday life in their own ways. Such fragmentation is very much bound up with the changing nature of consumption (see Lyon, 1994). Through consumption we can be who we want when we want, changing from one minute to the next.

The question that this chapter is concerned with is: how is post-modern fragmentation expressed in the 'real' world? This problem is inherently tricky insofar as some post-modernists may argue there is no such thing as the real world in the first place. There are only versions of that world and individual interpretations of it, rather than any 'real' sense of genuine reality. But before I consider this issue in more depth I want to establish a more accurate picture of what constitutes 'post-modern' culture. By doing so, it should be possible critically to evaluate post-modern contributions to contemporary social theory. Above all in this context, it is important to remember that post-modernism does not constitute a school of thought in the traditional sense, as you might consider the work of functionalists, Marxists or members of the Frankfurt School perhaps. Post-modernism is a broad umbrella term for commentators on the social world who have a variety of both positive and negative versions of what that world is all about. These versions may be very different and apparently contra-dictory but they all share a concern with some common themes.

In this context, McRobbie (1994) describes post-modernism as a breath of fresh air: 'It has spread outwards from the realm of art history into political theory and on to the pages of youth culture magazines, record sleeves and the fashion spreads of *Vogue*' (p. 15). McRobbie argues that post-modernism is very much bound up with the massive expansion, in recent decades, of the mass media, which, despite economic ups and downs, has continuously been able to create new markets. The net result of this 'implosion', according to McRobbie, is the dominance of the image:

> Images push their way into the fabric of our social lives. They enter into how we look and what we earn, and they are still with us when we worry about bills, housing and bringing up children. They compete for attention through shock tactics, reassurance, sex and mystery, and by inviting viewers to participate in series of visual puzzles. (1994, p. 18)

But McRobbie is also keen to point out that the pastiche and the ransacking and recycling we associate with post-modernism can actually just as easily amount to a vibrant critique as it can an 'inward-looking, second-hand aesthetics' (p. 22). The images we associate with post-modernism can never be unambiguously positive or negative. As far as McRobbie is concerned, it is naïve to talk about the end of the social or the end of meaning. People can actually use the diverse range of the media and its imagery to their own ends.

One author who is particularly useful in illuminating our under-standing of the popular cultural expression of post-modernism is Dominic Strinati (1995), who charts the various realms of popular culture in which post-modern fragmentation appears to exist, namely architecture, cinema, television, advertising and pop music.

Post-modern architecture, in contrast to its modern predecessor, which was functional and scientific, is playful, ironic and elaborate. Post-modern buildings are celebratory, not functional. They combine diverse elements of different time periods to create a dramatic surface impression, because surface impression is all. As such, Connor (1997) suggests that architecture represents the clearest place to examine the relationship between modernism and post-modernism, because categorical shifts are readily defined by architects. The post-modern movement is therefore characterized by hybrid languages of difference and plurality (Connor, 1997, p. 87). But the irony is that, in one sense, the difference we associate with post-modern architecture is in itself dehumanizing:

> The 'hybrid', 'complex' and 'dual-coded' language of postmodernist architecture ought to testify to a new sense of rootedness or locality, but when hybridization itself becomes universal, regional specificity becomes simply a style which can be transmitted across the globe as rapidly as a photocopy of the latest architectural manifesto. Paradoxically, the sign of the success of the anti-universalist language and style of architectural postmodernism is that one can find it everywhere, from London, to New York, to Tokyo and Delhi. (Connor, 1997, p. 87)

It is true to say also that when commentators talk about the post-modern city what they actually really mean is the expression of post-modern architecture. But there are exceptions. For example, Wynne and O'Connor (1998) argue that consumption is a particularly significant aspect of contemporary city life. Their point is that the commodification of culture is fundamental to an understanding of what constitutes the post-modern city. Cultural production, according to this view, is an increasingly significant aspect of city life. In particular, 'new cultural intermediaries' or producers are increasingly promoting cultural consumption as a key focus of city life. Cities like Leeds, keen to promote itself as a 24-hour city; Manchester, with its thriving gay village; and Glasgow, which was recently European City of Architecture and Design – all are looking towards new avenues of consumption to construct their identities. Lifestyles and the way in which lifestyles transform city cultures seem to be fundamental to what it means to be a post-modern city.

Many post-modern theorists have used Las Vegas as an illustration of what constitutes the post-modern city. Las Vegas, as McGuigan (1999) suggests, is a symbol of commodified fun, glitz and bright lights. Having visited Las Vegas myself recently, the most striking thing about the city is the juxtaposition of styles. The Las Vegas Strip is a concoction of magical environments, casinos which provide an escape from the real world and a ticket into the worlds of Treasure Island, Paris, Egypt, Venice and New York, amongst others. It is a world in which the commodity and the ability to spend money on the commodity for the commodity's sake become all. The post-modern city is not a functional city. It plays with the consumer's senses. The post-modern city, like the post-modern world, is, above all, experimental. Indeed, Dear (2000) goes as far as to suggest that Las Vegas and the casinos that populate it amount to a series of film sets 'on which ordinary people come to live, play and act out. . . . It is no longer possible to recognize the boundary between the screen and the street, between cinematic fantasy and the creation of the urban. Representations of cities are becoming cities. Life is becoming a virtual reality.' (p. 206).

Las Vegas is, of course, an extreme. But it also represents a world of extremes. To generalize from Las Vegas therefore can be and often is misleading. But what the Las Vegas example does provide is a microcosm of post-modern playfulness and entertainment. The world is changing and those changes are represented in the urban fabric of all our cities: in the form of themed pubs, cinema complexes, continental-style bars and eateries and in the juxtaposition of styles and the power of consumption that these symbolize.

The second area of post-modern culture identified by Strinati (1995) is post-modern cinema, which also prioritizes style ahead of content or substance. Whereas modern films may have adopted a predictable narrative style in the form of the classic Western or the Middle American romance, post-modern films prioritize spectacle and image at the expense of plot and social comment. You might therefore describe *The Matrix*, which constructs a world familiar and yet distant from our own, in which traditional notions of time and space are undermined, as post-modern in nature. However, many commentators argue that post-modern culture lacks originality. It simply reproduces elements from the past in a 'new' package. Certainly, *The Matrix* depends upon elements of traditional action films, but deals with them in original ways. Perhaps this is the essence of a post-modern film: the only sense of originality it can claim is built upon the foundations of the past. Pastiche is therefore an important aspect of post-modern film, as Connor (1997) notes. Terry Gilliam's strangely unusual and yet hauntingly familiar film *Brazil* therefore illustrates this point with the way in which it plays with history. It creates its own unique world but does so partly by parodying other films, including *Star Wars*. But perhaps, Connor makes his most important point when he says that 'it often seems though post-modernism in film is not a matter of a new dominant style so much as the corrosion of the very idea of such a dominant' (p. 199).

Jean Baudrillard (1993) discusses the impact of 'post-modern' cinema in some detail. He points out, for instance, that post-modern films, regardless of their quality, somehow leave us feeling completely indifferent. Very often they are reproductions of historical periods and also of films depicting those periods. A good example of this process might be *The Talented Mr Ripley*, which portrays the idealist hedonism associated with upper middle-class lifestyles in sun-drenched 1950s Italy. These sorts of film amount to flawless, hallucinatory 'artefacts'. They simulate reality.

Strinati goes on to discuss post-modern television. Much of contemporary television is indeed perhaps archetypally post-modern insofar as it so often appears to prioritize style and surface impression over substance. The programmes produced on British television by Chris Evans' company Ginger Productions, such as *Don't Forget Your Toothbrush* and *TFI Friday*, might therefore be described as postmodern insofar as they are very much style-led. The viewer is encouraged into the stylistic (and some would say ironically formulaic) world that Chris Evans has created. Douglas Kellner has considered the nature of post-modern television in considerable depth. For Kellner (1992), in post-modern television, 'image takes precedence over narrative, as compelling and highly expressive and non-realist aesthetic images detach themselves from the television diegesis and become the centre of fascination, of a seductive pleasure, of an intense but highly transitory aesthetic experience' (p. 146).

For the above reasons, television provides an especially useful illustration of post-modern culture. But according to Kellner it is misleading to suggest that post-modern culture is necessarily flat. In contrast, television can play an important role in the construction of identity, an issue to which I shall return later. Kellner illustrates this point with his discussion of *Miami Vice*, which, as he points out, is many critics' favourite example of post-modern television. Sure enough, *Miami Vice* prioritizes image at the expense of narrative plot. There is a plot there, but that plot is subservient to the pastel-coloured incubated world through which Crockett and Tubbs pass. This is a seductive and artificial world far removed from traditional images of police work. In this context, the story appears to be a mere afterthought. Kellner, however, argues that this emphasis on style and surface also incorporates meaning. This is not depthlessness then, but a political comment on the fragmentation and fragility of contemporary identities. The same might be said of the highly successful Mafia family drama *The Sopranos*, with its cinematic production values, and luscious soundtrack.

According to Strinati (1995), advertising also provides a graphic illustration of the impact of post-modern culture. In the modern world advertising was functional. Of course it tried to persuade, but it did so by celebrating the quality of the product or service concerned. Post-modern advertising, and apparently the vast majority of advertising we consume today, is far more dependent upon stylistic concerns. It appears to be about using the most impressive and memorable imagery to ensure that a product is retained in the consumer's mind. Strinati seems to be suggesting that advertising has, in effect, become a parody of itself. It is not about quality, but about which advertisement stretches stylistic boundaries. Advertising campaigns for Guinness have always been at the leading edge in this respect. One of its most recent commercials features a surreal sequence with surfers and white horses. The relevance of the images to the actual product concerned is negligible, but the production values are also incredibly high. The latter can also be said of another Guinness commercial, which is focused on an Italian village and which features a retired swimming champion racing to cover a particular distance in time to collect his pint of Guinness before it is completely poured; thereby maintaining a long-held village tradition. In effect, it is a race (which incidentally is rigged in favour of the swimmer) between the swimmer and the pint of Guinness. This commercial is unusual in the sense that it gives a post-modern gloss to a modernist frame. The village concerned gives the feeling of a scenic idyllic community set somewhere in the past: an escape from the harsh realities of the urban world. It is therefore a romantic vision, made possible by cinematic principles and not inconsiderable finance. In this setting a pint of Guinness would appear to be alien to your typical drinker. But far from it; the images created offer a means of escape: an unreal world accessible through the consumption of a commodity. In a previous incarnation Guinness was promoted as a healthy nutritious drink. Now it has become a lifestyle indicator.

The final area discussed by Strinati is that of popular music, which in its post-modern guise is very much about the mixing and matching of styles and genres. William Orbit's *Songs in a Modern Style* is a good example of this. Orbit takes a series of classical pieces of music and reinvents them in a contemporary electronic fashion. This reflects an apparent tendency in post-modern culture to borrow and regurgitate from the past. Orbit's is different in one sense: it provides a new take on old pieces of music, but in another it is lacking a certain sense of originality. It depends on the past. Other musicians referred to as 'post-modern' by Strinati include the Pet Shop Boys and Talking Heads. The latter incorporate a diversity of styles, including the exploration of 'world music', while the former adopt a very playful image which gives their own slant to what constitutes disco music. This constitutes a rejection of divisions between serious and fun pop music. Post-modern music plays with conventional categories. This is not functional music, but music that attempts to confound expectations. From another point of view, however, post-modern popular music might well be criticized for being unoriginal. The work of Oasis is a case in point. Many commentators in the popular press have remarked how the work of Oasis, one of the biggest-selling bands of the 1990s, amounts to little more than a reworking of the Beatles both musically and image-wise. Ironically, and intentionally so, the band's latest album is entitled *Standing on the Shoulders of Giants*.

Another illustration of post-modernism's apparent lack of originality is the increasing popularity of tribute bands. Bands such as Björn

Again and the Bootleg Beatles have been enormously successful in a culture that appears to be obsessed with regurgitating the past. Consumers of popular music often only appear to be comfortable with the predictable and the safe. Indeed, many bands who split up in the 1980s and early 1990s have since reformed and in doing so are very much dependent upon the good will generated by their back catalogues. Bands such as Culture Club, Blondie, the Human League and Duran Duran are cases in point. They are actively trading on fans nostalgic for their teenage years. Culture Club, Duran Duran and the Human League have even toured together with the clear intention of squeezing whatever was possible out of this desire for nostalgia. In this sense post-modernism is contradictory. It can reconstruct and reinvent the past in predictable ways, but it can also be innovative and obtuse. Many bands are pursuing new avenues of creativity. The boy and girl band may continue to play a key role in the charts, but many other artists are pursuing highly original avenues of expression. Radiohead, for instance, released their album *Kid A* without actually promoting any singles. The style of this record was entirely different to their previous releases and was in many senses uncommercial in nature, even insofar as it was made easily accessible on the internet. Certainly, as far as the band were concerned, originality rather than commerciality was the key.

Post-modern pop music, as is post-modern culture in general, is therefore remarkable for its eclectic nature. In this context, image is indeed prioritized over content. Hence many commentators have discussed the role of MTV as the archetypal media enactment of post-modernism. As a music channel, MTV clearly prioritizes image at the expense of narrative. In this sense, viewing MTV appears to be about a quick fix: consuming image after resplendent image, one after the other. Indeed, Tetzlaff (1986) sees MTV as a mirror image of the ideal post-modern text: 'Fragmentation, segmentation, superficiality, stylistic jumbling, the blurring of mediation and reality, the collapse of the past and future into the moment of the present, the elevation of hedonism, the dominance of the visual over the verbal' (p. 80). This quotation raises a key question: is post-modernism in some sense inauthentic? Does it promote a particular view of the world in which consumerism and the maximization of the present is all? Perhaps so, but the main idea to remember here is that a post-modern world is an eclectic world and one in which you as an individual are in constant danger of being overloaded:

> Eclecticism . . . of contemporary general culture: one listens to reggae, watches a western, eats McDonald's food for lunch and local cuisine for dinner, wears Paris perfume in Tokyo and 'retro' clothes in Hong Kong; knowledge is a matter for TV games. It is easy to find a public for eclectic

works. By becoming kitsch art panders to the confusion which reigns in the 'taste' of the patrons. Artists, gallery owners, critics, and public wallow together in the 'anything goes,' and the epoch is one of slackening. (Lyotard, 1984, p. 76)

Post-modern identity construction

Having outlined some of the cultural expressions of post-modernism, it would be useful to take one step back and to consider the broader context in which debates surrounding modernity and post-modernity have arisen. As I noted in Chapter 1, social theorists have always, in some form, been preoccupied with the question of social change. Ironically, this preoccupation has become at one and the same time more and yet less focused. It is more focused in the sense that social theorists have begun to concentrate on a specific debate as to whether the social world is undergoing some epochal change or shift. On the other hand, such a debate is so diverse and is constituted by such a variety of conflicting opinions that it is virtually impossible to make any real sense of what is actually being said. By focusing on a key theme, that of the post-modern identity, an issue which preoccupies so many post-modern theorists, we may be able to make more sense of this theoretical quagmire.

The question of identity construction is crucial to the debate over post-modernity in the sense that many theorists argue that social change is such that the nature of identity constructions are fundamentally different to what they were in the past. In other words, the nature of society is changing and as a result so is the nature of those people who populate that society. The overwhelming theme of post-modern conceptions of identity in general is that the onus for the construction of such identities increasingly falls on the shoulders of the individual. There is some resonance here with debates over the risk society, which I discuss in Chapter 7. Basically, the possibilities and choices facing the individual are notably more extensive in a post-modern world, and without the traditional supports we associate with modernity, such as strong family networks, community and organized religion, the individual is seen to interpret and negotiate the world individualistically and from one minute to the next. The individual is increasingly self-dependent, but increasingly vulnerable as a result. This issue, as I note in Chapter 8, is also closely tied up with the changing nature of the relationship between the global and the local. In a post-modern world an individual's identity is less likely to be locally based and more likely to be the product of global social connections. In effect, 'the level of time-space distanciation introduced by high modernity is so extensive that, for the first time in human history, "self" and "society" are interrelated in a global milieu' (Giddens, 1991, p. 32).

As one of those authors who doubts the extent to which we can call such a shift epochal or 'post-modern', Giddens prefers to talk about the impact of 'high modernity'. In this context, he suggests that the self becomes a 'reflexive project'. The individual finds him- or herself in a situation in which identities are constantly being renegotiated in light of the rapidity of social change. For Giddens (1991), then, in a changing world, we are not what we are, but what we make ourselves across time and space. In this environment identities are inherently insecure.

Debates over post-modernity become confusing because those authors who do talk about a radical change in the nature of the social world appear to be discussing the same sorts of trend as those who do not. The important thing to remember in this regard is that although such authors may well disagree as to the magnitude of the changes involved, those changes are still broadly speaking the same or at least similar. Many theorists of the post-modern argue that contemporary societies are increasingly directionless and so are identities as a result. The key point here then is that whereas life in modernity was very much about maintaining a strong sense of who and what you are, in a post-modern world people appear to be intent on actively avoiding such stability. In effect, as Bauman (1996) notes, in a post-modern world people appear to be concerned with actively avoiding commitment,

> And so the snag is no longer how to discover, invent, construct, assemble (even buy) an identity, but how to prevent it from sticking. Well constructed and durable identity turns from an asset into a liability. The hub of postmodern life strategy is not identity building, but avoidance of fixation. (p. 24)

In a world where culture is composed of isolated, disconnected parts, the construction of any form of coherent identity becomes increasingly difficult because in effect there are no secure foundations upon which an identity can be constructed. The individual is left to run riot in a constant struggle to locate him- or herself in a chaotic shifting cultural landscape. The individual resides in the spectacular present and his or her identity is inevitably and perpetually in a state of flux as a result. In short, there appears to be no such thing as a coherent core identity in a post-modern world. As such, many theorists go as far as to discuss 'the death of the subject' – the notion that in a post-modern society there can be no such thing as a unified identifiable self. If we reconsider the aspects of popular culture I outlined above, we can at least accept the possibility that we live in a culture full of signs, of imagery and of constant change. Given that such change is so important to how we might experience life on a day-to-day basis, the consumption of these signs, of the simulacra of popular culture, could be said to become the very source of our identity. Meanwhile, the so-called 'death of the subject', the fact that we can barely even identify any core identity anymore, means that people are becoming increasingly individua- listic and flexible, emotional and intent on being themselves. It should not therefore be assumed that the death of the subject is an unwanted consequence of social change. It gives the individual freedom as well as uncertainty:

> The post-modern individual is characterized by an absence of strong singular identity. . . . S/he is a floating individual with no distinct reference points or parameters. . . . The post-modern individual favours dispersion over concentration, the unrehearsed rather than the carefully organized. S/ he emphasizes choice, free expression, individual participation, private autonomy, personal liberation, without any need of universalistic claims or ideological consistency. S/he is . . . the disintegrating patchwork of a *persona*, with a disparate personality and a potentially confused identity. (Rosenau, 1992, pp. 54–5)

The focus on post-modern identity illustrates the complexities and paradoxes associated with post-modernism. The post-modern world is insecure and uncertain, 'the overwhelming variety of subject positions, of possibilities for identity, in an affluent image culture no doubt create highly unstable identities while constantly providing new openings to restructure one's identity' (Kellner, 1992, p. 174). An individual makes and remakes his or her identity, but ultimately and inevitably that identity is fragile.

Conclusions

What lessons can we learn from discussions of social theory's appar- ent infatuation with debates concerning post-modernity? Do these discussions really have any substance or do they in fact reflect the concerns of the people presenting such views more than the actual nature of social change itself? First, debates over post-modernism are debates over what may or may not be the most appropriate termino- logy to describe social change (Kellner,1992). But in that context, how should we evaluate post-modernity? Perhaps the most crucial point to consider is the degree to which post-modernists exaggerate the trends under discussion. There cannot be any doubt that we live in a rapidly changing world, but because post-modernists believe this to be self-evidently the case they may well exaggerate the extent to which such changes alter people's life experiences. In other words, they might be said to be predisposed to a vision of rapid social change. They exaggerate what might well be genuine patterns of social change, but the playful way in which they do so overplays their hand. The position which so many post-modernists adopt, one that rejects the possibility of human progress, by its very nature also dismisses the possibility of scientific advancement and the sorts of trends associated with debates concerning the emergence of a post-industrial society. The links between the cultural and the economic are therefore woefully neglected. Ironically this creates a vision of a world in which social change is predisposed.

One of the most outspoken critics of post-modernism is Alex Callinicos (1989), who draws attention to the degree of social change being monitored here. His position is clear: 'Now I reject all this. I do not believe we live in a "New Times," in a "postindustrial and postmodern age" fundamentally different from the capitalist mode of production globally dominant for the last two centuries' (p. 4). Callinicos's argument is that the debate over post-modernism actually tells us far more about the political disillusionment of the intelligentsia than it does about the changes they actually describe. In an apparently changing world which appears to be dominated by the superficial appeals of consumerism, intellectuals are struggling to retain some sense of their own identity. The political left and the role of intellectuals within the left is highly circumspect. Post-modernism is a means of expressing a deep disillusionment with this process, alongside what amounts to a declaration of defeat: an acceptance of consumer lifestyles. Post-modernism, then, is born from frustration and helplessness and a recognition that social scientists, in particular, can no longer claim to be capable of changing the world.

Beyond the above general concern about what intellectual trends might motivate a post-modern position, post-modern theory can also be criticized on several further counts. Above all, perhaps, many people who read original post-modern texts argue this approach asks more questions than it actually answers. It is almost as if to write a post-modern piece is to join a particular club or creed in which it is more important to portray a particular image or style than it is to say anything significant. Post-modernism is arguably far too abstract for its own good. As a result it is distanced from the very aspects of cultural life that it attempts to describe. In short, it often seems that post-modernists are simply trying to out 'post-modern' each other. The 'reasoning' for this might be that, as Lash (1990) argues, there is no sense in which we can distinguish between any form of reality; we can only identify representations of reality. In other words, anything goes in a world in which any opinion, point of view or perspective is as valid as any other. Most post-modernists would argue, then, that to present empirical evidence is a pointless waste of time. You cannot prove anything about post-modernity; you can only interpret it from your own personal and unique perspective.

Let us consider one example of an author who playfully uses a post-modern perspective to comprehend a particular aspect of contemporary social life in the above way. Morris Holbrook might be described as a consumer researcher. That is, he is concerned with consumption and consumers. In one particular article, Holbrook (1997) discusses his and his wife's decision to purchase a vacation property in Long Island, USA. Using his vacation experiences as a means of illustrating the fact that consumers seek consumption experience at the edge of adventure, Holbrook goes on to present a series of 'stereographic' picture postcards which depict aspects of his own family's consumption experiences. He does not claim that this material will help us to come to any broader conclusions about the nature of consumer society. Indeed, if he were to do so, he may undermine his very own 'post-modernness'. His analysis is an entirely idiosyncratic one. But as such, what does it actually achieve? It is introspective for post-modernism's sake. The mere implication that the reader should be interested in the first place is itself self-indulgent. The danger, then, is that to be post-modern is more about fulfilling a particular creed or academic style than it is about achieving real theoretical insights. In its more regrettable forms, post-modernism advocates pluralism and yet produces dogmatic pieces of indifferent rhetoric.

The implication of the above is that post-modernism amounts to an over-intellectualized movement that jumps far too easily to highly subjective and deeply questionable impressions of the world. As I suggested earlier the nearest a lot of post-modern work actually gets to providing evidence to back up claims about the fragmented media-saturated world in which we live is to gesticulate about the post-modern MTV viewer who passively sits in front of his or her screen, letting image after image wash over him or her. In this situation content is irrelevant. The consumer is satisfied with imagery that need not test his or her intellect, but simply feeds a need to consume the superficial. The problem with this image is, first, that it is imaginary. On what basis does representation purport to reflect how consumers really interact with MTV? As a text MTV may be quintessentially post-modern, but no assumptions should or can be made about how that text might be consumed. These things *do* require empirical investigation. That empirical investigation may not *prove* anything, but at least it can provide us with a means of extending the insights provided by theory, which can only take us so far alone. More pointedly, even if the portrayal of the MTV viewer is an accurate one, it may well be an atypical portrayal. In other words, very few people are likely to have access to the joys of MTV, and thus to generalize on that basis is misleading. Perhaps the more important point is that there are millions of 'consumers' out there who simply do not have access to the satellite and digital images that authors such as Jean Baudrillard (1983) are referring to. Some people do; others don't. And just because some people do have such access doesn't mean to say that we all necessarily live in a qualitatively different world as a result. This point may well reinforce suspicions that post-modernism is very much a middle-class phenomenon, a case of middle-class academics describing middle-class lifestyles. Mike Featherstone (1991) might well talk about the aestheticization of everyday life, but the degree to which such an analysis applies to the majority of post-modern consumers can only be doubted. Perhaps post-modernism is simply about the emergence of a new middle class.

One of the consequences of a post-modern mode of thought is the decline of the meta-narrative. This is related to the suggestion that modernity is about progress and that society is always advancing in some form or another. In short, post-modernity is associated with the demise of the Enlightenment project. Nobody believes any more that the world is moving towards some bright liberated future. From this point of view meta-narratives are redundant. We can no longer use totalizing systems of thought to explain the world and to predict the direction in which it is going. Systems of thought such as Marxism, psychoanalysis and Christianity no longer have any claim to the truth because there is no such thing as truth. It is for this reason, as I suggested above, that empirical exploration is apparently a pointless exercise. But critics of post-modernism have pointed out the underlying paradox of this line of thought. The very suggestion that meta-narratives have no role to play is a meta-narrative in itself, because it enforces a particular view of the world on those people who consume it. To assume that there is no such thing as truth and everybody's interpretation is equally as invalid as everybody else's is to create a totalizing system of thought. Baudrillard's discussion of the media is particularly over-arching in nature and presents a very opinionated and inclusive theory. He simplifes the phenomena he discusses because the notions that inform his analysis, such as the dominance of the media, are based on generalizations. And he does so in the name of post-modernism, or at least that label is attributed to him. Post-modernists, from this point of view, are imposing their own vision of the world upon us, consumers of social theory.

Students of social theory are often disappointed with post-modernism because it is so difficult to pin it down. Ultimately, however, the limitations of post-modernism actually represent its most important asset. The fact that we are describing not an actual school of thought but an umbrella term for a wide variety of theoretical twists and turns is in itself an advantage. Post-modernism represents a way of looking at the world which as theorists we can dip in and out of at our leisure. We might not accept the extremities of a post-modern position or indeed the apparent extremities of the language used to put that position across. But the key thing about post-modernism is that it has opened up social theory to a whole raft of theoretical issues that previously remained unexplored. The rise of consumption as a key focus of social theory (see Chapter 4) has much to do with post-modernists putting consumption on the theoretical agenda. The rise of cultural studies is also indebted, at least in part, to the post-modern turn in social theory, in the sense that post-modernism is more willing to accept cultural and popular cultural aspects of everyday life as meaningful in their own right. This book may never have been written but for the debates post-modernism has precipitated. However, ultimately, post-modernism has been hoisted by its own petard. Its free-for-all attitude to social theory as aligned with its precept that there is no such thing as absolute truth continues to create the impression, at least, of social theory for social theory's sake. A social theory that does not address the problems of the real world according to the social and political conditions that underlie that world is hardly worth its own weight in hyper-real TV guides.

The ultimate legacy of post-modern theory, then, is to undermine the notion of what it means actually to be a social theorist. If we accept the post-modern position that there is no such thing as reality, only representations of reality (Lash, 1990), and that we therefore cannot explain or understand the world in any meaningful fashion, then the social theorist is redundant. He or she has nothing meaningful to say. At the very least, post-modernism has forced social theorists to cower in a corner and contemplate their role in life. Moreover, any pretensions to political influence (despite some of the work being undertaken with the government by people such as Anthony Giddens) have had to be, at least for now, reconsidered. It is surely healthy for the social theorist to take a step back and consider the value of his or her work. If post-modernism has achieved this much, then it has achieved enough. Social theory may not be able to change the world or explain it, but at least with some more grounded conception of its uses it might at least provoke or enlighten (a word used advisedly) our understanding of the complex processes that lie behind our everyday lives. Post-modernism may not be the best way of understanding the sorts of social changes that are going on around us. On the other hand, it may represent the sort of metaphorical kick up the backside that social theory and social theorists so badly need.

Recommended reading

Fredric Jameson (1984) 'Post-modernism, or, the cultural logic of late capitalism', *New Left Review*, 146, 53–92. One of the single most important single articles on the question of post-modernism, this piece attempts to place post-modernism in the context of the changing nature of capitalism.

David Lyon (1994) *Postmodernity*, Buckingham: Open University Press. An ideal starting point which summarizes the main points of theoretical concern, including the key issue of post-modern consumption.

Pauline Marie Rosenau (1992) *Post-Modernism and the Social Sciences: Insights, Inroads and Intrusions*, Princeton: Princeton University Press. Once you have managed to get your head around the basics, this book provides an ideal means of extending your understanding of post-modernism, not least in the context of post-modern identity.

Dominic Strinati (1995) *An Introduction to Theories of Popular Culture*, London: Routledge. Includes an especially useful section on the cultural manifestations of post-modernism.

CHAPTER 6

A McDONALDIZED SOCIETY?

Regardless of whether we, as social theorists, choose to describe the world in which we live as 'modern', 'late modern' or 'post-modern', one thing is certain: social change is such that manifestations of consumerism are increasingly fundamental to the construction of our everyday lives. As I argued in Chapter 4, we appear to live in what is first and foremost a consumer society. It is all well and good to acknowledge this fact, but how can and do social theorists adapt such a proposition to the realities of everyday life? It is certainly tempting to assume that consumerism is omnipresent and that human beings simply consume what they are offered by the market; that, in effect, consumption provides a template according to which we construct our everyday lives. But such an analysis is far too simplistic to be entirely satisfactory. Consumer cultures and lifestyles are important, but can equally be said to be reflective of deeper integrative principles. In other words, social theorists need to acknowledge the fact that any explanation of social life has to contend with different layers of explanation, or at least with layers of explanation that can only be understood in relation to one another. One such example is the work of George Ritzer (1993, 1998), which at one level deals with the nature of contemporary consumer society, but at another addresses that society as being characterized by processes of rationalization, a notion originally discussed in the work of Max Weber (1992). Ritzer's work is therefore invaluable as an illustration of how classical social theory can be applied in contemporary contexts, and, perhaps more importantly, how social theory need not be abstract and remote, but can actively inform and critique what appear to be the most mundane aspects of everyday life.

Ritzer (1993, 1998) is best known for his theory of McDonaldization, which he sees as an attempt to investigate the changing character of contemporary social life. Ritzer argues that the fast-food restaurant is symbolic of some of the key aspects of social change which our society has undergone in recent decades. When studying McDonaldization, many students of social theory jump too easily to the misleading conclusion that McDonald's has somehow taken over the world. This may or may not be true, but Ritzer was more concerned with the way in which McDonald's and the experience of eating at McDonald's reflected some broader aspects of social change. He describes McDonald's as the 'paradigm case' of a broader process of

McDonaldization, 'the process by which the principles of the fast-food restaurant are coming to dominate more and more sectors of American society as well as the rest of the world' (Ritzer, 1993, p. 1). In particular, Ritzer noted how almost all social institutions, including education, sports, politics and religion, were adapting the principles of McDonaldization. In effect, then, Ritzer's theory of McDonaldization represents an attempt to bring Weber's work into the present day. For this reason, it is worth discussing what Max Weber was attempting to achieve in his own discussion of rationalization.

Weber and rationalization

The legacy of Max Weber is perhaps best remembered as that of somebody who understood the modern condition. Although many students may be most familiar with his work on the Protestant work ethic and questions of status and party, it is arguably Weber's discussion of rationalization that holds most resonance at the beginning of the twenty-first century. Many authors, such as Lash and Whimster (1987), Mommsen (1989) and Sayer (1991), have indeed gone as far as to describe Weber's work in this context as one of the single most important analyses of the constitution of modernity.

The core of Weber's argument is that modernity is characterized by the triumph of a rational way of thinking and acting upon the world, which amounted to a process of 'disenchantment'. In this sense, in contrast to Marx's work, as Sayer (1991) points out, capitalism is but one theatre in which the drama of rationality was carried out; it is the template within which the overall social consequences of rationalization were comprehended. A primary concern of Weber's work was therefore why the superstitious and spiritual character of traditional societies had been superseded, at least in the Western world, by a highly rational and calculated approach to the world. This apparently prioritized the achievement of an end rather than the human implications of how that achievement was brought about. In other words, a social system appeared to be emerging which neglected the very humanity which you might have assumed it would attempt to promote. In this rational world humanity is reduced to calculation, measurement and control. Weber therefore described a society preoccupied with reason, stability and discipline. The emergence of the Protestant religion and the Calvinistic quest for salvation and security generated a society dedicated to work and the transformation and control of the human environment; a world predicated on the need to progress. But of equal interest was the move towards individualism. Conducting his work in the nineteenth century, Weber recognized the way in which the nature of sociality or social relations was changing to the extent that human beings appeared to be individual units, often differentiated by their relationship to money (as Simmel, 1990, also pointed out), rather than according to their relationships with other human beings. In effect, for Weber the mystery of traditional society was lost in favour of a steel-hard cage of bureaucratic rationality where efficiency and predictability were more important than human creativeness and fulfilment.

The notion of formal rationality is particularly important to Weber. He felt that social structures had outgrown the individuals who occupied them and that the 'system' as a whole was so all-powerful that people's lives were now governed by a complex set of rules and regulations that took the humanity out of human life. In contrast to substantive rationality, a social system which would prioritize the needs of human beings rather than some abstract notion of what suits human beings as a collective, Weber felt that formal rationality represented the core of a new calculated social world in which fulfilment and satisfaction could only be achieved through rational capitalistic imperatives.

The problem for Weber was that the means were far more important than the ends in this calculated society. To illustrate this point, Brubaker (1984) provides a useful example. He points out that a population may actually need better health-care but, on the other hand, they may actually want TV sets, and in a rational economy the TV sets will be produced. The productive process and the social relations that emerge from that process are therefore entirely calculated – so much so that freedom is essentially the freedom to, at least in one sense, be controlled. As Brubaker (1984) argues, rationalization therefore involves 'the depersonalization of social relationships, the refinement of techniques of calculation, the enhancement of the social importance of specialized knowledge, and the extension of technically rational control over both natural and social processes' (p. 2). Brubaker goes on to identify three key aspects of rationalization in Weber's work. Weber argues that knowledge, and, in particular, scientific technological knowledge, has an increasingly important role to play in providing the basis for social action. The growing economic and technical basis of social life and the advance of bureaucracy demand specialized technical knowledge, access to which has, in turn, an important role to play in shaping processes of stratification and thus people's life chances. Human beings act according to conscious reflection about the probable consequences of their actions (Brubaker, 1984, p. 34). People are therefore instrumentally rational insofar as they act according to what will best serve their interests at that moment in what is such a rationalized bureaucratic world. For Weber, the world has been disenchanted and intellectualized and is the worse for it.

The second aspect of Weber's theory of rationalization which Brubaker discusses is that of impersonality, which is largely a consequence of a society that appears to pray at the altar of market relations. Specifically, Weber was concerned that the means of authority in a rationalized society were becoming increasingly abstract in nature. In a sense, Weber was describing an increasingly risky society where market forces are propped up by legal authority and impersonal forms of bureaucracy remain dominant. The abstract threats of bankruptcy and unemployment are constant and inevitable. A person's livelihood is not necessarily at threat due to his or her own actions, but as a result of the way the social system operates as a whole. For an individual's success to be evaluated, material wealth, rather than personal competence or achievement, becomes the only conceivable measure.

The third and perhaps most important aspect of Weber's theory of rationalization, discussed so effectively by Brubaker, is control. Weber's theory is a very critical one in the sense that he bemoans the ways in which this world of bureaucracy manipulates and dominates, not simply in the economic sphere, but in all realms of life. Above all, as Brubaker points out, Weber is concerned with the rational control imparted over men working in capitalist firms and bureaucratic organizations. In effect, social relationships are reduced to aspects of scientific, industrial or administrative processes and conformity becomes the name of the day. An individual performs a function in the capitalist system. It would be misleading to suggest that Weber totally dismissed the process of rationalization. He did indeed recognize its advantages in creating a far more efficient and effective economic system. But the price to pay for this system was dehumanization and the loss of freedom. In the modern world creativity and human fulfilment are things of the past. In Weber's world, human beings have become objects of a meaningless vocational culture (see Scaff, 1989). For Weber, rationalization cannot be 'cured' as such; it is, in a sense, irreversible. Any visions of a utopian world of human fulfilment are an illusion where rationalization is so well entrenched. In this respect, Weber was stridently anti-modernist. How was human progress possible in this 'polar night of icy darkness'? More importantly, perhaps, is Weber's analysis simply too negative and merely a product of his time? Meanwhile, Andreski (1984) has criticized Weber for being profoundly unclear in his conceptualization of rationalization. Weber

> was so full of ideas and in such a hurry to gather factual information to back them that he never formulated his theses carefully, never examined or weighed up arguments for and against, never made clear what were his premises or implications. . . . He ploughs through mounds of factual

information and churns up a flood of rule-of-the-thumb generalizations, explanations and suggestive comparisons. (1984, pp. 145–6)

Indeed, there might be a case for suggesting that Weber became obsessed with the concept of rationalization, whilst never developing it completely enough to be truly convincing. Indeed, as Turner (1992) suggests, there is some considerable evidence to suggest that processes of globalization and consumerism have helped to perpetuate a far less rigid social structure than that portrayed in Weber's work. From the opposite point of view, Weber could be said to have provided a legacy which other sociologists have inherited in order to describe and critique a world that is arguably far more rationalized than perhaps Weber would ever have imagined. In the century since Weber conducted his work, have human beings managed to overcome the constraints of rationalization? George Ritzer (1993) is adamant about one thing: the fact that they certainly have not.

The McDonaldization of Weber

Authors such as Scaff (1989) have argued that since Weber's work the impact of rationalization has actually intensified; spreading into all aspects of contemporary life such as the family, child-rearing, love and friendship, as well as being reflected in aspects of technology and communications, both of which are very controlled and dehumanized in nature. This is a theme taken up by Ritzer (1993), who uses the metaphor of McDonald's as an illustration of the highly controlled, bureaucratic and dehumanizing nature of contemporary social life.

Before going into detail about the way in which Ritzer develops Weber's ideas, it would be useful to consider a particularly graphic example of contemporary forms of rationalization as discussed in Ritzer's work. This helps to illustrate both the contemporary relevance of Weber's ideas and the way in which Ritzer attempts to apply them. Ritzer highlights the car industry as being a classic illustration of rational principles. The industry churns out millions of cars every year, apparently regardless of the impact upon the environment via pollution and road-building programmes. Quoting the particular example of the production by Ford of the Punto in the United States, Ritzer (1993) claims that Ford actually found in tests that the car's fuel system had a high chance of rupturing in a rear-end collision. But the car industry is notoriously competitive and as such Ford apparently decided to go ahead with production regardless. They duly calculated that approximately 180 deaths and roughly the same number of injuries would occur as a result of the fault. They estimated in turn that this would cost them $200,000 per person and that the cost to the company would be less than the $11 per car it would cost to repair the actual defect. This is a classic example of the apparently dehumanizing nature of rationalization and of the irrationality of McDonaldization. There may be a logical rational reason for making such a decision, but such a decision is entirely irrational when you consider the broader implications of that decision for the well-being, indeed the lives, of human beings.

So what exactly is McDonaldization, and how does it relate to Weber's discussion of rationalization? As far as McDonald's is concerned, Ritzer (1993) identifies four basic dimensions which lie at the core of the success story that is symbolized by Ronald McDonald: efficiency, calculability, predictability and control. First of all, McDonald's offers the customer efficiency. It apparently provides the most efficient way of fulfilling your appetite (even if only on a temporary basis). It provides an efficient means of satisfying our needs. Secondly, McDonald's provides food that can be easily quantified and calculated. It appears to offer value for money (e.g. through 'meal deals') for what, on the surface at least, appears to be a reasonably large meal. As Ritzer points out, in contemporary culture, 'Quantity has become equivalent to quality; a lot of something means it must be good' (p. 10). As consumers we are reassured by the sense that we are getting a good deal when the ubiquitous nature of McDonald's clearly illustrates that it is the company itself that is making the genuine profits. As Ritzer points out, there is another kind of calculation involved in visiting McDonald's, and that is to do with the preservation of time. Customers calculate the time they will save visiting McDonald's as opposed to, say, cooking the food for themselves. McDonald's, argues Ritzer, also offers us predictability. Wherever we go in the world we know a Big Mac will be the same. Neither time nor geography will change the ingredients of the Big Mac. But the predictability of McDonald's is again reassuring. We may not anticipate the most amazing culinary experience of our lifetimes prior to visiting McDonald's, but, on the other hand, we can feel safe in the knowledge that such a visit will hold no surprises. The food will be basic, but familiarly basic, and that in itself is enough.

The fourth characteristic of McDonald's which particularly intrigues Ritzer is control, and most notably the control exerted over those people working in McDonald's. The experience of working in McDonald's is highly prescribed and involves doing a limited number of tasks in a very particular way. Similarly, on entering McDonald's the customer is subjected to a highly controlled environment which positively discourages freedom of choice (e.g. again through the promotion of 'meal deals'); encourages a quick exit (e.g. through the provision of uncomfortable seats); and compels you to dispose of your own rubbish. But of most concern to Ritzer is the way in which non-human technology replaces human technology. The soft drinks dispenser, preprogrammed cash register and the frier which rings when the French fries reach optimum crispiness are all examples of how machines can apparently be more efficient than human beings. 'The result is that McDonald's is able to reassure customers about the nature of the employee to be encountered and the nature of the service to be obtained' (Ritzer, 1993, p. 11). On the downside, as Ritzer points out, both customers and employees are forced to work precisely in the way that the company wants them to work. The rational system that is McDonald's is, in effect, denying human reason.

But as I have already pointed out, Ritzer's discussion of McDonaldization extends far beyond McDonald's itself. For instance, Weber (1992) argues that the yearning for efficiency has turned into 'a near universal desire' (p. 35). Our society is effectively characterized by a mania for efficiency. Many sectors of society have had to become efficient to satisfy human beings who are accustomed to the efficiency of the fast-food restaurant. The fast-food restaurant did not, according to Ritzer, create this yearning, but it certainly helped to perpetuate it. Shopping is a case in point. The department store and the shopping mall represent highly efficient systems, as do shopping catalogues, internet sales and personal product scanners intended to make your shopping trip as efficient as possible. Similarly, Ritzer argues that the video shop symbolizes the way in which people are much more interested in efficiency than they are in risk-taking. After all, to stay at home and watch a video, fast-forwarding through the trailers, is much more efficient than having to travel miles to your nearest cinema.

In his discussion of calculability, Ritzer discusses numerous examples of the way in which quantity is used as a measure of quality. The package tour is one such example of a social phenomenon premised on superficial impressions of quality, whilst telling you next to nothing about the actual culture you are visiting. The same pattern is evident on our TV screens. In a style reminiscent of the Frankfurt School (see Chapter 2), Ritzer criticizes television schedules for being determined by TV ratings rather than quality. His suggestion that European television is of a better quality than its American counterpart has more recently been undermined by the emergence in Britain of digital television, which again is apparently more about attracting an audience in whatever way possible than it is about presenting quality television, as Ritzer himself predicted. This emphasis on quantity is also reflected, according to Ritzer, in what he calls junk-food journalism, which is more about sensationalism and edibility than it is about depth of analysis. Perhaps, more importantly and indeed worryingly, education is also becoming an increasingly quantifiable experience. The preoccupation with grades and league tables in schools has meant that less attention is arguably being paid to the quality of the experience and more to the end product of that experience. This trend is equally in evidence in universities, where the excellence of teaching is judged on a numerical scale as part of a 'Teaching Quality Assurance' and where one of the prime means of students' ability to judge the relative merits of different institutions is a somewhat spurious process of concocting league tables. These tables, published by national newspapers, are based on somewhat unpredictable criteria which none the less give the impression of an authoritative measure of standards.

Ritzer portrays a world founded on predictability. He therefore describes international motel chains such as Holiday Inn and Quality Inn as pioneers of the rationalization process; their success being based on the fact that their customer knows exactly what service will be provided regardless of the location. Ritzer also goes on to discuss the rationalization of the film industry, and, in particular, the phenomenon of the sequel, which aims to satisfy consumers by using the comfortable familiarity of a tried and tested recipe. Such predictability ensures profits for the film studios because it plays on the consumers' desire to feel secure and in control of their cinema viewing: 'Like a McDonald's meal, many sequels are not very good, but at least the consumers know what they are getting' (Ritzer, 1993, p. 89).

Tourism is again a focus for Ritzer's critique of the predictability of contemporary social life. The amusement park, for instance, provides a highly predictable environment characterized by what Ritzer (1993) describes as 'almost surreal orderliness' (p. 92). Employees of parks such as Disneyland and Walt Disney World apparently look alike and behave alike. Meanwhile, sport, which you might intuitively expect to be unpredictable, is becoming increasingly predictable at the behest of the television companies: the tie-break in tennis being a classic example of the way in which even sports have had to become more predictable in order to satisfy the needs of the TV consumer. Basically, then, Ritzer argues we live in a world that offers no surprises. Such predictability is closely related to the issue of control.

Ritzer points out that people are the greatest source of uncertainty and unpredictability in a rationalized system, and that therefore efforts to increase control are more often than not directed at them. The process of McDonaldization is very much bound up with the need to exert control over employees and customers. Perhaps the most important way of achieving such control, and of removing an element of unpredictability, is by replacing human beings with technology. By this, Ritzer (1993) means technological materials, skills, knowledge, rules, regulations, procedures and techniques, as well as machines and tools:

The basic idea, historically, is to gradually and progressively gain control over people through the development and deployment of a wide variety of increasingly effective technologies. Once people are controlled, it is possible to begin reducing their actions to a series of machine-like actions. . . . With the replacement of humans by machines, we have reached the ultimate stage in control over people – people can cause us no more uncertainty and unpredictability because they are no longer involved, at least directly, in the process. (pp. 100–1)

Ritzer acknowledges that technologies are not implemented solely for the purpose of control and that factors such as increased productivity are also important. However, you only have to consider the prevalence of controlling technologies to realize how important they are to the make-up of contemporary society. Ritzer argues again that the amusement park is an especially graphic example of this aspect of McDonaldization. Employees in the various Disney parks appear to be subjected to a series of rules and regulations that could be said to reduce them to robots. Alongside the 'human robots', life-like talking automatons reinforce this feeling. Any humanity appears to be removed from aspects of performance by a rigid programme designed to limit human error. Visitors to the parks are arguably equally controlled in the sense that they are forced to obey non-human technologies which inform them of routes they are obliged to take. According to Ritzer, the shopping mall is also an example of a highly controlled environment in which consumers are subtly 'encouraged' to behave in certain ways. The mall provides shoppers with a safe and secure environment, but the cost to be paid for that environment is its essential lack of humanity. Indeed, Ritzer (1993) goes as far as to refer to those consumers who wander the shopping mall hour after hour as 'zombies' (p. 111). Medicine is also an area of our lives that can be interpreted as becoming increasingly controlled. Ritzer accuses GPs, for instance, of being little more than dispatchers who send patients on to the appropriate machines and specialists. From this point of view the physician has less and less control or influence over decision-making, which, in turn, is increasingly a prescribed technological matter. More and more bureaucratic layers control the medical profession; the privatization of health in Britain being a crystal-clear example here. Meanwhile, for the customer, health provision becomes an increasingly impersonal experience. As technology develops, the world in which we live is apparently becoming increasingly controlled to the extent that 'more and more of people's ability to think will be taken from them and built into the technology' (Ritzer, 1993, p. 120).

Ritzer's primary concern with the above aspects of McDonaldization is that rationality is essentially irrational, and he sees this irrationality as amounting to a fifth dimension of rationalization. In other words, despite pretensions to be otherwise, McDonaldization is actually inefficient, unpredictable, incalculable and promotes a loss of control. The so-called 'improvements' to social life that these aspects of rationalization are intended to achieve often produce the opposite effect. Automated teller machines (ATMs) are a classic example of this. Apparently intended to save time, energy and effort, they seem to encourage longer queues than in the traditional banking hall. According to Ritzer, then, any improvements or efficiencies characterized by rational systems tend to benefit those touting rationalization, rather than those using the systems. It may, for instance, be efficient for a supermarket if we scan our own foodstuffs; but it is not necessarily the most efficient way of doing things for ourselves. But Ritzer's main concern is that McDonaldization has meant that people are losing control over the system which is controlling them. Ritzer therefore mirrors Weber's discussion in arguing that human beings are threatened by an iron cage of rationalization.

Expressing America; Expressing McDonaldization

Ritzer (1995) develops the above theories in his critique of the global credit card society. His achievement here is, again, a significant one, insofar as he manages successfully to bring social theory to life in a contemporary context. While on the surface criticizing the role of the credit card in the maintenance of contemporary consumer society, at a deeper level Ritzer describes a more general process, 'the American express'. He is therefore concerned with the dramatic pace of social change, particularly as it pertains to changes in the nature of consumption. He sees the credit card as providing a key foundation upon which such changes can take place. In short,

> Credit cards are a key feature of modern society, and an examination of them allows us to see clearly some of the essential features of the modern world. In the end, this study of credit cards leads us to some of the most essential problems of modern society – crime, debt, threats to privacy, rationalization, dehumanization, and homogenization. Thus, the credit card is both a key component of the modern world and a marvellous window into it. (Ritzer, 1995, p. xii)

This last point is in itself of interest insofar as it raises some very pertinent questions about the nature of social theory. Ritzer takes Simmel's impressionistic sociology as his guide, insofar as he admires the philosophy underlying Simmel's work: that the intense scrutiny of a particular element of society can lead towards a broader understanding of the social world in general. The suggestion here is that every aspect of social life is somehow related to every other aspect of social life and that by looking very closely at the social impact of the credit card we can come to broader conclusions about the underlying make-up of society. According to Ritzer, then, the credit card takes social theorists to the very core of modern consumer society. In particular, it represents a vivid illustration of the 'oppressive and deforming impact of large-scale social structures on individuals' (p. 3). The credit card and the consumer society in general are, from this point of view, equally as fascinating in this respect as more traditional sociological phenomena such as capitalism and bureaucracy. In a way then, Ritzer is asking sociologists to be more imaginative by addressing the issues of social change and social problems from unique and atypical perspectives.

As far as the credit card is concerned, Ritzer suggests that the consumer society is obsessed with spending. This is no better illustrated than in the form of the global demand for credit encapsulated in the credit card, which itself plays a primary role in the perpetuation of rationalization. The world of consumerism provided by the credit card, and, in particular, credit card loans, is instantly served up to the consumer in what Ritzer describes as a highly rationalized assembly-line fashion. The end result of all this is a society that is spiralling into dehumanizing debt and which is doing so in the name of rationalization. The credit is quite simply 'the ideal tool to allow for smooth movement between rationalized systems' (Ritzer, 1995, p. 177).

A cynic might criticize Ritzer for cashing in on the McDonaldization industry (what we could refer to as McMcDonaldization) in his more recent book, *The McDonaldization Thesis* (1998), which amounts to a collection of related (and at times disparate) essays dealing with various aspects and applications of McDonaldization. But the real benefit of this contribution to debates surrounding McDonaldization is that Ritzer broadens his analysis to address what he calls 'the new means of consumption', the link with McDonaldization being firmly established in this context as an exploitative process which includes some consumers whilst excluding others. In so doing, he incorporates the insights of a diverse range of theorists, including Karl Mannheim (1929, 1935) and Jean Baudrillard (1983). As far as Mannheim (1929, 1935) is concerned, Ritzer is particularly fascinated with the implication of his work that McDonaldized systems are dehumanizing in the sense that they threaten the human ability to think in intelligent ways. McDonaldization encourages mindlessness, and this is an attribute of modernity which Mannheim develops in his work. In Ritzer's reading, Mannheim is concerned that human beings have a declining ability to think rationally. In a sense, then, his work is more subtle than Weber's, or at least more pertinent to the debate over McDonaldization. In Mannheim's analysis it is not simply human values that are threatened by McDonaldized systems; of more concern, and quite rightly so, is the tendency of those systems virtually to eliminate human thought. The key notion here is one of stratification:

> The utility of Mannheim's theorizing is enhanced in this realm because . . . he points to the fact that one's position in the organizational heirarchy affects one's ability to think. Those at the top are able to limit the effect of external constraints on them, while actively imposing such constraints on those below them in the organization. The result is that the further one descends in a McDonaldized organization, the less the ability of employees to think through their actions on their own. (Ritzer, 1998, p. 25)

This element of stratification means that Mannheim's contribution to the debate over McDonaldization is, in one sense, more sophisticated. For him rationalized systems have a personal dimension. On the other hand, however, insofar as he claims planning can provide a means of offsetting disenchantment, Ritzer argues that Mannheim underestimates the eroding effect of rationalization, which in fact is revitalized by such planning. I do not want to go into any further detail about Mannheim's contribution to the debate over McDonaldization, other than to say that Ritzer concludes that in many ways Mannheim's conception of rationalization is more manageable than Weber's. It can be criticized for being a product of its time, but it still manages to provide an alternative perspective on McDonaldization which Ritzer is correct in encouraging us to pursue. Ritzer remains convinced that Weberian theory should continue to be the prime source of theoretical debate concerning McDonaldization (his view of planning being Mannheim's main weakness), but Mannheim's work provides a useful addition to the debate none the less.

Of equal interest here are Ritzer's efforts to relate McDonaldization to post-modernism: pointing out that modernism and post-modernism amount to alternative ways of looking at contemporary phenomena and that rationalization is a process most closely associated with modernism. If rationality is associated with modernity, it follows that irrationality should characterize post-modernity. In this context, Ritzer considers how far we can accept that McDonaldization is actually declining in the apparently fragmented world in which we live. Are the dominant rational systems which Weber describes in the process of being swamped by irrationalities? Far from it, argues Ritzer. He believes very strongly that McDonaldization will remain triumphant, and that, regardless of some irrational characteristics we might associate with post-modernism, rationalization remains all-dominant:

The triumph of McDonaldization means, by definition, the continuation, even acceleration, of modernity. . . . If history is any guide, McDonaldized systems will survive, even proliferate, long after we have moved beyond postmodern society and scholars have relegated postmodernism to the status of a concept of little more than historical interest. (Ritzer, 1998, p. 191)

Ritzer's handle on alternative ways of conceptualizing social change, and in particular that of post-modernism, is intriguing and is, in turn, witness to his unswerving belief in the immense and all-powerful influence of rationalization. But also of interest to the scholar of social theory is how Ritzer goes about addressing this issue methodologically. Ritzer freely acknowledges that there simply has not been any 'scientific' research into the topics he is addressing. Fast-food restaurants, credit cards and consumption in general have not proved to be of fundamental sociological concern, at least to American sociologists, and this despite the United States apparently being the world leader in consumerism. His contention, then, is that because of this, American social theorists have actually become desensitized to consumption as a key social phenomenon to the extent that, in contrast to their European colleagues, they have almost taken it for granted as the American way of life. Many American social scientists, argues Ritzer, perceive questions of McDonaldization and consumption to be too trivial to be worthy of their attention, and as such reflect the broader productivist bias which has characterized the history of social theory, as I point out in Chapter 4.

In contrast to much traditional social theory, Ritzer therefore argues that his work is inevitably journalistic or at least depends very much on journalistic sources, quite simply because there are no other recent sources available. It might be suggested that in this instance Ritzer 'doth protest too much'. He shouts rather too loudly about how what is really important is not the empirical input of the ideas he deploys, but the extent to which those ideas prove useful to those who read them. He therefore self-consciously draws attention to the (perceived) inadequacies of his own work and to the suggestion that such work is barely theoretical at all. I know of colleagues who have sneered at Ritzer's work because it just isn't serious enough. It does not behave in the way in which people believe social theory should behave. It is not abstract or especially systematic and as such does not present itself as having access to a privileged interpretation of the world. Yes, it interprets and analyses, but it does so in a way that negates the privileges that tend to be associated with a knowledge of social theory. As such, it raises issues about the broader role of social theory and whether social theory has to rise *above* the everyday. I will return to this theme later in this chapter.

Before concluding this particular section, it is worth pointing out that in his most recent book, *Enchanting a Disenchanted World* (1999), Ritzer's focus on the consumer society emerges as an increasingly pivotal aspect of his analysis. His thesis is that the settings in which we consume are becoming ever more fundamental to the way we live, to the extent that the social world appears to be structured to 'lead and coerce us' into the world of 'hyperconsumption' (p. x). Consumption is omnipresent. We are, in effect, 'consumed by consumption' (p. xi). The new means of consumption such as the casino, mega-mall, theme park or themed restaurant therefore take on an almost enchanted, religious quality. Spectacular spaces of consumption (symbolized above all perhaps by the consumerist nirvana of Las Vegas) also operate as highly effective rationalized selling machines. Post-modern forms of consumption have, from this point of view, re-enchanted the process of consumption. They have made consumption impulsive, mysterious and emotional, to the extent that the consumer is actively seduced by it. The post-modern world of consumerism in which we live is therefore both exhilarating and deeply threatening: a world of the spectacular juxtaposed against the abiding question of how to 'live a more meaningful life within a society increasingly defined by consumption' (p. 217). Rationalization continues to play a key role in this aspect of social change.

The McDonaldization of McDonaldization

The irony of Ritzer's theory of McDonaldization and the reception of his ideas in general is that they have appeared to have given rise to an industry in itself. In one sense, then, the theory of McDonaldization has been McDonaldized or at least brought into the rational world of social theory and debate. Ritzer himself has written prolifically on the subject of McDonaldization, as have his critics. Indeed, unusually for such a recent and in some ways down-to-earth social theory, Ritzer has stimulated and given new life to a classical piece of social theory, Weber's theory of rationalization, which clearly has contemporary resonance. The two collections that immediately spring to mind in this regard are *Resisting McDonaldization*, edited by Barry Smart (1999a) and *McDonaldization Revisited*, edited by Mark Alfino, John S. Caputo and Robyn Wynard (1998). In his introduction to the former, Smart (1999b) draws attention to the way in which Ritzer's theory manages to help delve beneath superficial aspects of the global consumer society. But Smart also goes on to question how far we should accept the proposition that McDonaldization represents the most appropriate means of coming to terms with social change, or indeed of coming to terms with the impact of globalization. Indeed, Smart even debates the extent to which the notion of McDonaldization is simply and no more than a device for making Weber's theory of rationalization more timely and more palatable to students. In this sense, Ritzer might be said to be McDonaldizing social theory: he may be criticized for making social theory consumable, predictable and convenient. McDonaldization may well be, from this point of view, the fast-food of social theory. Perhaps unfairly, Ritzer could actually therefore be *criticized* for developing Weber's ideas in a contemporary context; for elaborating Weber's ideas, but not actually presenting something genuinely original. More importantly, from a critical point of view, Smart believes that Ritzer fails to come to terms with the degree of complexity of the social processes he discusses. For instance, he does not discuss the mechanisms which are deployed actively to persuade people that rationalization is actually good for them, and in particular to buy into the family identity of McDonald's:

> The problem identified above arises from conceptual slippage, from Ritzer's failure to adequately differentiate between complex processes of modern rationalization and their uneven consequences, and from a parallel tendency to conflate discussion of McDonald's the fast-food business with 'McDonaldization' as a complex social and economic process. (Smart, 1999b, p. 17)

I want to address the above issues by briefly considering two further critiques of Ritzer's work. The first of these is Douglas Kellner's (1999) chapter on 'Theorizing/Resisting McDonaldization' in the Smart collection. Kellner commends Ritzer for popularizing Max Weber's theory of rationalization, and, indeed, goes as far as to say that 'Ritzer has touched upon upon some vital nerve centres of the contemporary era' (p. 187). In particular, Kellner notes that the mode of theorizing which Ritzer adopts is under considerable attack from post-modern quarters, insofar as it encompasses 'such a diverse field of topics and artefacts [which] exemplify the sociological moment of illuminating abstraction, of generating a concept so broad as to conceptually grasp and interpret a wealth of data in a way that theorizes defining and constitutive features of the present moment' (p. 186). But Kellner's main criticism of Ritzer's work is that it does not sufficiently develop a cultural dimension, and that the process of rationalization as expressed in McDonald's itself is not distinguished clearly enough from the broader impact of McDonaldization.

Kellner's concern, then, is that Weber underestimates the subjective aspects of the process of rationalization and therefore valorizes its socio-economic aspects at the expense of the hedonistic and fun-orientated cultural aspects of the processes Ritzer describes (see

Chapter 5). From a post-modern point of view, McDonald's has drawn its customers into a world of hyper-real commodification, crossing the modern/post-modern divide with its 'phantasmagoric advertising and commodity spectacle' (Kellner, 1999, p. 191). More presciently, Kellner argues that approaches to McDonaldization need to be more systematic than is the case in Ritzer's work. Ritzer's discussion of McDonaldization is provocative from this point of view, but underestimates the potentially positive features of McDonaldization. There are times, as Kellner points out, when rationalization is a good thing. When travelling in unfamiliar countries we may actually benefit from the comfort of efficient, calculable, predictable and controlled systems. Similarly, within universities, for instance, bureaucratic rationalization can play a positive role in people's lives: 'it can promote the forces of domination and hierarchy, but it can also empower individuals against institutions via standardized practices and regulations' (Kellner, 1999, p. 201). There is arguably an in-built assumption in Ritzer's work that McDonald's is driving a process of homogenization which in turn is destroying any possibility of individuality and diversity. As far as Kellner (1999) is concerned, this underestimates the 'proliferation of difference, diversity, variety and hetereogeneity' (p. 202) that characterizes post-modernity. There may indeed be evidence for suggesting that processes of McDonaldization and globalization, fundamental to Ritzer's work, actually extend the degree of consumer choice and thus the freedom available to the consumer (see Chapters 4 and 8).

The question of consumer freedom and hence the extent to which Ritzer provides a balanced view of rationalization is fundamental to critiques of his work, as is the suggestion which I have made in my own work that Ritzer's theory does indeed lack any empirical foundation beyond its journalistic one (see Miles, 1998b). At times, therefore, Ritzer's work appears to adopt an unbending theoretical perspective on the social world that is supported by countless examples of self-supporting impressionistic illustration. In other words, Ritzer could be said to present selective illustrations of his position; positions which have no real empirical value. I am not suggesting that Ritzer's work does not have any basis in reality – clearly it does – but perhaps that basis is a rather blinkered one that would benefit from more considered empirical insight.

What I want to suggest here is that the McDonaldization thesis is simply too totalizing to be entirely acceptable. It undervalues the ability of human beings actively to interpret McDonaldized systems. In other words, McDonaldization exists, but, inasmuch as it does exist, people often relate to it subjectively. I personally address this issue in an article in the Alfino et al. collection (Miles, 1998b). This article reports upon an empirical project which was concerned with the relationship between youth consumption and identity. The research, which involved my working as a shop assistant in a well-known high street sports store, simultaneously raised several points of concern directly relevant to Ritzer's concern with rationalization. This provided the opportunity for me to take on the role of a covert participant observer, during which I observed the sports store as a site of consumption. A particular concern of mine was how far this setting truthfully reflected the sort of analysis Ritzer presents. As I noted above, Ritzer describes shopping as an increasingly efficient process, and it was indeed true to say that, as part of a chain of virtually identical stores, consumers are able to buy their preferred goods in a highly efficient and predictable environment. The uniform ways in which shop assistants are dressed and trained also reinforce the validity of Ritzer's position. There is no room for the shop assistant, or indeed the shopper, to display any individuality in this context. The sports store is an example of a dehumanized social space. In particular, the actual decision of the consumer to purchase a pair of training shoes is far from a free one. It is actually very controlled in the sense that it is determined by all sorts of intervening factors, including the layout of the store as well as the impact of the mass media, fashion and advertising.

On first sight, the above description appears to fit in nicely with Ritzer's conception of McDonaldization. But the problem is that this is where Ritzer's ideas begin to falter. He does not adequately consider the way in which consumers, and in this case, young people, actively engage with and negotiate rationalized systems. The theory of McDonaldization appears to be accurate, on the surface at least, but people are more than capable of using the rationalized nature of the consuming experience to their own ends. In fact, people can actively embrace the principles of rationalization because it can actually give them a sense of control (Miles, 1998b, p. 59). As far as young people in particular are concerned, then, consumption might be said to provide a means of stability in what for them is so often such an insecure, risky world (see Beck, 1992) in terms of educational and employment prospects (see Roberts, 1995). In these circumstances, and in a world where they share less and less by way of common biographies, young people are out to find any little piece of stability they can possibly get. The suggestion here is that in this context consumption and the rationalized principles associated with it allow young people to cope with the sorts of stresses and strains associated with life in a risk society. They actively use the controlled environment of the sports store, and of consumer culture in general, to provide them with a stability that simply is not possible in other realms of their lives. Ways of consuming are potentially highly prescribed, but such prescription is often a help rather than a hindrance:

Upon entering the sports store the young people I observed were able to forget, indeed, escape from, their everyday concerns. They became immersed in another culture, a culture symbolised by the street life portrayed by MTV. In a world characterised by insecurity and uncertainty as to the future, as well as the present, young people can open this 'window of stability' and enter a whole new world – a world in which, regardless of family background or work prospects, they can be treated as equals, in the sense that they have equal access, depending upon resources, to the cultural capital of consumption. (Miles, 1998b, p. 61)

What I want to suggest in the above context is that Ritzer's vision of rationalization is an over-deterministic one. Above all, his theory underestimates the role which individual agency plays in the interpretation of social structures, a topic which continues to fascinate social theorists (e.g. Archer, 1995). In other words, rationalization, although it exists, is not as much of a one-way process as Ritzer appears so fervently to claim. Rationalized social systems operate, and to an extent young people, and people in general, are controlled by them, but not to the same degree that Ritzer suggests. In short, 'Ritzer cannot be forgiven for presenting a theory which misunderstands a consumer society in which the complexities of structure and agency are played out and negotiated by consumers throughout the course of their everyday lives' (Miles, 1998b, p. 65). Ironically, then, rationalization can itself be negotiated in a rational and reflexive fashion.

Conclusions

Regardless of those complaints presented by his detractors, Ritzer's contribution to contemporary social theory is undoubtedly an enormous one, even though his approach may not be original, in the sense that his whole theory rests on foundations provided by Max Weber, and his contributions to debates over modernity and postmodernity are not without their limitations. The pros and cons of Ritzer's work and how it illuminates our understanding of an apparently rationalized world can indeed be debated endlessly. Authors such as Ray and Reed in their book *Organizing Modernity* (1994) have indeed argued that rationalization is simply not as all-embracing as many commentators have tended to suggest. Where rationalization does exist, it is arguably tempered by an active and informed public motivated by the possibilities inherent in the rational negotiation of values in modern societies. As such, Hage and Powers (1992) have argued that the long-term impact of rationalization has been diluted, notably in the context of changing relationships to and in the workplace. In this context, Hage and Powers prefer to discuss the notion of 'complexification', the idea that, far from being rationalized, the workplace, one of the main arenas in which we construct social relationships, is characterized by increasingly creative occupational specialities. In other words, human beings are not dehumanized by social change, but are positively liberated by it. Complexification involves individuals acquiring more and more knowledge so that they can respond optimally to highly individualized circumstances, which therefore puts increasing emphasis on individual personality and individual control.

Alternatively, at a deeper level, it might be argued that human beings are all subjected to an illusion of flexibility. We feel we are liberated by a rationalized consumer society, but that society dehumanizes us through what is no more than a superficial impression of consumer freedom. We feel we can be who we want through what we consume, when in fact we are simply being what the social system wants us to be: consumers. The validity of either of the above perspectives will continue to be debated. If nothing else, we should commend Ritzer for highlighting the need to pursue such a debate.

Perhaps contemporary society is simply far too complex and paradoxical for such a strict reading of the McDonaldization thesis to be acceptable. The opportunities available to us in a consumer society are at one and the same time constraining and enabling. Ultimately, Ritzer's work does at times disappoint, perhaps most markedly in his analysis of the ways in which the effects of rationalization might be offset. Ritzer suggests visiting a greasy spoon café once a week, sending all junk mail back to the post office and not paying to watch any films with roman numerals in their title. The triviality of these suggestions is testament to the deeply embedded nature of social life and to Ritzer's concern that these trends are far from being reversed and are actually intensifying. But on the same token, they also reflect a theory that is in some senses politically impotent. In this respect, Barry Smart's (1999b) contention that Ritzer's work suffers from not adopting a more Marxian political economy approach is potentially valid. Similarly, Kellner (1999) criticizes Ritzer's neglect of the economic basis of rationalization and how people subjectively use McDonaldized systems. But putting the above debate to one side, Ritzer's ultimate achievement is to revitalize a piece of social theory in an applied and, perhaps above all, accessible context. Social theory that relates to the real world in practical and understandable ways should not be dismissed on the basis that it is journalistic. The contention here is that social theory remains just that, theory, unless it is applied in real-life contexts to which people reading that theory can relate. In this respect, Ritzer's work is a phenomenal success and should be commended.

There should be no doubt that Ritzer over-extends the McDonald's metaphor, such that those who attempt to use his theory often flounder as to its broader social significance. This is a great shame for a theory which in so many other respects succeeds in achieving what appears to be so problematic for so many other theorists: making social theory 'real'. The world in which we live today is very much different to that which Weber inhabited, and in this respect Ritzer's contribution to social theory is as much a tribute to the abiding value of Weber's work, and classical social theory in general, as it is to the value of the McDonaldization thesis itself. But if the legacy of both theorists is to be realized, then social theorists ultimately need to construct a balanced vision of a rationalized world which, potentially at least, offers subjective opportunities as well as objective controls.

Recommended reading

Mark Alfino, John S. Caputo and Robin Wynard (eds) (1998) *McDonaldization Revisited: Critical Essays on Consumer Culture*, New York: Praeger. One of the, if not *the*, best of the collections discussing the implications of the McDonaldization thesis.

Rogers Brubaker (1984) *The Limits of Rationality: An Essay on the Social and Moral Thought of Max Weber*, London: Allen and Unwin. One of the most informative of those works attempting to come to terms with Weber's theories, and particularly his conception of rationality.

George Ritzer (1993) *The McDonaldization of Society*, London: Pine Forge. A contemporary classic. A much criticized, but provocative and thought-provoking example of what social theory can achieve.

George Ritzer (1998) *The McDonaldization Thesis*, London: Sage. A useful addition to Ritzer's original work which broadens its theoretical basis whilst focusing more specifically on the question of 'the new means of consumption'.

CHAPTER 7

A RISK SOCIETY?

It would be no exaggeration to suggest that debates over 'risk' and the emergence of a 'risk society' represent one of the abiding obsessions of both social science and the media at the beginning of the twenty-first century. It is certainly true to say that you cannot pick up a newspaper or watch the news on the television without being told about which life-threatening disease, impending environmental disaster or moral danger currently threatens the very core of your everyday life. AIDS is a global disease which apparently threatens us all, hurricanes are forging their path across the earth's surface as we speak, and we simply cannot let our children play on the streets, because to do so would be to put their very lives at risk. But are these risks genuine and do they, in themselves, constitute a whole new type of society or social experience? In this chapter I will outline social scientific debates surrounding the risk society, whilst considering the ways in which such risks are manifested on a daily basis. The core of this debate resides in the following question: how legitimate are the risks that apparently face contemporary society and individuals who live in that society? Do they in fact exist at all, or are they simply a manifestation of a wider malaise which is itself symbolic of the uncertainty and insecurity characteristic of the broader experience of late modernity? In short, do we live in a 'risk' society'?

Risk society and social change

Like post-industrial society theory, work on the risk society tries to come to terms with the long-term impact of social change. It represents an attempt to understand the trajectory of the future in light of recent aspects of social change. In other words, it is concerned with how human beings understand and act upon the social world that surrounds them, which in itself represents an outcome of historical change and transformation. The suggestion here, then, a suggestion that could be said to underlie the rationale for this book as a whole, is that human beings are not simply the product of the current circumstances or surroundings in which they find themselves; those circumstances are the complex product of a vast array of events and historical coincidences. It is not that individuals are simply the product of some form of global conspiracy, but that their experiences, and, in turn, the construction of their identities, represent the end result of their personal and social interpretation of social change. They can play their own chess moves, but only according to the rules that have already been laid down for them in the broader context. In other words, social life is built on historical foundations and upon the relationship between the individual and society or through the ways in which structure and agency are played out.

As I noted in Chapter 1, a whole host of authors have contributed to the above debate, and many have recognized that the very notion of risk lies at the heart of what it means to live at the beginning of the twenty-first century. Indeed, three of the most important and influential contemporary social theorists, Ulrich Beck, Mary Douglas and Anthony Giddens, are also theorists of the risk society. But before I discuss these particular authors' specific contributions, I want to consider the reasons why risk has apparently become such an important focal point for the sociological imagination.

Lupton (1999) points out that the meanings and use of risk are associated with the emergence of modernity and of industrialization, which itself incorporates capitalism, the institutions of surveillance and nuclear weaponry. If we accept that notions of modernity are concerned with the idea of human beings somehow taking control of the physical world in the name of progress, then you could argue that risk is the negative consequence of such sentiments and possibly the price to pay for humanity naïvely thinking that such control was possible in the first place. Lupton goes on to argue that the contemporary obsession with the concept of risk has its roots in the changes inherent in the transformation of societies from pre-modern to modern and then to late modern or post-modern (see Chapter 5). This reflects a growing sense that the early promises of modernity have failed to materialize and that science and medicine are more than just straightforward vanguards of progress (Lupton, 1999, p. 11). Many authors have pointed out that post-modernity is characterized by fragmentation, uncertainty and the sweeping away of tradition, and in these circumstances the validity of science is increasingly undermined:

> All of these changes are seen as contributing to a particular way of understanding the self and the world that differs dramatically from earlier eras. For the individual, it is argued, these changes are associated with an intensifying sense of uncertainty, complexity, ambivalence and disorder, a growing distrust of social institutions and traditional authorities and an increasing awareness of the threats inherent in everyday life. (Lupton, 1999, pp. 11–12)

In other words, as Jarvis (1998) suggests, the more we come to know about the world, the more uncontrollable and unpredictable it appears to become and the more we come to question the value of science as a means of monitoring such unpredictability. The media have a particular role to play in this process. News is transmitted into our living rooms almost before it happens. It is so immediate and all-consuming that the actual extent of the risks that surround us arguably becomes grossly exaggerated, while our faith in those who control risks becomes dissipated:

> . . . news tells us of a world of challenge, of risk; it all helps to reproduce a picture of a world that is constantly troubled and troublesome, a world that may be fascinating but is also dangerous. Sociologists and historians may protest that muggings are not a recent phenomenon, and that the groups and individuals who most fear violence are not those most likely to suffer from it, but none of this alters the perception that we live in a world of risk. Once we perceive risk and danger as being potentially ever-present, they become real for us: the representation and reality subtly blend together . . . the media world operates as a 'spectacular' reinforcement of tendencies already there in late modernity, in which the world we transformed returns to trouble us, and to play with our reflexive sense of who we are and where we are going. (Jarvis, 1998, p. 313)

Perhaps the most graphic illustration of the power of the media and the knack they appear to have in magnifying the degree of risk is the BSE crisis which occurred in Britain in the mid- to late 1990s. The work of Barbara Adam (1998) is particularly effective in highlighting the role that the media played alongside the British government and science in the mismanagement of risk (see also McGuigan, 1999). During this period the government continually gave the public mixed messages about the threat BSE held in terms of the relationship with the contraction of CJD by humans, simply because experts are experts and as such are bound to disagree with each other (Giddens, 1998). Media reportage of these pronouncements and discussion of contrary governmental/scientific expert advice added fuel to a fire which soon leaped out of control. The problem in this respect, as Adam (1998) points out, is that science can never be as precise as we actually want it to be:

> Where scientists are resistant to come up with quantification and facts, journalists and politicians tend to do their job for them: the vague and propositional language of science gets translated into politically and economically acceptable certainties and assurances [when in actual fact] indeterminacy and uncertainty stare us in the face wherever we look and search for reliable information. (pp. 166–7)

What remains interesting about the BSE crisis is that the media defined when it should have been a matter for public concern. They also defined the parameters for the debate whilst arguably exaggerating the degree of risk in order to sell newspapers. These circumstances could only intensify public mistrust of science and hence the fear of risk. The feeling that we have very little control over our futures was clearly intensified by the contradictory complexity of the debates surrounding BSE when the audience wanted exactly what it could not get: straightforward answers. As McGuigan (1999) and Macnaghten and Urry (1998) argue, this confusion represents one of the prices to pay for a civilization which appears to be extremely attached to short-term economic imperatives. In this context, Breen (1997) also points out that the welfare state, the nuclear family and firms are becoming less effective in offsetting risk away from the individual, resulting in a situation where labour market risk, in particular, is liable to affect those least powerful far more than those in power. This point represents a grave sociological concern, as does the fact that

> a role is played by the selectivity of the mass media, which present certain improbabilities – when they do occur – in an all the more striking manner; while others, especially those without news value, are not publicized, or only within the context of everyday incidents, that is to say of normalized probabilities. (Luhmann, 1993, p. x)

Regardless of the degree of actual risk, there is no doubt that the media are at least partly responsible therefore for the fact that there is, as Furedi (1997) notes, a growing hostility towards scientific advance, and, in turn, a growing concern about the claims made on behalf of knowledge. At its most blunt, the argument here is that whereas historically risk was 'natural', nowadays it is manufactured. Humanity has simply over-stepped the mark and nature has apparently taken revenge on the apparently arrogant undertones of humanity. This is, however, an extreme, one-sided and conservative argument and one that underestimates the social influences underlying our perception of risk (see Furedi, 1997). To suggest that risk is simply determined by the mishandling of scientific advance is far-fetched in the extreme and suggests that we are all equally in danger of risk. It is certainly true to say that the degree of that risk is very much dependent on the individual's power and influence (Furedi, 1997, p. 58). More specifically, there is evidence of an increasing mistrust of expert systems as arbiters of risk. Technological expertise appears to be becoming increasingly specialized to the extent that science appears to be little more than a rather disconcerting debate between experts with different views who have limited comprehension of the effect that these views may or may not have on the population at large. In this respect, it may not be an increase in risk, *per se*, which is fuelling the sense of insecurity that appears to characterize our society, but rather an increased concern that we are not being given the full story by those professionals in a position to allay such fears. As Furedi (1997) suggests,

> A tendency to mistrust scientific claims has helped to fuel public unease about the consequences of technological developments. Many of the panics about environmental and health-related issues demonstrate an explicit rejection of the claims of scientists on the subject. Mistrust of science is one of the most visible elements in the growth of risk consciousness itself. (p. 130)

Furedi's analysis of such scepticism is of particular interest insofar as what it tells us about the general mentality associated with late modern society. In particular, social life at the beginning of the twenty-first century appears to be characterized by scepticism and cynicism. As Furedi suggests, human beings appear to have lost faith in themselves to the extent that it is almost as if we feel we are only capable of damaging the world in which we live. Many things that have been created by human beings, such as nuclear power or, at a more abstract level, the capitalist system, as expressed through the market, are largely perceived in negative terms. In a world where the future is apparently so uncertain, we appear to have been lulled into a sense of precaution and fatalism: '. . . since society reminds us that it is our powerlessness that we have in common, suffering seems to be the main inspiration for the sense of community. It is a collective sense but the collective sense of resignation' (Furedi, 1997, p. 175).

The implication of Furedi's work is that all concerns about risk are imagined and simply the product of this 'culture of fear'. It is highly debatable as to whether or not this position is sustainable. Indeed, the irony is that it is scientific advance which has created a situation in which the world's relationship with nature is particularly precarious. At one level we can therefore identify large-scale risks such as the threat of nuclear war, or environmental disasters such as Chernobyl which may have occurred in one place, but the effects of which spread throughout Europe, indeed the world. The risk society is an international society where actions in one country affect the well-being of the rest of the world, through exhaust emissions, for example. But it is not simply the actual threat of risk that is the core to this sense of foreboding. In some respects a risk society is a paranoid society in the sense that it is a society that appears to be more sensitive to risk than ever before. Environmental risks are perceived as a global threat. We cannot control the globalization; neither can we control risk.

This, then, provides the context within which the notion of risk has become a keyword, synonymous above all with the uncertainties associated with rapid social change. Human beings seem to be desperately trying to control the uncertainties that surround them, whilst simultaneously conceding that such forces are in actual fact beyond their control. Thus authors such as Frank Furedi (1997) talk about the existence of a 'culture of fear', insofar as although people may live longer than they did and be healthier and wealthier than they were in the past, such advances have come at a cost and the social, economic and scientific advances which made these developments possible have actually created new and, in actual fact, bigger problems and fears. This apparently creates a distinctly inhuman environment in which human beings are having to learn to constrain themselves and their actions; an environment in which human beings are increasingly passive. Indeed, 'in a world awash with conditions and impending catastrophes, [the individual] is doing a job by just surviving' (Furedi, 1997, p. 12). The world has changed at such a dramatic rate and the global forces at work in ensuring such change are so far beyond individual comprehension that both the present and the future have become terrifying and stress-inducing and are manifestly beyond the realms of human control.

It should be becoming increasingly evident that notions of risk are closely related to other areas I have discussed and will discuss throughout this book. In particular, it will soon become clear that the debates addressed by commentators on risk are closely linked to questions of post-modernity, which also centre on the contention that the experience of society has changed radically in recent years. As I pointed out above, the emergence of a risk society represents modernity's attempt to free itself from the contours of industrial society. But these changes are not simply social in nature; they actively change the nature of the individual's experience of everyday life, as a discussion of the work of Beck, Douglas and Giddens will now illustrate.

Ulrich Beck and *Risk Society*

First published in English in 1992, Ulrich Beck's book *Risk Society* has had a major impact on social scientific conceptions of risk and more broadly on sociology as a discipline. As far as Beck is concerned, risk is the defining characteristic of our age. In developing his ideas, Beck is particularly fascinated with the notion of reflexive modernization, the paradoxical process by which social change is such that the individual experiences an increasingly risky life, and yet at one and the same time is increasingly free from the constraints of social structure. Beck (1992) therefore defines risk as '. . . a systematic way of dealing with hazards and insecurities induced and introduced by modernization itself. Risks, as opposed to older dangers, are consequences which relate to the threatening force of modernization and to its globalization of doubt' (p. 21). Beck goes on to discuss the long-term transition from a pre-industrial, through an industrial to a risk society. Each of these societies contains risks and hazards, but in markedly different forms. In particular, the risk society is characterized by the fact that such hazards are induced, or at least are perceived to be induced, by human beings. Thus, at an environmental level older dangers such as excrement on the streets of nineteenth-century London were immediate and real, but could be dealt with reasonably easily. In late modernity risks are more likely to be abstract in nature and far less easily resolved, in the case of the threat posed by BSE to livestock, consumers and farmers, for instance. In *Risk Society* Beck argues that we no longer live in a safe, predictable world. The contemporary world is now characterized by its uncertainties and the risks these uncertainties bring with them, risks which operate at a global environmental level, as well as a more immediate personal level. In particular, Beck argues that modern life brings with it irreversible globalized threats to the lives of animals, plants and human beings.

Beck (1992) contends that it is possible to identify a new mode of socialization, a 'metamorphosis' or 'categorical shift' in the make-up of the relationship between the individual and society. In a class-based modern society everybody apparently dreamed about maximizing the size of their own particular slice of the communal pie. In a risk society people are far less optimistic and are more concerned with surviving than succeeding. What is now important, then, is the prevention of the bad rather than the achievement of the good. In effect, therefore, the successful production of wealth has been superseded by the production of risk. The subsequent quest for safety has become the central tenet of contemporary society. For this reason, society is no longer a class society, because everybody, no matter their class, is subject to the ravages of risk. Beck (1999) therefore discusses the distinction between a first modernity and a second modernity. He describes the former as the modernity based on nation-states where the notion of immediate territories and communities plays a fundamental role. But the stabilities of this period associated with progress are undermined in a second risk-based modernity.

It is arguably Beck's work on the individualization of risk that is of most interest to the sociologist. Beck believes, as Lash and Wynne (1992) point out, that modernization involves not only structural change but also a changing relationship between social structures and social agents. Historical changes are such that the individual appears to be less constrained by social structures and yet ironically more constrained by his or her private whims and fears. People are having to be increasingly independent, but such independence comes at a cost. Social life appears to be more flexible on the surface, but is in actual fact in many respects ever more constraining. It is constraining in respect of the psychological impact upon the individual. As Beck (1992) puts it,

> . . . social problems are increasingly perceived in terms of psychological dispositions: as personal inadequacies, guilt feelings, anxieties, conflicts and neuroses. There emerges, paradoxically, a new immediacy of individual and society, a direct relation between crisis and sickness. Social crises appear as individual crises, which are no longer (or are only indirectly) perceived in terms of their rootedness in the social realm. (p. 100)

In particular, the modern world is so complex that the 'harmful, threatening, inimical lies in wait everywhere, but whether it is inimical or friendly is beyond one's own power of judgement; thus we depend on experts, and our "cognitive sovereignty" is threatened' (p. 53). We feel helpless and at one and the same time dependent upon, and yet sceptical of, the knowledge of experts. Technology and science may in one sense be liberating but in another they take control out of the individual's hands while creating more personal pressure for him or her to try to maintain such control.

All this may appear to be theoretically opaque, but Beck is in actual fact highlighting in a very graphic fashion the essential irony of social change: that despite processes of individualization human beings are increasingly subject to external forces, and arguably standardization. Beck therefore argues that this creates an institutional dependency on the part of the individual, who becomes increasingly susceptible to personal crises. Thus, the everyday experience of advanced modernity is characterized, for Beck (1992), by the fact that

> each person's biography is removed from given determinations and placed in his or her own hands, open and dependent on decisions. The proportion of life opportunities which are fundamentally closed to decision-making is decreasing and the proportion of the biography which is open and must be constructed personally increasing. Individualization of life situations and processes thus means that biographies become self-reflexive; socially prescribed biography is transformed into biography that is self-produced and continues to be produced. (p. 135)

Beck (1992) argues that this creates, on the one hand, an ego-centred world-view on the part of the individual, but, on the other, an increased dependence on institutions. In order for an individual to be a 'success' in the above conditions, he or she may be increasingly dependent upon the vagaries of the labour market. This opens the individual up to an increased risk of failure, in the sense that any failure is perceived on his or her part as implicating personal inade-quacies. Risk is therefore played out institutionally and yet dealt with at an individual psychological level to the extent that 'the apparent outsides of the institutions become the inside of the individual biography' (Beck, 1992, p. 130). The psycho-social implications of a risk society are clearly massive. If social change creates a set of circumstances in which the individual is increasingly vulnerable, then is society serving any purpose at all?

Beck develops these issues whilst emphasizing a more global dimension in his collection of essays *World Risk Society* (1999). In this book Beck goes as far as to argue that risks have become a major force of political mobilization, 'often replacing references to, for example, inequalities associated with race, class and gender' (p. 4). The effect of globalization, according to Beck, is that areas of politics that were previously disparate are being united on a global scale, and they are being united by questions of risk. Subsequently, personal biographies as well as world politics are getting increasingly risky in what is a world of 'manufactured uncertainties' (p. 5). The uncertainty and insecurity of contemporary life is an issue that concerns Anthony Giddens, whose work I shall consider next.

Anthony Giddens, fate, risk and security

Many of the themes raised by Beck are debated in the work of the British sociologist Anthony Giddens (1991), who also recognizes that 'science and technology are double-edged, creating new parameters of risk and danger as well as offering beneficent possibilities for humankind' (pp. 27–8). Giddens (1990) identifies four key aspects of risk in his earlier work on modernity:

1 The increasing role of surveillance in society as expressed through the control of information and people. This apparently extends the threat of a totalitarian power base.
2 The emergence of an era of 'total wars' which superseded the age of the more limited wars that preceded it. Thus, the threat of nuclear war leaves a shadow hanging over the modern world, above and beyond the increased fatalities associated with war during the twentieth century in general.
3 The threat encapsulated in the uncertainty and unpredictability of economic change.
4 The subsequent threat of ecological disaster and decay caused by the erraticism of capitalism and its propensity to create inequality. Capitalist accumulation is therefore perceived to be a major cause of environmental degradation (see also Kivisto, 1998).

The risks inherent in the move towards high or late modernity are not seen to be inevitable; they are *potential* consequences. (With ten years' hindsight, however, it could be argued that many of these risks have become *actual*.) Nevertheless, as Kivisto (1998) points out, there is no mistaking the pessimistic tone in Giddens' work.

> On the other side of modernity, as virtually no one on earth can any longer fail to be conscious, there could be nothing but a 'republic of insects and grass', or a class of damaged and traumatized human social communities. . . . Apocalypse has become trite, so familiar is it as a counterfactual of day-to-day life; yet like all parameters of risk it can become real. (Giddens, 1990, p. 173)

In some respects Giddens' pronouncements are slightly more sober in his later work *Modernity and Self-Identity* (1991), in which he prefers to describe living in the world produced by high modernity as tantamount to riding a juggernaut. For Giddens, risk is an orientation forced upon us by the abstract systems of modernity which in turn highlights the unpredictability of social change. In a way, the risk society makes the effects of social change ever more immediate, because we are forced to deal with social change and its negative as well as positive ramifications, at every turn. Because there is no real consensus as to what constitutes 'truth' or who can deliver it, the individual is constantly having to make complex everyday judgements. In effect, he or she can barely trust the authenticity of his or her surroundings. There are no right answers to the dilemmas of everyday life, whether or not we should eat genetically modified food, for instance, and as such we live in a world of chance and risk.

Although in many respects similar to that of Ulrich Beck, in some ways Giddens' conception of risk is perhaps more sociological and at times less environmental in nature. In particular, Giddens provides us with several insights as to the relationship between risk and identity, the latter being an especially important focus for contemporary social theory in general. As such, when talking about increasing 'reflexivity', the idea that societies have been forced to reflect on themselves and back on how and why they have developed in the way they have, Giddens is more concerned about personal, individual self-reflexivity, while Beck prefers to emphasize social reflexivity (Kumar, 1995, p. 145). Giddens therefore talks about the implications for identity of a radicalization of modernity (as opposed to its transformation). He believes not that risk is necessarily markedly greater than it may have been in the past, but that its impact on identity is more profound. We perceive risk to be greater than it is in reality. In contemporary society an individual effectively treads a tightrope between risk and opportunity. The individual is obliged to choose between a vast array of

lifestyle choices to the extent that everyday life amounts to an amalgamation of risk calculations. Indeed,

> The development of relatively secure environments of day-to-day life is of
> central importance to the maintenance of feelings of ontological security.
> Ontological security, in other words, is sustained primarily through routine
> itself. . . . The protective cocoon depends more and more on the coherence
> of routines themselves, as they are ordered within the reflexive project of
> the self. (Giddens, 1991, p. 167)

Giddens therefore argues that the concept of risk has become
fundamental to how both lay actors and technical specialists organize
the world. In particular, the fact that the media and mediated experience nowadays play such a fundamental role in people's everyday
lives means that the individual is in perpetual danger of being
overwhelmed by the perception of risk, which has in itself become
a way of life. Crucially then, Giddens (1991) argues that the self
becomes a reflexive project. Risk opens the individual up to uncertainty. It forces him or her to live an uncertain life, because there are
so many other choices that an individual might have made, and have
made more appropriately, from one life-situation to the next. Giddens
(1998) has also talked about risk in the context of some of his more
recent work on social democracy and 'The Third Way', in which he
argues that risk can be utilized as a positive force:

> A positive engagement with risk is a necessary component of social and
> economic mobilization. Some risks we wish to minimize as far as possible;
> others, such as those involved in investment decisions, are a positive part of
> a successful market economy. . . . We all need protection against risk, but
> also the capability to confront and take risks in a productive fashion.
> (pp. 63–4)

Giddens' theory of risk has important implications for our understanding of the value of social theory, particularly in terms of his
argument that social change and institutions affect everyday life
and selfhood, but are also shaped by individual actions (see Lupton,
1999, p. 73). Giddens' notion of the 'duality of structure' is therefore
paramount here: the idea that structure and agency are mutually
dependent; that structure makes action possible, that it is the medium
of action, but at the same time it is reproduced only in and through
action. In other words, structure is both enabling and constraining. It
is the medium and outcome of action. As such, McGuigan (1999)
points out that the tension between existential anxiety and ontological
security lies at the heart of Giddens' theory, but is far from free of the
structural constraints imposed by society as a whole. Most importantly, it would be misleading to draw a picture of the individual as

being perpetually insecure; rather, he or she is, generally speaking, ontologically secure, and the anxieties and fragilities of the late modern world only directly affect him or her on a momentary basis. When they do so, however, the issue of risk plays a paramount role in balancing the relationship between structure and agency.

Mary Douglas, risk and culture

If one principle underlies this book as a whole, it might well be the suggestion that insightful social theory should not exist in a theoretical vacuum. Rather, it should reflect and explain active changes in our lived cultural experience. As sociologists, we need to be critically aware, and explicitly so, about those approaches which fail to help us comprehend how societies affect individuals and how individuals affect societies. The ways in which social structures determine an individual's experience can only tell us half the story. Human beings are creative and responsive agents of the social world and the individual is the product of a balance between structural influences on everyday life. The impact of the capitalist economy on people's lives is therefore, for instance, of paramount concern. Social theory can only be of value if we use it as a means of understanding the relationship *between* the individual and society, and more specifically if we use it to address aspects of our own experience of that society. Social theory should not exist in a theoretical vacuum, but nor should it exist in a political one. In this context, Mary Douglas's (1992) cultural conception of risk may prove especially useful.

Mary Douglas argues that risk and danger are culturally conditioned ideas shaped by the pressures of everyday life. Risk has apparently become central to our social lives precisely because of the move towards a global society. We are liberated from the constraints of local community but at one and the same time are bereft of traditional forms of protection and support. Nobody can apparently agree as to what is and what isn't risky (see Douglas and Wildavsky, 1982). Douglas (1992) therefore suggests that risk fulfils the forensic needs of a new global culture, the shift to a world community having constructed a new set of political priorities. As such, she describes risk as a generalized 'weapon of defence' which 'fills the needs of justice and welfare' (p. 15):

> Of the different types of blaming system that we can find in tribal society, the one we are now in is almost ready to treat every death as chargeable to someone's account, every accident as caused by someone's criminal negligence, every sickness a threatened prosecution. . . . Under the banner of risk reduction, a new blaming system has replaced the former combination

of moralistic condemning the victim and opportunistic condemning the victim's incompetence. (pp. 15–16)

Risk fits the bill in that it provides a neutral vocabulary for the conception of social change. Risk is forward-looking and provides a means of assessing the dangers ahead, whilst simultaneously serving the needs of what is an increasingly individualistic culture.

Risk, then, provides a discourse within which the individual can look forward to being protected. At a day-to-day level, if we think about risk enough and if we describe every social experience we come across as risky, we can convince ourselves that things will ultimately get better. Discourses surrounding risk, notably as they are played through by the media, are not about community but about the protection of the individual and of individual rights. This is what Douglas refers to when she talks about the political dimension of risk. Risk therefore helps to prop up a culture in which the liberty of the individual remains a political priority, not to say a political vote winner. The politicization of risk is not apparently a process that has been thrust upon the populace, but one that they gratefully collude in. Risk is not a 'thing' in any real sense, but a highly artificial way of thinking about the world. Perhaps Douglas and Wildavsky's (1982) most important point, then, is that risk is a collective construct. Risk is not an objective calculation of reality that needs to be confronted but a matter of social organization, and its management is an organizational problem. As Douglas and Wildavsky argue, 'Standing inside our own culture, we can only look at our predicament through our culturally fabricated lenses' (p. 194). By looking at young people's specific experiences of risk it may be possible to highlight the fact that the impact of the so-called 'risk society' is primarily a psycho-social one.

Young people at the forefront of risk

Young people have often been portrayed by sociologists as somehow being at the cutting edge of social change, as representing some barometer or measure of the social changes that surround them and impact upon their lives (see Miles, 2000). This is no more readily illustrated than in the context of young people's relationship with a risk society. In this respect, the work of Andy Furlong and Fred Cartmel (1997) is of particular relevance. Furlong and Cartmel argue that young people have become especially vulnerable to the heightened sense of risk and the individualization of experience that have characterized the move towards high modernity: 'Young people today are growing up in a different world to that experienced by previous

generations – changes which are significant enough to merit a recon-
ceptualization of youth transitions and processes of social reproduction' (p. 6). In a world where traditional forms of social support appear
to have broken down, Furlong and Cartmel argue that young people
are facing a greater diversity of risks and opportunities than ever
before. Family, work and school provide more unpredictable and less
secure environments than they would have done in the past, and
journeys into adulthood are therefore becoming increasingly precarious: 'Moreover, because there are a much greater range of pathways
to choose from, young people may develop the impression that their
own route is unique and that the risks they face are to be overcome as
individuals rather than as members of a collectivity' (p. 7).

Whilst individualization may appear to be liberating on the
surface, it actually undermines the ontological well-being of the
individual. The individual is, in other words, less and less certain
about whether his or her actions are appropriate. He or she is more
and more likely to feel like the world is quite literally spiralling out of
control. At this point what on the surface may appear to be an
objective risk actually becomes a cultural one, in the sense that the
individual interprets the degree of risk on the basis of the cultural
understanding he or she has of his or her surroundings. It is in this
sense that a risk society becomes a paranoid society. The actual
objective level of risk, as Furlong and Cartmel observe, has changed
little. It is the subjective and cultural perception of these risks that has
grown out of all proportion. In this context, young people's identities
are inevitably and increasingly fragile. To back up this proposition,
Furlong and Cartmel describe a situation in which patterns of education and employment have changed radically in recent years. Young
people are apparently having to stay on in education for longer and
longer periods in order to compete in what is an increasingly trau-
matic environment. They may crave the independent lifestyle that
their first job may or may not bring them, but in reality they are forced
to prolong the transition through training schemes, courses and
temporary forms of employment. Indeed, during the 1980s and 1990s
youth unemployment in Britain grew at a sharper rate than that of
other age groups, to the extent that we can no longer barely even
identify a 'youth' labour market (Roberts, 1995). Transitions into
adulthood have therefore been extended, partly reflecting the
increased difficulties young people are having actually entering the
labour market, which in itself makes education an increasingly attrac-
tive prospect. This, in turn, results in young people being dependent
upon their families, but often in this context on themselves, for longer
periods than was previously the case.

Ironically, perhaps, the most appealing avenues for escape in the
above circumstances are risky forms of behaviour such as drug-taking

and alcohol consumption which simply serve to accentuate the risky and unpredictable nature of youth lifestyles in a changing world. Kelly (1999) applies these sorts of ideas to Australian youth. He therefore discusses the problems facing governments who seek to regulate populations of youth within the context of a risk society. Noting that young people are increasingly obliged to take part in a lifelong reflexive 'do-it-yourself' project of the self, Kelly suggests that they are having to deal with 'institutionally generated risk environments'. In particular, the problems and issues associated with transformed labour markets and globalized economies appear to suffocate the individual, who is left to muse about how he or she can possibly cope in such circumstances. Kelly argues that the transformed nature of transnational economic and cultural flows and the apparent opening up of space through information and communication networks have important implications for young people. Indeed, he goes as far as to describe young people as occupying 'wild zones': transformed spaces where there is a deficit of state, market and self-regulation. As a result, many young people who are able to do so flee to 'tame zones', which are more economically, politically and culturally secure. In this context, Kelly argues that the apparent ungovernability of youth has led to more sophisticated attempts at regulation and surveillance of youth. As a result, programmes which seek to regulate those at risk, such as a Vocational Education and Training (VET) agenda in Australia, have emerged. VET therefore represents 'an attempt to reconfigure the practices which regulate youth (as transition) in the spaces transformed by processes of reflexive modernization' (Kelly, 1999, p. 206). Intending to provide pathways between schooling and training and employment, VET illustrates how governments are having to respond to the changing needs of young people in a risk society. Whether initiatives such as this and 'The New Deal' in the UK are successful is a matter for intense debate, but at the very least they represent a recognition of the particular difficulties and pressures young people face at the turn of the twenty-first century.

It is also important not to forget that children are in some respects equally threatened by the uncertainties of a risk society. Indeed, the issue of child safety raises some key concerns about the authenticity of the risk society. An article by Scott et al. (1998) deals with this issue particularly well in pointing out that children represent the focus for a great deal of social anxiety around which has emerged a 'protective discourse' (Thomson and Scott, 1991). However, there may be a strong argument for suggesting that the discourse surrounding childhood risk has grown out of all proportion to the actual risks those children face. There is no doubt, as Scott et al. (1998) point out, that adults do need to 'protect' children. In this context sexual anxiety and risk is especially prominent and media coverage is particularly adept at exaggerating the degree of risk involved here. For example, Scott et al. quote an edition of *Woman's Hour* on BBC Radio 4 on 30 January 1998 in which gardening was promoted as a safe child-friendly activity because 'you can't let them play outside in the street anymore – they may get molested' (p. 693). Notions of 'stranger danger' represent an evocative and common media image, while there may be a strong case for arguing that parents are over-protecting their children as a result. The consequence of risk perception is that children's lives are constrained insofar as they are forced to become increasingly dependent on adults. There has been a massive decrease in the number of children going to school on their own in the last thirty years, for example. Meanwhile, children are apparently being frightened by the threat of events that apparently have very little chance of actually happening. The anxiety generated by risk and the media portrayal of risk may indeed

> curtail children's activities in ways that may restrict their autonomy and their opportunities to develop the necessary skills to cope with the world. . . . In trying to combat sexual risk while safeguarding childhood 'innocence', what is gained on the swings of protection may be lost on the roundabouts of confusion, vulnerability and dependency. (Scott et al., 1998, pp. 701–2)

Both children and young people are undoubtedly rendered psycho-socially vulnerable in a risk society. The irony of social change is that despite young people appearing to be at the forefront in terms of maximizing the advantages to be had in the communications and technology revolution, below the surface they are having to cope with all sorts of unprecedented tensions. It is these tensions that social theories such as risk are trying to comprehend.

Conclusions

The question that still remains is whether or not the risk society is really as bad as some of the above commentators might suggest. It is certainly true to say that Ulrich Beck in particular presents an extremely pessimistic view of the society in which we live; a world threatened by environmental and personal collapse. But do we really spend every minute of our day dreading the impending doom of our futures? In his book, John Adam (1995) points out that the same objective reality that Beck describes has generated an entirely different interpretation. Adam therefore discusses the work of Wildavsky (1988), who describes an environmental age in which many commentators have argued that technology has become a weapon of enslavement. Wildavsky goes on to point out that many of the world's environmental scares have been grossly exaggerated (notably by the media) or even non-existent. From this point of view it could be argued that it is the alarmist nature of consumers of risk, rather than the risk itself, that is the fundamental characteristic of life in a changing world. What is interesting then, as Adam points out, is that both Beck and Wildavsky have cultural interpretations of risk; the latter seeing physical nature as robust and human nature as resilient and adaptable. Wildavsky's work can therefore be described as that of an individualist, as compared to the egalitarian nature of Beck's work. Indeed, these two authors' approaches to risk illustrate the way in which the same evidence can apparently be interpreted by different authors in very different ways. Indeed, the whole debate surrounding risk illustrates the critical benefits of social theory and of sociology in general. Social theory may not provide all the answers, but what it does do is provide a framework within which you can come to your own conclusions.

It is particularly important that social theory is not simply descriptive about social phenomena such as risk, but that it adopts a critical approach to aspects of daily life and the ways in which such life is constructed. Indeed, 'The question is rather what we can learn about normal processes in our society from the fact that it seeks to comprehend misfortune in the form of risk' (Luhmann, 1993, p. viii). Perhaps in the context of risk the most important lesson to learn about 'normal processes' in our society is that 'It is thus at best an abbreviated (practical but indispensable) way of putting it when we say that modern technology is "risky". Only communication about technology and – above all – the communication of decisions about the deployment or nondeployment of technology is risky' (Luhmann, 1993, pp. xii–xiii).

The emergence of a risk society, if such a thing exists, might well tell us more about the increasing influence and normalization of high technology than anything else. The world may not be any riskier than it was in the past, it's just that the means of communicating that risk are now more omnipresent. We feel that we live in a technological world and assume that that world is inevitably riskier than the world we used to know. The risk society arguably has very little to do with actual changes in the nature of social life, but more to do with unsubstantiated fears about the rapidity of social change.

What is especially important here, then, is who communicates notions of risk and why they do so. Taylor-Gooby (1999) argues that questions of risk have become crucial to government thinking. He argues that the insecurities of the late modern world as expressed through unemployment, new technology, globalization and the breakdown of the family are counter-balanced by people being better educated and more often than not better off than they ever have been before. Despite the risks facing them on a day-to-day level, people are therefore arguably more confident in managing their own affairs and more critical of government interference. In a risk society, then, state provision is more about creating space for individual opportunity. But the problem is, as Taylor-Gooby points out, that those who are most at risk and those least able to take advantage of individual opportunity and choice are the poorer members of society: 'Risk, then, affects some people harder: they live in the wrong part of the country, they have least skills. Risk society is an individualistic idea which fails to see there are entire groups with difficulties in finding and keeping work' (p. 17).

In a sense, risk society is not as remote or as out of control as a lot of the rhetoric that surrounds it, and certainly its political appropriation, might imply. Taylor-Gooby points out that governments, as they are liable to do, emphasize opportunities and freedoms. They use the discourse that risk provides to promote the idea that the risk society we live in is an opportunity society; that it is reasonable to punish those people who fail to take such opportunities through, for example, the withdrawal of benefit. The problem with a risk society is that life is riskier for some members of society than for others. Sometimes risk results in genuine and unavoidable exclusion; something that should be recognized if governments are to play any role at all in making people's lives less risky than they already are.

In conclusion, debates over the emergence of a risk society raise all sorts of issues and highlight all sorts of concerns pertinent to life at the beginning of the twenty-first century. However, risk is also a discourse that can be used as a political and ideological tool. Douglas's (1992) argument that risk fulfils the forensic needs of a new global culture is in this respect a highly pertinent one. In many ways people in general, as well as politicians, use discourses of risk to cope with the uncertainties that apparently confront them on a daily basis. By using risk we can convince ourselves that we as individuals can at least assess the dangers ahead. Even if we don't control risk at the moment, we can at least look forward to a future in which we might be able to do so. Risk, in effect, helps to convince us that things *will* get better. The problem with such a discourse, however, is that it is very much dependent on an individualistic conception of social life, premised as it is on the notion that the individual and the individual alone takes the burdens of a risk society on to his or her shoulders. This is not to suggest that risk is somehow thrust on to us and that human beings have no control in this respect. Far from it; we appear to be actively colluding in the maintenance of the very risks about which we so vehemently object. In this sense we might well agree with Urry's (1998) contention that we live in a risk culture as opposed to a risk society. Risk is a global experience and we collude in that experience on a global basis.

As far as social theory is concerned, this debate clearly illustrates the continued significance of discussions concerning structure and agency, which should continue to dominate the thoughts of social theorists. But it also illustrates that social theory can change the world as well as simply describe it. Discourses surrounding social theory *do* have a political influence. This is an important point to remember. Social theory can be more than simply descriptive. It can actually be used pro-actively (and sometimes detrimentally) to change, or at least change conceptions of, the world. Beck (1999) argues that 'Risk science without the sociological imagination of constructed and contested risk is blind' (p. 4). This much may be true. Equally blind is a social theory that does not take into account the myriad ways in which its theories can be applied, and the way in which the very application of that theory can change the world which it is attempting to comprehend. As far as the risk society is concerned, such a discourse may galvanize the very stresses and strains characteristic of contemporary social life which it is actually trying to describe. The theory itself plays an active role in convincing us that the stability of our everyday lives is increasingly under threat. Theory itself is potentially ideological. It feeds and revitalizes the very phenomena which it is seeking to analyse. In other words, when post-modernists argue that sociology can no longer change the world, but can only describe it, they may actually be saying something that is potentially dangerous. They may be underestimating the impact of social theory. Sociologists and social theorists may not be able to change the world for the better, but if they are not careful they may well change it for the worse.

Recommended reading

Ulrich Beck (1992) *Risk Society: Towards a New Modernity*, London: Sage. Perhaps the most influential and insightful analysis of the risk society. This book put risk firmly on the sociological agenda and helped to establish it as a key theoretical concern in a changing world.

Mary Douglas (1992) *Risk and Blame: Essays in Cultural Theory*, London: Routledge. An impressive and insightful, if at times somewhat complex, discussion of the cultural contexts in which risk operates.

Andy Furlong and Fred Cartmel (1997) *Young People and Social Change: Individualization and Risk in Late Modernity*, Buckingham: Open University Press. A useful and considered analysis which gives applied insight to the practicalities of young people, who are left to deal with the consequences of a risk society on a daily basis.

Anthony Giddens (1991) *Modernity and Self-Identity: Self and Society in the Late Modern Age*, Cambridge: Polity. A wide-ranging work in which Giddens addresses a host of theoretical aspects of social change. The impact upon self-identity is arguably the most stimulating dimension of his analysis.

CHAPTER 8

A GLOBAL SOCIETY?

Of all the themes covered in this book, globalization might well, or at the very least should, represent *the* most pressing of concerns for contemporary social theorists. Authors such as Hogan (1996) and Wiseman (1995) have none the less described globalization as an 'awful' and 'ugly' word bound up in complex processes and aspects of social change, but also in theoretical trends and fashions. Despite and perhaps because of the plethora of work that continues to be published in and around the area of globalization, the term itself remains highly contested and ambiguous. As Hogan goes on to note, it is this very ambiguity that has ensured its longevity. Globalization remains an open-ended and, at times, confusing notion, and one that can only continue to provoke debate. It is the social theorist's responsibility to conduct that debate on as secure foundations as possible.

This chapter will attempt to clarify the debate over globalization and in doing so try to identify what 'global' issues, above and beyond the hyperbole, are justified in preoccupying the contemporary social theorist. Social theorists have long been concerned with social change on a world-wide scale. Weber's analysis of processes of rationalization and Durkheim's discussion of suicide rates world-wide immediately come to mind (see Waters, 1995). More recently, Immanuel Wallerstein's (1993) work on the emergence of a 'modern world-system' has been especially influential. But only in the last ten to fifteen years or so has the debate converged on such a prevalent discussion about the specific characteristics of globalization. Despite such convergence, there remains no single definition of globalization. To attempt to provide such a definition would simply serve to underplay the degree of complexity involved here. But one thing is for sure: there is a strong case for arguing that the tensions which exist between the global and the local have an increasingly fundamental impact on the construction of social life. A broad spectrum of theoretical concerns, including risk, post-industrialism, mass society, McDonaldization, post-modernism and consumerism, are all moulded, at least in some form, by processes of globalization. Indeed, as Short and Kim (1999) point out, globalization is so influential that we may actually have to reconsider the post-modern contention that meta-narratives no longer hold water in a world of rapid social change (see Chapter 5). Might there be some credence in the argument that globalization itself constitutes some form of a meta-narrative? Is globalization, in effect, the primary force behind social change at the beginning of the twenty-first century?

What is global? What is globalization?

Before we can consider the implications of globalization for social theory in general, we need to think about what actually constitutes the 'global'. Short and Kim (1999) suggest that globalization constitutes an aspect of *globalism*. Globalization therefore refers to the stretching of a whole swathe of economic, cultural and political activities of a similar nature across the global landscape. Second, a discourse of globalism has also emerged, insofar as the very notion of globalization has become popularized, to the extent that it is often difficult to distinguish between myth and reality. For this reason it is very important to construct a carefully considered account of globalization which avoids exaggerating the sorts of social patterns under discussion (Short and Kim, 1999).

The sociological concern with globalization therefore reflects long-term changes in the social world with which social theorists have long attempted to grapple. Many social theorists have talked about the increasing interdependence of societies on a world scale on both an economic and a cultural basis. As far as the actual experience of social life is concerned, this is perhaps most closely bound up with the issue of identity. Perhaps above all, the social sciences and social theory are associated with a concern with the transition to a modern society; in other words, the processes that led to a move from a traditional, largely rural, agricultural, religious and small-scale society to a society centred on large urban areas, democratic political institutions, the application of science and technology, massive population growth and concentration and, above all, cultural, political and religious heterogeneity. This transition incorporated fundamental changes in the nature of identity. In a traditional society identities were more likely to be very fixed, solid and stable. A person's role in life was very likely to be determined by his or her birth. An individual was born into a community with a fixed set of beliefs and was more than likely to die in that community, having spent most of his or her life trying to maintain it. Traditional identities can therefore be seen to be unproblematic. As an individual you were *given* an identity and that identity wasn't very likely to change very much over the course of your life-time. In contrast, modern identities are essentially problematic. If we accept that one of the primary characteristics of modernity is the effort on the part of human beings to control and transform their physical environments, then the same can be said of identity. The *experience* of modernity appears to be very much about a constant struggle to control that identity. Modernity constitutes a very much more transitory experience than anything that may have preceded it. In particular, as Marx notes, the dominance of the market is such that 'all that is solid melts into air'. Modern identities are highly contradictory. People's identities appear, from one point of view, to have been liberated by modernity. Their identities are now ascribed, not prescribed. But there is a price to pay for such liberation and that price is risk and uncertainty. In the modern world identity is problematic. The problematization of identity is captured most graphically in the work of some post-modernists who argue that the world has undergone some form of an epochal change which incorporates what they often refer to as 'the death of the subject' (see Chapter 5). The argument here is that there is no longer any such thing as a core self and that individuals adopt a broad spectrum of identities from one moment to the next. In this context, identities are less and less localized. Local sources of identity may continue to be important, but tend to be so in relation to the global. In a sense, then, in a global 'society' identities are increasingly mediated, and this is why cultural aspects of globalization are so important to social theorists. I will return to this point later. But broadly speaking the debate over globalization and its many forms recognizes the fact that events farther away from our actual day-to-day activities have an increasing influence on our lives and on our identities. This point is summed up nicely by Giddens (1991): 'Globalization can . . . be defined as the intensification of worldwide social relations which link distant localities in such a way that local happenings are shaped by events occuring many miles away and vice versa' (p. 64).

As I have already noted, there are a variety of different types of globalization, be they economic, cultural or political. Globalization is a multi-dimensional phenomenon and as such incorporates a series of complex linkages between categories that sociologists have previously worked so tirelessly to separate (see Tomlinson, 1999a). There are, in effect, as Allen and Massey (1995) suggest, many 'globalizations', including the globalization of telecommunications, of finance and of culture. On the economic level the actions of transnational companies are seen to be central to the globalization of production. Companies no longer base their decisions to locate on a national basis, but often decide where the best place to do so is on a global scale. Meanwhile, the world's financial markets are connected through rapid developments in information technology which have meant that capital and resources can be switched around the world at a touch of a button. Though the above sorts of aspects of globalization are virtually invisible to the individual, the implications of such a process are very real and as such less and less remote from real life. As more and more companies work on a global basis, crucial decisions might be made about the viability of a person's job thousands of miles away, and as such the person or persons responsible for making those decisions are likely to be more hard-headed and less sentimental than if they were part of the local community. Meanwhile, at the beginning of the twenty-first century the desire or want to travel abroad has apparently become a right or a need. As global consumers it is almost as if we expect to travel abroad, consuming global cultures in the process.

A key development here then has been the receding influence of the nation-state, which is itself intimately tied up with what some authors have described as either 'time-space compression' or 'time-space distanciation'. Thus, David Harvey (1989), who relates his discussion of time-space compression closely to that of post-modernity, considers the ways in which global capitalism has immensely speeded up in recent decades, resulting in massive disruptions and implications for political-economic practices, the balance of class power, and social and cultural life in general. The acceleration in production and the associated accelerations in exchange and consumption have apparently resulted in an increasingly volatile and ephemeral market. Our culture, then, is increasingly unstable and disposable to the extent that we live in a world where we throw away 'values, lifestyles, stable relationships, and attachments to things, buildings, places, people, and received ways of doing and being' (Harvey, 1989, p. 286). The problem with all this, as far as Harvey is concerned, is that we may not be able to cope as easily with such rapid social change as we might think. Globalization as expressed through time-space compression has created an ever more stressful world.

The notion of globalization does indeed indicate the emergence of a world 'in which different institutions function as parts of one system and distant peoples share a common understanding of living together on one planet' (see Lechner and Boli, 1999, p. 1). Globalization is concerned with the consciousness that such processes precipitate; it represents the linking together of social institutions, culture and consciousness upon economic and political foundations. The problem for social scientists is that they have traditionally struggled to apply broad theoretical conceptions to the actualities of everyday life. This problem is accentuated in a global context. However, it may be possible to begin to address this problem if more emphasis is placed on cultural dimensions of globalization. As Robins (1997) argues, 'Globalization is ordinary: we are all now exposed to, and increasingly aware of, its consequences. We are all immersed in the globalization process' (p. 12). We encounter globalization in the form of global brands, global cuisines, global alcohol, global clothes and fashion, global electronics and global cars. Our everyday experience of globalization is therefore arguably, more than anything, cultural in nature.

Cultural globalization

In light of the above, I want to suggest that the most interesting and potentially most important aspect of globalization, in the creation of what Urry (1998) and Ohmae (1990) describe as a new golden age of 'borderlessness', is in fact cultural. In other words, cultural dimensions of globalization represent the most enlightening means by which social theorists can come to terms with the nature of social change, which, as I pointed out above, is characterized by an apparent undermining of traditional conceptions of society. It is the social theorist's job to understand what the consequences of globalization actually are for what people think, believe, do and create (see Hogan, 1996; Robertson, 1992). In other words, there is a suggestion that sociologists have tended to struggle when attempting to come to terms with the cultural meanings that are actively invested in aspects of globalization. As such, there is an immediate need to rise above conceptions of the economic and political dimensions of globalization in order to address what globalization really means for human beings and their everyday lives. Equally importantly, a discussion of globalization will serve to illustrate how what appear to be even the remotest aspects of social change have an active role to play on how we as individuals actually experience everyday life. We may not feel we have much control over the rapid pace of the social changes that surround us, but such changes actively impinge on who and what we are from one day to the next. Tomlinson addresses the issue of cultural globalization in his book *Globalization and Culture* (1999a), in which he acknowledges that the notion of culture is as elusive as that of globalization. But the main reason for focusing on the cultural dimension of globalization is that it taps into such a cross-section of social experiences. The cultural sphere constantly mirrors and interacts with the multi-dimensional aspects of globalization I mentioned above. As Tomlinson (1999a) points out,

> . . . we have to unravel from the complexly intertwined practices of the cultural, the economic and the political, a sense of the purpose of the cultural – that of making life meaningful . . . the emphasis [should be] on meanings as ends in themselves, as distinct from simply instrumental meanings. (pp. 18–19)

In effect, Tomlinson calls for a study of the ordinariness of globalization. Culture therefore connects large-scale social change and the immediacy and intimacy of everyday life. The cultural dimension highlights the dialectical nature of globalization and, in turn, the fact that globalization is not necessarily controlling, but may also interact with the local: '. . . globalization promotes much more physical mobility than ever before, but the key to its cultural impact is in the transformation of localities themselves' (Tomlinson, 1999a, p. 29).

Despite the above, and as I pointed out earlier, it is very important that we do not get carried away with the rhetoric that surrounds globalization. In particular, it is absolutely crucial that we do not overemphasize the degree of social and cultural change involved here. As Robins (1997) points out, it is important to acknowledge the fact that globalization does not supersede and replace *everything* that existed beforehand. Globalization, and cultural globalization more specifically, represents an 'accumulation of cultural phenomena' (p. 19). Cultural expressions of globalization exist alongside local and national cultural forms. In turn, as both Robins (1997) and Hannerz (1992) note, how a person experiences and responds to globalization will depend on his or her own social, economic and political circumstances and those of the locality in which he or she lives. Any discussion of cultural globalization therefore needs to be a careful one. Perhaps the best place to start in this respect is the global media.

Mass-mediated global culture

The globalization of culture represents one of the abiding representations of the late twentieth century and continues to be equally as powerful at the beginning of the twenty-first. The mass media play an especially important role in this process. As Atkinson (1999) points out, the mass media have an enormous amount of power in determining how we perceive foreign cultures with which we have no direct contact. In many respects, then, the mass media have the power 'to play God' in actively intervening in how the West relates to the rest of the world; the massive humanitarian response to the Ethiopian famine in the mid-1980s being a case in point (Atkinson, 1999, p. 102). It is also a particular concern of Atkinson's that Western agencies produce and transmit 90 per cent of the world's news, and a distorted version of such news at that.

In some respects, however much we may not like it, the media baron Rupert Murdoch, owner of News Corporation, represents the absolute personification of globalization. The main flow of globalization arguably takes place via the transmission of global media, which tend to be dominated by massive multinational corporations and media barons such as Murdoch, who own newspapers, television stations, and even whole sports (through television contracts), on a world-wide basis. The problem here is that the mass media are so ubiquitous that we have come to take them for granted. More importantly, we not only take global culture for granted, but also those processes that underlie global culture. Globalization does not just happen; it is arguably the product of an expansionist economic strategy, and, as Robins (1997) notes, international consumer culture lies at its core. Consumers of the mass media do not constantly marvel at the wonders of globalization. They simply do not have to because it has become a constant aspect of their everyday lives. The point here is that human beings have arguably come to take global-ization for granted. Globalization has become a way of life. This was no more in evidence than during the Gulf War, when CNN's reporting of events, though dramatic, actually appeared to be rela-tively routine. This was a routinized mass-mediated reality. Friedland (1999) therefore points out that CNN not only came to report the news, but actually shaped events and became part of them. In effect, 'The Gulf War . . . demonstrated how world television could be bent to follow lines favorable to the dominant Western nations that were the base of that system' (p. 297). By 1992 CNN International was able to reach a global audience of 53 million viewers. It prides itself on providing 24-hour news from any point on the globe at any time. Consumers appear to live in a global culture where they have almost immediate access to events going on in the world at any given time and at a touch of a button.

For the above reasons, global changes in the impact of television have preoccupied many theorists of globalization. Indeed, Barker (1999) goes as far as to suggest that 'television has become a leading resource for the construction of identity products . . . meanings which people produce interactively with television texts are woven into their identity products' (pp. 3–4). Barker argues that television is actually *the* major source of global cultural capital because it allows us to become 'global armchair travellers'. It allows us to perceive the worlds of others and to reconstruct those worlds in the context of our own. Television has therefore precipitated a state of affairs in which identities themselves are not culturally bound. In a global 'society' identities are borderless.

Glocal homogenization?

But the big debate here centres on whether cultural globalization is actually undermining the richness of cultures world-wide in prefer-ence to a process of homogenization; a process arguably underpinned by the global media. You only have to consider the symbols of global capitalism to have some sympathy for this point of view: Coca-Cola, IBM, McDonald's, American Express, Microsoft, Pepsi, are all brands that appear to symbolize the global dominance of consumer capitalism. This issue is, or at least was, perhaps best taken up in the work of those authors concerned with the process of cultural imperialism: the process by which Western culture has apparently come to dominate the world. The notion of cultural imperialism, as Tomlinson (1991) notes, reflects the concern on the part of neo-Marxists that the mass media are implicated in a 'large totality of domination' (p. 20). In this sense, the term 'cultural imperialism' is a Marxist one. However, in discussing cultural imperialism, Tomlinson is more concerned with the process of cultural homogenization. He is careful to point out that people do not suffer from some form of false consciousness in this context, and that cultural homogenization is not a bad thing in itself. Globalization, from this point of view, is about the spread of uniformity. However, it would be misleading to suggest that that uniformity is necessarily bad. As such, Barker (1999) argues that the globalization of television is not best understood as a process of cultural imperialism. Cultures are being homogenized, but there is also evidence of heterogenization and localization which operate simultaneously. The notions of imperialism and homogenization suggest a one-sided relationship. This, according to Barker, is misleading. The notions of globalization and hybridity are therefore more appropriate in this context. At the very least we can say that globalization has ensured that identities are increasingly complex, and that television has played a role in complexifying these identities.

Globalization is very much about the paradoxical tensions that exist between the global and the local. Therefore, global culture is inherently unstable and uncertain, and the effects of globalization are ambivalent (Bauman, 1998a). The discussion of the concept of 'glocalization' reflects such tensions. As Beck (2000) points out, globalization and localization amount to two sides of the same coin; a coin whose effect is inevitably unequal: 'For globalization splits the world's population into the globalized rich, who overcome space and never have enough time, and the localized poor, who are chained to the spot and can only "kill" time' (p. 57).

American culture is most often criticized in the above regard. Much in the style of members of the Frankfurt School, critics have found an easy target in the vulgarities of American popular culture (see Chapter 2). From the production point of view, as Barker (1999) points out, US corporations dominate the global communication industries. The influence of Bill Gates, the world's richest man and the owner of Microsoft, is a case in point. Even industries such as the computer industry and the internet, which may on the surface appear to be liberating, may in actual fact be highly controlling, insofar as they actively accentuate global economic inequality. And it is Americans who are in control. Many social theorists are therefore concerned with the process of Americanization, whereby American culture is apparently being transformed into a global culture. The United States seems to have succeeded in perpetuating a vision of American consumerist culture as an emancipatory force characterized by rugged individualism. This image has been carried along global channels of cultural flow. Indeed, Burnett (1996) notes that it has been estimated that in the 1990s American mass media products accounted for 75 per cent of broadcast and basic cable television revenues world-wide, and 55 per cent of all film screenings. Meanwhile, 55 per cent of all home video rentals are of American origin and American books make up 35 per cent of the world market. From this point of view, the globalization of culture is more than simply the spread of com-munications on a global scale, but a further expression of American economic and cultural dominance.

This American dominance is exemplified by the power and influence of CNN. The network propagates a very American-centric vision of the world and arguably does not take into account the diversity of languages, cultures and perspectives that exist world-wide. Likewise, Serge Latouche (1996) argues, the West in general spreads propaganda via its media, 'an insidious "gift" which wit-nesses to the over-flowing vitality of hyperdeveloped societies, but strangles all cultural activity among the passive recipients of its messages' (1996, p. 21). In this context, Latouche discusses the example of the African adoption of French television. He points out that France provides African television with a free television service amounting to about 5,200 hours of programming every year. Above and beyond any economic benefits this may have for France, Latouche suggests that as a direct result of this deal, no real African audio-visual industry has been developed. This is an example of the economic consequences of cultural globalization and vice versa, and an illustration of the power that some Western countries have over less developed parts of the world. Ironically, then, even actions that appear to be counter-acting the disadvantage that these countries feel actively extend that disadvantage both culturally and economically. From this point of view, the West is actively destroying the ethnic diversity of the third world. In this context, Ulrich Beck (2000) points out that if any term has become most associated with globalization, then that term is 'McDonaldization' (see Chapter 6). In effect, cultural symbols and ways of life have converged around uniformity.

The implication of the above is that the distinctive features of indigenous cultures throughout the world are gradually being eroded by Western and more especially American culture, a process, as

Ritzer (1993) points out, which is extended by the world-wide dominance of the credit card (see Chapter 6). As far as Britain is concerned, Marling (1993) argues that the American way permeates every aspect of our everyday lives. However, perhaps the most important point to make in this respect is the following:

> Despite the fascination with Uncle Sam's credit cards, fast food, white-walled tyres and Virginia tobacco, which might be said to be a by-product of American television, there's a cynicism, even a loathing, of real American intervention, of the political Big Brotherhood. American *cultural* influence, in other words, may be wide, but it isn't very deep. (p. 123, emphasis in the original)

Similarly, Featherstone (1995) argues that the suggestion that the United States lies at the centre of cultural globalization is a difficult one to sustain. Clearly, the United States remains a global player, but other centres such as Japan and East Asia are also becoming ever more influential in this regard. Indeed, Japanese products, and, in particular, Japanese electronics, have certainly reached a global market, but they have not needed to do so on the back of any conception of Japanese culture. They have done so because consumers want to buy Japanese products.

As Tomlinson (1999a) points out, although the debate surrounding cultural imperialism still rages, it is a position that is far less fashionable now as we enter the twenty-first century than it was in the 1970s and 1980s. Indeed, as Tomlinson himself notes (1999b), authors such as Giddens (1991) and Bauman (1998a) actually argue that globalization illustrates the decline of the West rather than its triumph. Communication technology isn't the exclusive preserve of the West. It ambiguously counter-imposes enablement and disempowerment (Tomlinson, 1999a, p. 27). What might be said to be happening here, then, is an actual erosion of the influence of the West through a process of *modern* globalization. Tomlinson's reading of Giddens is such that globalization has apparently become so influential that its Western underpinnings are no longer as significant as they were. In other words, the West has itself squandered its own unique cultural underpinnings. What it is to be 'Western' is no longer as clear as it used to be. Globalization is not a one-way process; it is culturally negotiated. In these circumstances the cultural dominance of the West is increasingly diluted.

From the above it is clear that debates over cultural globalization are clearly therefore many-faceted. Another author who discusses the make-up of global popular culture is Street (1999), who points out that the reception of 'global popular culture' and the meanings invested in it will vary considerably with time and place. There is a particular danger in assuming that American popular culture, for instance, is received uniformly. Street uses the diverse ways in which jazz was consumed in the Soviet Union, as anything from the worst possible representation of capitalist excess to the authentic voice of an anti-capitalist culture, to illustrate this point. As such, Street argues that sociologists have tended to underestimate the processes that create global forms of popular culture in favour of a superficial analysis of texts and their interpretation. In other words, we need to look more closely at the way culture is actually produced. Street is therefore concerned that 'the rhetoric of global culture has become detached from the material and institutional conditions that underlie the appearance of globalization' (p. 79). This rhetoric has led us to assume certain things about globalization, and those assumptions are usually negative in nature. The suggestion that global companies are actually responding to market changes should not therefore be dismissed, nor should the role of national mediating institutions be underestimated. In short, analyses of globalization need to be more subtle and reflexive than they have been in the past. In particular, they need to account for the obvious tensions that appear to exist between the global and the local. In this context, Beck (1992) actually argues that global capitalism needs to maintain local diversities, insofar as

> A single world culture pushed to its outer limits, where local cultures die out and everyone consumes, eats, sleeps, loves, dresses, argues and dreams in accordance with a single schema (however neatly divided by income group) would spell the end of the market, the end of profits. A world capitalism shaken by sales crises has a special need for local diversity and contrast, as a means of surviving through product and market innovation. (p. 46)

The local damage caused by global capitalism will continue to rage. But ultimately it is very tempting to accept Kumar's (1995) suggestion that over-optimistic post-modern perceptions of globalization are simply blinded to the exploitation of such localities as a means to an economic end. Quite often, then, any relationship between the global and the local, in the case of tourism for example, will involve compromise and exploitation. The unfortunate conclusion probably has to be that the global, and, in particular, global capitalism, is the stronger player in this relationship. McGrew (1992) therefore notes that rather than representing the present epoch as the dawning of a 'global civilization', it might be more accurate to refer to globalization as the final consolidation of a 'capitalist world society'. Ultimately, one factor alone has a primary influence on the everyday experience of the world's population, and that factor is encapsulated in the continuing power and control exerted by global capitalism. It is symbolized by the image of the Asian piece-worker earning next to nothing in the name of the West.

Consuming food cultures

As a means of addressing the above issues I want to consider one particular aspect of cultural globalization, not because it is any more important than any other, but because it highlights some of the above issues so graphically. The globalization of food is characterized at an economic level by the massive growth, in recent decades, of world agricultural production, alongside a long-term decline in international food prices (Watts and Goodman, 1997). But the effect of global systems is not as straightforward as this statement might imply:

> The food economy is on the one hand increasingly differentiated in new sorts of ways at the level of consumption – some within the LDCs [Less Developed Countries] are eating better at a time when others are descending into a universe of ever-greater food insecurity, millions in California go hungry while others consume 'designer' organic vegetables shuttled around the world . . . a reflection of deep polarities within the world economy at large. (Watts and Goodman, 1997, pp. 2–3)

It might be argued that such polarities are best expressed through the medium of consumption. In short, those countries wealthy enough to consume at high levels, are able to consume a wide variety of different foods according to the ups and downs of food fashions. For such countries food is indeed global (Marsden et al., 2000). But in this respect globalization is very much a lifestyle phenomenon. For instance, the glut of global media and information may well influence the types of foods that become popular in one country as opposed to another.

One author who considers the global consumption of food in detail, and who does so from a cultural point of view, is James (1996). James points out that food consumption in contemporary Britain is often about juxtaposition. The juxtaposition of the Indian restaurant and the Chinese takeaway on the high street, but also of the cuisine itself: the exquisite curry followed by the British tradition of the after-dinner mint. The key question, for James, is whether or not in this context food can still act as a marker of local cultural identity. She therefore considers whether the confusion of culinary signposts actually constitutes a breakdown in markers of distinctiveness that may distinguish one individual or culture from another. In turn, is British identity as we know it being radically modified? In short, the global nature of food consumption is said, from this point of view, to reflect the increasingly precarious and temporal nature of global identities. On the other hand, there are aspects of global food consumption which indicate globalization is often just as much about continuity as it is about change.

James argues that shared forms of consumption mark our differences from others and between cultural orders. In this sense, the relationship between global food consumption and identity construction is a paradoxical one. It provides a flexible source of identity which is actually based on inflexible cultural stereotypes. James therefore charts the considerable changes that have occurred in the nature of British cooking since the 1950s. Chinese, Indian, Spanish and French cuisine, amongst others, constitute a regular part of the British diet. And yet alongside this development, the tension between the global and the local is illustrated by a concurrent movement towards 'a more localized, even parochial, taste in food' (James, 1996, p. 81). The plethora of culinary television shows and newspaper columns often appear to be reasserting what constitutes 'genuine' British food, in the form of, say, cheese, wine or bread.

James goes on to discuss and apply in some detail Hannerz's (1990) work on cosmopolitanism, which she adapts in the form of a discussion on the global nature of food. James therefore identifies four contemporary discourses of food which shape global and local identities simultaneously:

1   Global food: a discourse in which food appears to be increasingly transnational. Food is not locally based but homogeneous, any differences between regions being played down. This trend reflects a process of what is in effect food imperialism (or indeed 'McDonaldization') in which the identities available through food are safe, predictable and conventional.

2   Expatriate food: a discourse in which the heterogeneity of cuisines and their cultural and local diversities are emphasized. In this context, James discusses the example of the author Peter Mayle's book *A Year in Provence* (1992), in which food plays a key role in actively changing his identity and in creating for him a new sense of the authentic local. The book therefore reflects a wider trend towards the consumption of foreign lifestyles and quality. This approach therefore celebrates the subtleties of and differences between global and local cuisines.

3   Food nostalgia: a discourse in which the local is vigorously defended against the threat of global standardization. In other words, this discourse represents a desire to protect the authenticity of the local food, such as obscure brands of British cheese or sausage for instance. It represents a call, above all, to save British

culinary tradition. However, as James points out, this discourse, like that of the expatriate discourse, is a peculiarly middle-class one which has very little to do with the mass consumption of food. Rather, it is about who can afford to eat what. Food nostalgia (as a reaction to globalization) may therefore actively sustain older class divisions. Globalization, in turn, may be just as much about reinforcing the old as it is about introducing the new.

4   Food creolization: this discourse refers to the mixing and matching of food cultures through single meals and often single plates and palates: a blending of international styles and tastes. For instance, a labour migrant unable to find the necessary ingredients may have to make the best of those ingredients available: memories of 'home' being re-created locally through food. The creolization of food, argues James, may also represent a new mark of Britishness, with its emphasis on 'posh' but convenient food.

What does all this add up to? Above all, it is important to note, as does James, that the four discourses engaged with here are overlapping, and, as such, globalization is far more complex than it may appear to be on the surface:

> In embodying identities in a multiplex fashion, [these discourses] offer ways of embracing Otherness, of confronting the global through localized, even personal, food styles and, conversely, a way of living a local life with and through global imagery. . . . The globalization of food is not, therefore, just a matter of the movement of food stuffs between nations; nor is it simply the amalgamation or accommodation of cuisines. It is a complex interplay of meanings and intentions which individuals employ subjectively to make statements about who they are, and where and how their Selves are to be located in the world. (James, 1996, p. 92)

The globalization of food incorporates a whole raft of social, economic and cultural relationships all of which highlight the apparent immediacy of globalization and the way in which it actively impinges on people's (and, in particular, consumers') identities. It refers to the global impact of capitalism, but also to the influence that impact exerts on people's everyday lives. However, it is also very important to remember that that impact varies spatially and socially and that in some respects, notably in the guise of food consumption, globalization may be a largely middle-class phenomenon. The danger here, then, is that the social theorist makes certain assumptions about globalization precisely because he or she is viewing that change through middle-class lenses.

Conclusions

There can be no doubt that aspects of globalization are increasingly playing an active role in the construction of social life on a day-to-day basis. The above example of global food consumption illustrates that at the very least from a Western point of view this is certainly the case. The effect of globalization on more distant lands is more questionable. For one, they are well beyond the scope of most of our immediate experiences. But as Spybey (1996) suggests, we undoubtedly share some experiences on a global scale. Although, owing to its paradoxical nature, it is important not to be swayed either way by arguments as to the positive and the negative impact of globalization, there is a nagging concern that, at least in some respects, the positive impacts of globalization are inevitably spatially specific. Globalization, in short, is more likely to benefit the haves than the have nots, both geographically and socially. This raises some important issues for the social theorist adapting his or her work for application in the sphere of social research: how can globalization, if we accept it exists, be harnessed to the greater good? It might indeed be argued that social theory is ultimately redundant if it is not harnessed in order actively to do something about improving our understanding and experience of the everyday world, and in particular the sorts of inequalities that are associated with globalization.

As I mentioned above, in one sense the whole debate over globalization undermines the very essence of what it means to be a social theorist. The very meaning of globalization centres on the fact that people and networks of communications are connecting in ever more unexpected ways; ways which are more and more unlikely to operate on a national basis. Urry (1998) describes this as the 'hollowing out' of traditional societies. Global flows combine and cross to alter fundamentally our experience of time and space. Immediate local space is therefore simply transitory and cannot any longer determine who it is we are. Rather, we pick and choose elements from the disjointed offerings that confront us from day to day.

The above trends are intensified by, for instance, the preponderance of cross-border travel, notably in Europe, and the global refugee problem, both of which problematize the notion of society. Societies no longer, according to Urry, speak in a single voice. Urry uses a quotation from Rose's work which lucidly sums up the problem, in that although 'our political, professional, moral and cultural authorities still speak happily of "society", the very meaning and ethical salience of this term is under question as "society" is perceived as dissociated into a variety of ethical and cultural communities with incompatible allegiances and incommensurable obligations' (Rose, 1996, p. 353). Urry (1998) does not suggest that a new social, the global, has replaced, the old, the societal. The national is still very important to most people's everyday lives. But perhaps what is more important is the fact that inhuman objects are becoming increasingly important to the construction of human identities. Technology, imagery, symbolism, machinery, are especially important in this regard. An illustration of this point is that it has recently been estimated that around 50 per cent of the British population own a mobile phone. This is an astounding figure which illustrates very vocally the way in which place and space have been opened up in a global age. Urry's argument is that in these circumstances any power that human beings do have is less and less likely to be human in nature:

> There is then no distinct level of social reality, if this implies that there are social entities which are the particular and unique outcome of humans acting in and through their particular powers. In particular, since all apparently social entities in fact involve networks of connections between humans and these other components, then there are no such entities as human societies. If there are no humans anymore, so there are no (human) societies. There is, one might say, 'no such thing as society'. (Urry, 1998, p. 15)

Bearing the above in mind, I want to conclude this chapter by returning to what continues to be a very pressing issue for social theorists concerned with globalization, namely: the impact of globalization on the changing nature of identity. In his book, *Identity Crises* (1998), Robert G. Dunn talks about the destabilization of identity. He means by this that contemporary identities are indeed being culturally transformed as a result of economic and technological transformations associated with an ever-expanding capitalist society. This process, largely bound up, in turn, with the process of commodification, is also clearly associated with 'a new globalization of capital and communications and information technologies, and the emergence of new kinds of politics and social movements [which] underlie the demarcation and formation of a new multilayered cultural terrain' (p. 107). Consumption clearly plays an important role in the construction of global identities.

The processes of globalization I have discussed above put a particular strain on national identities, because, as Urry (1998) suggests, the terrains upon which those identities are secured are no longer as stable or predictable as they would have been in the past. Urry therefore wonders how far the very notion of 'society' is practicable in a world where social barriers are apparently and constantly being broken down. Can societies any longer be referred to as being bounded in any real sense? The notion of risk which I discuss in Chapter 7 is important here insofar as risk is not state- or society-specific; it permeates the globe. Everybody, regardless of national borders, is subjected to risk, and what therefore emerges is more of a 'risk culture' than a 'risk society'. In other words, the notion of society implies a far more structured kind of social experience than is currently the case. There are, from this point of view,

> no social structures either in the sense of social interactions of presence and absence, or in the sense of enduring social relations which people bear. . . . whatever the limits of the 'societal' model, there do seem to have developed an extraordinary array of processes which undermine whatever had remained of a societal conceptualization of what it was to be a human being at the end of the twentieth century. (Urry, 1998, pp. 3–4)

The massive interest in questions of globalism and globalization, both academically and in the mass media, are testament to this argument.

In the above context, the continued attractions of consumer culture encourage a state of affairs in which the individual is arguably more likely to associate him- or herself with a global brand and a cosmopolitan way of life than the characteristics historically associated with a particular nation or region. In short, the new global culture 'is at present a predominantly commercialized culture, devoid of origins or place' (Dunn, 1998, p. 135). But the paradox here, as Dunn points out, is that, despite the globalization of commercialization, such aspects of social change continue to operate alongside cultural values, traditions and ways of life. Local cultures are inevitably reconstituted in new ways, and this has important implications for the nature of identity. Western cities, in particular, become increasingly diverse, both ethnically and socially, and identities reflect such cosmopolitanism. This in itself can only be a positive thing. Conversely, contemporary societies are characterized by a breakdown of authority. We live in a far more eclectic 'society' than we did in the past and are therefore increasingly uncertain as to what we should and should not do. Global consumerism appears to fill that void, but it also provides new sources for the construction of identity:

> The destabilization of identity and values stemming from economic and technological change has generated multiple and contradictory responses to the decline of modern authority, both conservative and progressive, creating a novel and ambiguous ideological landscape. The decline of the older exclusionary hierarchies of modernity and the seeming exhaustion of modern culture have created possibilities for a genuinely global and universalistic culture built on recognition and inclusion of difference. (Dunn, 1998, p. 141)

The debate over globalization raises all sorts of concerns which are fundamental to what it means to be a social theorist. The influence of globalization and the social, economic and (arguably) especially cultural processes it engenders clearly have a very significant impact on the nature of social life. As Short and Kim (1999) argue, a global consciousness has become more and more fundamental to our everyday lives. Technological change associated with the internet has extended this process. As Short and Kim go on to suggest, however, the discourse that surrounds globalization has also come to play an important political role. Indeed, there is a danger that the hyperbole that surrounds this issue could be used to justify wage cuts and changes in labour conditions in the name of the competitive global market. In this sense, as Short and Kim point out, globalization is presented as a sort of uncontrollable global force that leaves social tradition and locality in its wake. The global economy may well have its economic benefits, but there is also a distinct danger that globalization becomes an excuse for economic exclusion. The third world, in particular, appears to be in a no-win situation in which what the Western world gains in surplus, the third world loses in wage differentials (see Latouche, 1993). The third world is constantly fighting a losing battle to pay off global debts, whilst failing to address the economic shortcomings of its locality. Globalization therefore treads a dangerous path. At one and the same time it appears to be both a liberator and an imprisoner. Globalization may indeed be the trendiest of academic issues, but it also affects the way in which we live in all sorts of complex and subtle ways. It does so unevenly, however. Indeed,

> We need to conceptualize globalization less as a wave sweeping all before it, and more like a leopard-spot pattern, with small islands of wealth and global connectivity interspersed with marginalized areas and populations. . . . The popular discourses of globalism have exaggerated the islands rather than the seas of poverty and marginalization. (Short and Kim, 1999, p. 6)

Authors such as Short and Kim and Abu-Lughod (1991) criticize discourses surrounding globalization for tending to be biased towards core countries and, in turn, for being speculative, over-abstract, hazy and vague. This is no more true than in the case of cultural globalization. There is therefore a significant need for more grounded empirical work on the question of globalization (Short and Kim, 1999, p. 8). The problem with debates over globalization is that globalization itself is a highly generalized social process (Waters, 1995).

So what are the implications of this realization for social theory and more broadly for sociology as a discipline? One thing is for certain: sociology needs to be less parochial in nature. Although sociology has to come to terms with the impact of globalization on a local level, it also has to cater for the diversity and complexity of the broader social processes involved. In effect, social theory and sociology need to work in tandem:

> Globalization can offer the expansion of possibilities for sociology partly because it expands this marketplace for narratives, but not merely so. Globalization connects the local and national structures, on which sociologists are already experts, within emerging supranational flows. Sociology is strategically, possibly uniquely placed to provide the local interpretations of globality which will be necessary if the inhabitants of the planet are to understand why their local and national political systems are approaching ineffectivity. (Waters, 1995, p. 163)

To conclude, one author who has recently addressed the role of sociology and social theory in a changing world is Immanuel Wallerstein (2000), who argues that since the 1960s globalization has utterly transformed the context in which sociology operates. Yet despite this, as far as Wallerstein is concerned at least, 'globalization' is simply a buzz-word and continues to be meaningless as an analytic concept. It simply is not precise enough to be of genuine analytical value. However, what it does do, at a more general level, is acknowledge the realization that something very new is actually happening, a feeling of new-millennium angst and uncertainty. This uncertainty is reflected in the directions in which sociology and social theory have had to go. The social sciences, more generally, have had to concede that social phenomena are infinitely complex, as are the explanations for those phenomena, and as such cannot be easily explained. In this context, 'What we need is some calmer reflection about the possibilities and priorities of social thought and about the organization of our scholarly activities' (Wallerstein, 2000, p. 29). But if this transition is to be a success, it is the division that operates between science and philosophy, according to Wallerstein, that needs to be addressed. A wholesale reunification and re-division of social science is therefore necessitated, 'so as to create a more intelligent division of labour, one that would permit significant intellectual advance in the twenty-first century' (p. 33). Above all, social science is distorted by the fact that it is itself not global. On the whole it is conducted by an élite band of people in the richest corners of the globe. If the impact of globalization is going to be realized, Wallerstein's contention is that world social science has to be nothing less than transformed. This he accepts is a monumental task and perhaps an impossible one, but it is none the less necessary. Ultimately, social science and social theory are as much part of the world which they inhabit as they are a critical reflection upon that world.

The theme of globalization will continue to be important to social theorists because it relates so closely to so many of the core issues with which they are more generally concerned. It may be an exaggeration to describe globalization as a new meta-narrative. Its impact is too spatially varied for this to be the case. However, the contention that globalization is, in fact, the primary force behind social change at the beginning of the twenty-first century is a serious one and should be critically interrogated. The tendency for many social theorists to take globalization for granted is actually witness to the continued influence of the concept and the fact that it reflects the accelerating pace of social change on the global stage. If social theory is able to adapt to the complex demands of a global social-scape, then it needs to learn to be more flexible than is currently the case. It needs to consider far more reflexively the role of social theory in an ever-changing world, and whether or not, indeed, social theory can do anything at all to change that world for the better.

Recommended reading

Ulrich Beck (2000) *What is Globalization?* Cambridge: Polity. A detailed and enlightening discussion of globalization by one of the foremost social theorists of our time.

Frank J. Lechner and John Boli (eds) (1999) *The Globalization Reader*, Oxford: Blackwell. An impressive collection with a broad cross-section of important articles on all the major dimensions of globalization.

John Tomlinson (1999) *Globalization and Culture*, Cambridge: Polity. A theoretically informed and well-developed discussion of the specifically cultural implications of globalization.

Malcolm Waters (1995) *Globalization*, London: Routledge. An interesting and thought-provoking work particularly useful in its discussion of the relationship between the global and the local. A good place to start.

CHAPTER 9

THEORIZING FOR 'REAL'

The ability to theorize about social life is a skill and one that many people never actually manage to command. But the simple recognition that social theory is a skill and not something that needs to be rote learned is a significant achievement in itself. Learning 'theory' or the body of knowledge associated with a specific theorist is not an end in itself, but a means to an end: the skill of critiquing theories and, more importantly, the ability to actually and actively theorize. *Social Theory in the 'Real' World* has attempted to illustrate that social theory can have interesting things to say about the world and is about far more than the partially relevant theories of long-dead classical theorists. Indeed, the book's abiding philosophy is that social theory is only exciting if you make it exciting. If social theory seems boring, it is because, more often than not, those people who study it are reluctant to make the necessary effort to apply it to real-life situations. It may seem somewhat pretentious to say so, but it is worth suggesting that by discovering social theory you may even discover a small part of yourself. The benefit of social theory lies in its potential for shedding light upon circumstances that you may have previously taken for granted. Such insight can potentially tell you as much about yourself as it does about the world in which you live.

In this concluding chapter I want to outline some of the major themes that have emerged from the book as a whole, indicating as I do so the apparent status of social theory as we enter the twenty-first century. What state is the endeavour of social theory actually in, and where might or should it go in the near future? There does seem to be plenty of evidence to suggest that the world is, indeed, undergoing considerable social change, but what does this change mean for social theory itself? The first issue I therefore want to consider briefly is whether the degree of social change perceived by the social theorists I have discussed during the course of this book is genuine or whether it says more about the process of theorizing than it does about the social change it is attempting to theorize.

Continuity or change?

Many of the theories I have discussed have been concerned with the degree to which social change constitutes an epochal shift. In other words, is the world in which we live now so radical and so different to the one in which we used to live that it justifies us in talking about a whole new type of society? This debate is perhaps most closely associated with discussions over post-modernism. In this context many authors prefer to talk about late or high modernity than post-modernity. In effect, they regard social change as representing a continuity with the abiding aspects of modernity. The interesting thing about this is that despite disagreeing about the magnitude of the change involved, theorists often appear to be talking about virtually the same themes. In this sense, whether or not such change constitutes an epochal shift can amount to a matter of opinion. Such divergence in opinion represents one of the abiding appeals of social theory. But there is also a more serious concern that we should consider as critics of social theory. There may be a case for arguing that social theorists are predisposed or pre-programmed to exaggerate the degree of social change they are trying to account for.

The world is constantly changing, but there is a danger that because as individuals we are part and parcel of that change we assume that it is happening at a faster rate than any previous period in history. And there is also a danger that social theorists focus on any patterns of change whilst either consciously or sub-consciously excluding contradictory evidence of continuity. The work of Daniel Bell (1973) provides a case in point. Bell is no doubt perfectly justified in drawing attention to key aspects of social change in employment patterns, for instance. But such changes co-exist with continuities. And even if a number of social realms can be seen to have been affected by social change, we should not jump to the conclusion that in tandem these trends constitute a whole new society. In short, social theorists are human beings and, like many human beings, are attracted to the melodramatic. You might criticize George Ritzer for using the self-consciously melodramatic label of 'McDonaldization', which hints at massive social change, but which, under the surface, perhaps says more about the continuity of social change than its radical transformation. Social theorists are likely to focus on the transformative nature of the changes which they chart. There is certainly no intention on the part of such theorists to mislead, but the reader of social theory should come to his or her own conclusion as to how far the changes charted by such theorists amount to a radical break with the past.

In considering the dilemmas involved in charting social change, and, in particular, the fact that social theorists are, at least in some form, part of that change themselves, it is worth considering whether or not social change is predictable enough to be theorized in the above sorts of ways. In particular, can projective social theories which are concerned with the way in which the social world will develop in the future really be effective? The important thing to remember here is that social theory cannot provide all the answers. A social theory that accurately predicted the future would be a disappointment in the sense that it may well not provide an effective enough platform for continued debate. A social theory should be evaluated not according to the extent to which it accurately predicts change, but rather according to how far it stimulates debate about that change. Perhaps we should not therefore talk about 'good or 'bad' social theories but about theories that either do or do not serve to bring the sociological imagination to life (see Mills, 1959).

Theorizing the ordinary

Reading social theory is in one sense a very personal experience. No social theory will, or even necessarily should, say the same things to different people. This is what I mean when I say that social theory should, if anything, be most remarkable for what it says about your own everyday life. Applying aspects of social theory to your own experiences is a fundamental aspect of your evaluation of a theory. It is therefore worth reiterating the suggestion that in developing a theoretical mind-set the mundane or the everyday is especially important. Throughout the book I have attempted to illustrate in particular how aspects of popular culture are especially important from a theoretical point of view. They are important because they appear to be trivial and therefore are particularly susceptible as arenas of ideological intent. We may feel we are being exploited or alienated in the workplace, but are less likely to feel that way in our own time. In effect, then, aspects of social change which are under-pinned by power relationships, and in particular the relationships we associate with the development of capitalism, are potentially reinforced in the most trivial aspects of our everyday lives during which our 'guard' is most likely to be down. This realization reflects the changing nature of social theory in general and in particular the increasing recognition that cultural aspects of life are worth considering in their own right. It is partly for this reason that the realm of consumption is one of the fastest-growing areas of social theory, and this reflects the realization that consumption is more than merely the trivial by-product of production.

The implication of the above is that everybody everywhere is implicated in the process of social change. Broad patterns of social change have a real impact upon each and every one of our lives on a daily basis. But this point itself raises an important class dimension to debates concerning the role of social theory. If social change affects us all regardless of our class background, then how effectively does the social theorist deal with such change? In short, the vast majority of (if not all) social theorists are middle class. They have a peculiarly middle-class vision of the world. This is not necessarily a bad thing, but it may mean that their vision of the world is an inherently biased one. It is in this context that Callinicos (1989) accuses post-modernism of saying more about the disillusioned nature of the post-modernist than it does about social change itself. Many post-modern theorists talk about the aestheticization of everyday life, for instance (see Featherstone, 1991). They discuss the way in which consumption plays such a key role in people's lives and how consumers are able to pick and choose their identities from the menu of life. But again, such sentiments tend to be generalized ones that fail to deal with the complexity of social change. For instance, it is true to say that consumption and consumer culture have an important role in constructing people's identities. But the way in which they do so may be radically different from one person to the next. Somebody without adequate resources may indeed have an intimate relationship with consumer culture precisely because he or she is unable to access that culture. Meanwhile, the post-modernist's own point of view may be the product of his or her own sense of identity, or indeed of a sense that his or her academic identity is in some way being undermined by the ramifications of social change. My point is that social theory does tend to focus on the broad brushstroke at the expense of detailed analysis. Social theory is by definition social, but as a result can underestimate the degree of personal complexities underlying broad patterns of social change. Like the rest of us, social theorists live social change and they do so through their own eyes. Those eyes may not be reflexive enough to take into account how the same patterns of change may affect people's lives in radically different ways.

Social theory as rhetoric

It is absolutely essential that social theory does not degenerate into meaningless rhetoric. As I mentioned above in the context of McDonaldization, there is a constant danger that consumers of social theory are won over by the superficial appeal of a theory. Globalization is a good example of how a particular theoretical perspective has become a sociological buzz-word. The same applies to many of those theoretical themes I have addressed in this book, such as risk, post-modernity and consumption. It is almost as if theorists feel obliged to address such issues in some guise regardless of their actual salience.

During the course of this book I have discussed the work of Georg Simmel as an example of impressionistic social theory. Simmel's contribution to social theory is a considerable one, but his work, or at least the implication of his work, should be considered with a note of caution. Impressionistic social theory is one thing; theory that has no real basis other than the mutual affirmation of fellow theorists is another. In other words, it is important that social theories are based in some sort of practical context rather than in an ocean of rhetoric. Social theorists should be particularly wary of technological determinism. Authors like Daniel Bell and even Ulrich Beck could be criticized for exaggerating the technological factors underpinning social change to such an extent that social change ends up being assumed as opposed to analysed. The buzz-word is the adversary of reflexive social theory. It may appear to provide shelter in times of uncertainty but ultimately that shelter will never withhold the shower of criticism that will befall it. Students of social theory should therefore be prepared to critique theories that hide behind the security of a particular theoretical school or approach that has more credibility than the theory itself. More specifically, they should be very wary of reading off too much from patterns of social change that appear on the surface to be self-evident, but which in fact may be less certain than they intially appeared. For example, many journalists are currently preoccupied with the proliferation of the internet and how it appears to be transforming our relationship with technology and in many cases with the workplace. But the internet is still in its early days and its long-term effects are uncertain. A social theorist should not be dragged along by the hype associated with the internet, which, as I suggested above, may actually engender more stimulating lines of thought in the context of who does *not* have access to the internet than to who actually does. The truth beneath the hype may actually tell us more about the nature of social change. At the end of the day current discussions concerning the internet may simply tell us more about the influence that the mass media have on the culture in which we live.

The 'real' world

Bearing in mind my warning about being too swayed by theoretical fads and buzz-words, it is worth considering in some detail an issue which I touched upon in Chapter 5, namely the extent to which in a so-called 'post-modern' world it is even possible to study or theorize about any such thing as the 'real' world. This issue accounts for the italics in the book's title. Post-modernism has undermined the whole business of social theory and has forced social theorists to reconsider their contribution to 'knowledge' creation. This is not in itself necessarily a bad thing. Any theoretical development that forces social theorists to be more reflexive has to be positive.

Modern social theory was concerned with discovering and charting reality. Post-modernists often argue that there is no adequate means for representing reality, and some even deny there is any such thing as reality at all (Rosenau, 1992, p. 110). In this context, Rosenau discusses Baudrillard's (1988) work, in which he argues that there is no 'real' world and that the apparently archetypally 'unreal' Disneyland is in fact authentic because it doesn't *pretend* to be real. It is rather an amalgamation of images or 'simulacra'. Reality, then, is only how we as consumers of reality actually perceive it. We construct our own universes in our own minds and through our own individual experiences. To try to define some form of generalizable real world on this basis would therefore be foolhardy. Other post-modern theorists have pointed out that reality is a linguistic convention. There is no reality beyond language. Reality is little more than a linguistic habit (see Flax, 1990; Rosenau, 1992). But perhaps the most convincing argument of all those raised by Rosenau is that this whole debate over whether or not there is any such thing as an independent reality is little more than a game played by intellectuals who are conveniently insulated from the savage realities of the 'real' world. Perhaps post-modern intellectuals know absolutely nothing about the harsh lessons inherent in the real world and thus can only conceive of it as a mental construction. This latter position is the nearest to my own. There is a constant danger that social theory becomes so self-obsessive and so removed from the actualities of everyday life that it becomes completely impotent. It is in danger of making itself so remote, so abstract and so exclusive that reality becomes something that nobody wants to explore beyond the surface: not because it does not exist, but because it simply is not worth worrying about to that extent. The effect of post-modern thought on social theory in general has been an exciting one. But as Thomas and Walsh (1998) point out, ultimately sociology (and as such social theory) is the product of modernity. It is the product of a world in which human beings are at least to some extent concerned with understanding and making sense of the world around them. Such an understanding may not make the world a better place in which to live, as theories such as those presented by George Ritzer and members of the Frankfurt School tend to suggest, but at least it represents an acknowledgement that our own individual lives can, in whatever limited way, be improved. This in itself may or may not be realistic, but it does not condemn us to a life of doom and despair. Contemporary society is undoubtedly very complex and cannot be understood in its entirety. But ultimately, as

Thomas and Walsh point out, a post-modern sociology is an impossibility. If we accept that grand narratives no longer have a role to play in an ever-changing world, then the development of a post-modern sociology which takes on post-modern thought and all its contradictions wholeheartedly would simply replace one set of meta-narratives with another. Rather, we need to develop a sociology and a social theory of post-modernism (see Lash, 1990). As social theorists, we need to understand the complexities of the world around us reflexively, without adopting an epistemological position that predetermines our conception of that world.

Dunn (1998) argues that the current state of the world in which we live has created a particular problem for social theorists. In short, 'The dominant modes of theorizing today are often unduly conditioned by the workings of contemporary culture itself, uncritically reproducing the basic structures, conditions, and values of consumption society' (p. 221). In other words, the consumer society in which we live so infuses every aspect of contemporary life that it actively limits the terrrain in which theorists work, 'reframing the problems they work on, and relocating the "subjects" they study' (p. 221). *Social Theory in the 'Real' World* has self-consciously adopted a cultural perspective on social change. Dunn argues that the world is such that it is actually very difficult to avoid doing cultural analysis, which itself reflects the politically correct middle classness of those undertaking theoretical exploration:

> Thus, while a concentration on culture represents an appropriate response to a culturalization of society, this concept has become too exhaustive (and exhausted), too overworked and encumbered by special intellectual and political preoccupations, absorbing that which surrounds it in a fashion reminiscent of the larger society. Accordingly, we should question whether theory has lost a desired critical perspective in becoming too identified with the actually existing society and culture. (p. 222)

In this context, Dunn expresses his concern that the material and historical conditions underlying cultural production and transformation are undermined. I share this concern. None of the theories discussed in this book holds any water without appropriate consideration of its economic and social undercurrents. More than anything, social theory should be 'social'. This is not a book about cultural theory but one that argues that culture is the manifestation of social change. In other words, structural change is expressed through the individual's interaction with social institutions. Individuals are active negotiators of social structures and the primary realm in which they do so is the cultural one. It is for this reason that the relationship between structure and agency, as I pointed out in Chapter 1, is so important. In this respect, culture is just as much a product of social relations as it is 'constitutive of these relations' (Dunn, 1998, p. 224). Dunn advocates a focus on questions of identity and difference. I would agree with this sentiment, but would add the caveat that contemporary social theory should focus on the question of identity as it is actively played out in the actual life of the person using or reading that theory in what has to be an imaginative and reflexive fashion. An individual's identity is played out through his or her ongoing relationship with social change. Our identities are a complex product of the subjective and the objective and represent the means by which we consciously and unconsciously navigate the complex uncertainties associated with the relationship between structure and agency.

Imaginative theory

The fundamental conclusion of this book is that social theory can only really be of value if it is used in an imaginative and creative fashion. Social theory is not a passive pursuit, nor does it or should it represent a static body of knowledge. A student of social theory will get very little out of social theory if he or she expects to be energized by simply reading and internalizing what a particular theorist has to say on a given topic. Social theory is near to useless as a source of reference. It does not provide a magic box of answers or solutions; it provides a resource from which you can develop your own interpretations, ideas and insights. Social theory only comes to life when the reader puts his or her own life into it. Imagination is therefore the key.

A reflexive social theorist is not satisfied with what a theory tells him or her, but is concerned with adapting that theory in original ways. There are a number of options in this respect. It is a particular concern of mine that when thinking about social theory there is an inherent danger of being unnecessarily constrained by disciplinary boundaries. In short, the most effective or stimulating way to theorize is not always within the constraints of a particular disciplinary tradition. We, of course, all have or are undertaking some form of training associated with a particular discipline, even if that training is undertaken off our own backs. However, this should not prevent us from exploring ideas more immediately associated with other disciplines. The question of identity, for instance, is of fundamental importance to theorists from all sorts of disciplines. To depend on the insights of one disciplinary approach would be to cut off numerous, and potentially profitable, avenues of exploration. However, the fact is that disciplinary boundaries are for all sorts of professional reasons jealously guarded and protected (see Archibald, 1976). It takes the most imaginative of minds to overcome such barriers. But one way to do so in a theoretical context may well be to identify 'mediation phenomena', important foci for debate that apparently fall in the voids between disciplines (see Holland, 1977). Theory is not a strait-jacket and neither should be the disciplinary contexts in which theory operates. Unfortunately, disciplinary traditions are such that the onus is on the reader of social theory to make the necessary connections beyond the often blinkered boundaries presented to him or her by his or her own discipline. In this context, Stones' (1996) call for a 'past-modern' sociology is of considerable interest. There is, indeed, a need to find a middle way between 'sociological modernism' and what Stones describes as 'defeatist postmodernism'. The former under-estimates the complexity of the social world and overestimates the ability of the sociologist to construct a 'true' understanding of that world, whilst the latter sees sociological analyses as being no more than a mere fictional account. As such,

> sociology needs to provide itself with guidelines on how to traverse the bridges and the junctions that connect the insights of ontology and high theory to the empirical evidence necessary to make claims about the real world of any one moment. . . . we need to maintain a clear sense of the real, but . . . we also need to acknowledge the complexity of that real and the enormous demands of subtlety that this imposes upon anyone wanting to come anywhere near an apprehension of it in a given time and space. (Stones, 1996, p. 1)

There may or may not be any such thing as a 'real' world'. But that world is *real* to those people who live in it; for that reason it is the social theorist's responsibility to construct a debate which is concerned with moving beyond common-sense interpretations of that world.

Social theory in practice

The relationship between theory and practice or theory and research will continue to be a fundamental concern to sociologists and social theorists alike. Social theory should surely not exist in complete isolation. Not only should it reflect on 'real' life, but it should also arguably have practical implications and influence. One author who considers this question in some depth is Derek Layder (1998), who outlines what he calls an 'adaptive' approach which attempts to fulfil the needs of both theorists and researchers alike. Layder acknowledges the damaging tendency of theorists to 'do' theory and

172 Social theory in the real world

researchers to 'do' research. He therefore advocates bridging this gap
through the adoption of a new set of rules of sociological method:

> Adaptive theory both shapes, and is shaped by the empirical data that
> emerges from research. It allows the dual influence of extant theory
> (theoretical models) as well as those that unfold from (and are enfolded in)
> the research. Adaptive theorizing is an ever-present feature of the research
> process. (p. 133)

As far as Layder is concerned, then, adaptive theory takes into
account the ·complexity of the social world and the multifarious
interconnections that exist between social activities and social
organization. In this context, Layder and I concur that acknowledging
such complexity does not in any way deny that as social scientists we
can at least seek what he calls 'best approximations' to the truth (p.
142). We should not abandon the quest for knowledge, but seek to
make that quest more sophisticated and reflexive. 'Adaptive' theory is
adaptive in the sense that it is capable of adjusting to what emerges
during the course of data collection. It is not constrained by some
over-arching theoretical position or agenda. However, at the same
time it acknowledges that some theoretical positions do exist prior to
that data collection, and they therefore have to respond and adapt
accordingly. As such,

> extant 'theoretical elements' are never simple empiricist 'reflections' of
> data, they are intrinsically capable of reformulating ('adapting' or 'adjust-
> ing') themselves in response to the discovery of new information and/or
> interpretations of data which seriously challenge their basic assumptions.
> Such reformulations may involve only minor modifications, but they may
> also require fundamental reorganization, such as either abandoning one
> existing category, model or explanation, or creating new ones, depending
> on the circumstances. (pp. 150–1)

The key theme here is that social theory should be reflexive, as should
the social theorist, who needs to be prepared to adapt his or her
theory to the world he or she is researching, which, in turn, is
inevitably and perpetually adapting to itself. In this sense it is not
always appropriate to adopt an entirely objective perspective on the
social world. Our experience as human beings is necessarily
subjective and should not be denied.

An underlying concern about social theory is whether or not it has
or indeed should have any political influence. As Antonio and Kellner
point out, any intention to understand society in its totality and to use
this type of theory to serve radical or reformist movements is undermined by post-modern thought. Social criticism, from this point of
view, has been paralysed by the fragmentation of social life where

any desire for a collective project becomes untenable. The danger is that the above discussion about the status of social theory and of sociology in a so-called 'post-modern' world ensures that social theory is mute; that social theorists can only have opinions about the world, and that these opinions are no more valid than anybody else's: that social theory has no political role to play. This position is an extreme one, and one that should not necessarily lead us to the conclusion that the social theorist should hide away in his or her shell conscious of his or her inability to change or improve the world. Social theorists should avoid the temptation to strip their theories of political content. If we accept the argument I have presented throughout this book that the primary role of social theory is to provoke thought and debate, then political intent (regardless of its actual impact) should be a priority and not an embarrassment. Value freedom is in itself a chimera, and even if it can exist, it ultimately does little more than lull the theorist into a false sense of security based on a superficial veneer of theoretical validity. Social theory should encourage debate, not paralyse it. The work of the Frankfurt School may be politically questionable, but its extremely subjective nature brings alive ideological questions about popular culture. The suggestion that social theory can itself change the world in some fundamental fashion is, of course, itself highly questionable. But the danger is that if social theorists deny the validity of the human subjectivity engendered in politics, then theories they develop will amount to little more than bland, unintelligible and meaningless descriptions. Subjectivity and passion are what bring social theory to life. The end product of that theory may be indigestible, but it is paradoxically in the indigestion that the pleasure of the meal actually lies. I am not advocating a complete disregard for a balanced and considered perception of the social world; far from it. Value judgements are only reasonable when they are based on some observable reality. But ultimately we construct that reality through our own relationships with the social world.

The issue of globalization provides a particularly telling illustration of the benefits of theory that acknowledges the theorist's own perception of the world. An individual may decide to study processes of globalization for a number of reasons. These may include the fact that this topic constitutes a buzz-word and that he or she is personally motivated by the political dimensions of globalization. But to deny these motivations is to deny the very core of what it means to be a human being. As I pointed out in Chapter 1, a social theorist has to take certain precautions in studying his or her subject matter. He or she has to take some measures to stand outside of that subject matter. The social theorist has to look at social phenomena through sociological eyes. But this in itself should not obliterate the essence of that theorist's desire to address questions of globalization in the first place. I do not believe a social theorist can get *too* involved in his or her subject matter. What I do believe is that a social theorist can get so involved that his or her work is no longer theoretical. It is here that a balance needs to be struck. Social theory should not be motivated solely by politics and it should not deny the value of the sorts of measures outlined by Bauman (1990), such as the use of responsible speech, if social theory is to have anything significant to say. But ultimately a social theory without passion is arguably an empty social theory.

Regardless of the question of subjectivity, social theory should surely at the very least purport to highlight some of the power inequalities that underlie social life. Perhaps social theory cannot claim to liberate but at the very least it can inform, and that constitutes the fulfilment of a political goal in its own right. The discussion of risk and its impact on the political agenda in Chapter 7 is a good illustration of this point. Social theory cannot change social policy alone, but if we begin to recognize its prescience, then it may have more relevance to policy implementation than we might ever have imagined. An effective and thought-provoking social theory is often a vocal one and one that has a point to make. A less interesting social theory is one that concedes defeat to the speed of the change that influences it. A social theory can be politically charged, but to be effective it has to have solid foundations upon which to base such an argument. Above all else, students of social theory need to be critical. If the political extremities of a particular theory or school of thought are what best stimulates such criticism, then so be it. Social theory should be utilized as a tool for stripping away the layers of common sense.

Concluding comments

Social theory will never be truly satisfying. It was never intended to satisfy, but rather to rouse and provoke. It is absolutely inevitable that some people have never been and will never be stimulated by social theory. But it is also absolutely imperative to remember that this unfortunate fact is quite often more about the inadequacies of the theories or theorists concerned than the inadequacies of the person or persons reading or interpreting those theories. When theory becomes especially difficult to comprehend, the last thing the reader of that theory should do is to blame him- or herself.

Social Theory in the 'Real' World has tried to clarify some of the complexities that social theorists have struggled with for over a century and which they will no doubt continue to struggle with for decades, if not centuries, to come. Social theory *is* having to adapt to the rapidity of the social changes that are happening around it. But ultimately change is not such a bad thing. Social theory should help us to understand such change, as opposed to making us more scared of it than we were in the first place. And if social theorists can use change as a means of sparking off new avenues of exploration and of stimulating critical and reflexive thought, then they have succeeded. In the end, reality is what we as human beings make of it. Social theory cannot make reality for us. But what social theory can do, if we allow it the room to do so, is to clarify the complexities of contemporary social life; it can highlight the limitations of common-sense views of the world and suggest alternatives. Social theory can only ultimately achieve such an aim if we, as the 'consumers' of social theory, take it out of the abstract world which it has tended to occupy for so long and return it to the realities of our own everyday lives. The impact of social theory can only be 'real' if we actively and self-consciously endeavour to make it so.

REFERENCES

Abu-Lughod, J. (1991) 'Going beyond global babble', pp. 131–8 in A.D. King (ed.) *Culture, Globalization and the World-System*, Basingstoke: Macmillan.

Adam, B. (1998) *Timescapes of Modernity: The Environment and Invisible Hazards*, London: Routledge.

Adam, J. (1995) *Risk*, London: UCL Press.

Adorno, T.W. (1989) 'The culture industry reconsidered', pp. 128–35 in S. Bronner and D. Kellner (eds), *Criticical Theory and Society: A Reader*, London: Routledge.

Adorno, T.W. (1991) *The Culture Industry: Selected Essays on Mass Culture*, ed. J.M. Bernstein, London: Routledge.

Alfino, M., Caputo, J.S. and Wynard, R. (eds) (1998) *McDonaldization Revisited: Critical Essays on Consumer Culture*, New York: Praeger.

Allen, J. and Massey, D. (1995) 'Introduction', pp. 1–5 in *Geographical Worlds*, Buckingham: Open University Press.

Amin, A. (1994) *Post-Fordism: A Reader*, Oxford: Blackwell.

Andreski, S. (1984) *Max Weber's Insights and Errors*, London: Routledge and Kegan Paul.

Ang, I. (1985) *Watching Dallas*, London: Routledge.

Archer, M. (1995) *Realist Social Theory: The Morphogenetic Approach*, Cambridge: Cambridge University Press.

Archibald, W. (1976) 'Psychology, sociology and social psychology: bad fences make bad neighbours', *British Journal of Sociology*, 27, 2, 115–29.

Arnold, M. (1932) *Culture and Anarchy*, Cambridge: Cambridge University Press.

Atkinson, P. (1999) 'Representations of conflict in the western media: the manufacture of a barbaric periphery', pp. 102–8 in T. Skelton and T. Allen (eds) *Culture and Global Change*, London: Routledge.

Baert, P. (1998) *Social Theory in the Twentieth Century*, Cambridge: Polity.

Barker, C. (1999) *Television, Globalization and Cultural Identities*, Buckingham: Open University Press.

Baudrillard, J. (1983) *Simulations*, New York: Semiotext(e).

Baudrillard, J. (1988) *America*, London: Verso.

Baudrillard, J. (1993) 'The Evil Demon of Images and the procession of simulacra', pp. 194–9 in T. Docherty (ed.) *Postmodernism: A Reader*, Hemel Hempstead: Harvester Wheatsheaf.

Baudrillard, J. (1995) *The Gulf War Did Not Take Place*, Sydney: Power Publications.

Bauman, Z. (1988) *Freedom*, Buckingham: Open University Press.

Bauman, Z. (1990) *Thinking Sociologically*, Oxford: Blackwell.

Bauman, Z. (1995) *Life in Fragments: Essays in Postmodern Morality*, Oxford: Blackwell.

Bauman, Z. (1996) 'From pilgrim to tourist – a short history of identity', pp. 18–36 in S. Hall and P. du Gay (eds) *Questions of Cultural Identity*, London: Sage.

Bauman, Z. (1998a) *Globalization: The Human Consequences*, Cambridge: Polity.

Bauman, Z. (1998b) *Work, Consumerism and the New Poor*, Buckingham: Open University Press.

Beck, U. (1992) *Risk Society: Towards a New Modernity*, London: Sage.

Beck, U. (1999) *World Risk Society*, Cambridge: Polity.

Beck, U. (2000) *What is Globalization?* Cambridge: Polity.

Beeghley, L. (1997) 'Demystifying theory: how the theories of Georg Simmel (and others) help us to make sense of modern life', pp. 267–72 in C. Ballard, J. Gubbay and C. Middleton (eds) *The Student's Companion to Sociology*, Oxford: Blackwell.

Bell, D. (1973) *The Coming of Post-Industrial Society: A Venture in Social Forecasting*, New York: Basic Books.

Bell, D. (1976) *The Cultural Contradictions of Capitalism*, London: Heinemann.

Bell, D. (1991) *The Winding Passage: Sociological Essays and Journeys* (2nd edn), New Brunswick, NJ: Transaction Books.

Bernstein, J.M. (1991) 'Introduction', pp. 1–25 in T.W. Adorno, *The Culture Industry: Selected Essays on Mass Culture*, ed. J.M. Bernstein, London: Routledge.

Best, S. and Kellner, D. (1991) *Postmodern Theory: Critical Interrogations*, Basingstoke: Macmillan.

Block, F. (1990) *Postindustrial Possibilities: A Critique of Economic Discourse*, Berkeley: University of California Press.

Bocock, R. (1993) *Consumption*, London: Routledge.

Bourdieu, P. (1984) *Distinction: A Social Critique of the Judgement of Taste*, London: Routledge and Kegan Paul.

Bowlby, R. (1987) 'Modes of shopping: Mallarmé at the Bon Marché', pp. 185–205, in N. Armstrong and L. Tennenhouse (eds) *The Ideology of Conduct*, New York: Methuen.

Breen, R. (1997) 'Risk, recommodification and stratification', *Sociology*, 31, 3, 473–89.

Bronner, S. (1994) *Of Critical Theory and Its Theorists*, Oxford: Blackwell.

Brubaker, R. (1984) *The Limits of Rationality: An Essay on the Social and Moral Thought of Max Weber*, London: Allen and Unwin.

Bryman, A. (1995) *Disney and His Worlds*, London: Routledge.

Burnett, R. (1996) *The Global Jukebox: The International Music Industry*, London: Routledge.

Callinicos, A. (1989) *Against Postmodernism*, Cambridge: Polity.

Campbell, C. (1987) *The Romantic Ethic and the Spirit of Modern Consumerism*, Cambridge: Polity.

Campbell, C. (1995) 'The sociology of consumption', pp. 96–126 in D. Miller (ed.) *Acknowledging Consumption: A Review of New Studies*, London: Routledge.

Chaudhary, V. (2000) 'Fans tackle club over broken "bond" deal', *The Guardian*, 29 February: 5.

Connett, D. and Tomas, J. (1996) 'A golden goal', *The Observer*, 27 October: 10.

Connor, S. (1997) *Postmodernist Culture: An Introduction to Theories of the Contemporary*, Oxford: Blackwell.

Craib, I. (1992) *Modern Social Theory: From Parsons to Habermas*, Hemel Hempstead: Wheatsheaf.

Craib, I. (1997) *Classical Social Theory*, Oxford: Oxford University Press.

Dant, T. (1999) *Material Culture in the Social World*, Buckingham: Open University Press.

Davies, H. (1995) 'Merchandise United', *The Guardian*, 4 April: 1–3.

Dawe, A. (1978) 'Theories of social action', pp. 88–119, 362–417 in T. Bottomore and R. Nisbet (eds) *A History of Sociological Analysis*, London: Heinemann.

Dear, M. (2000) *The Postmodern Urban Condition*, Oxford: Blackwell.

de Certeau, M. (1984) *The Practice of Everyday Life*, Berkeley: University of California Press.

Douglas, M. (1992) *Risk and Blame: Essays in Cultural Theory*, London: Routledge.

Douglas, M. and Wildavsky, S. (1982) *Risk and Culture*, Berkeley: University of California Press.

Dunn, R.G. (1998) *Identity Crises: A Social Critique of Postmodernity*, Minneapolis: University of Minnesota Press.

Edwards, T. (1997) *Men in the Mirror: Men's Fashion, Masculinity and Consumer Society*, London: Cassell.

Featherstone, M. (1991) *Consumer Culture and Postmodernity*, London: Sage.

Featherstone, M. (1995) *Undoing Culture: Globalization, Postmodernism and Identity*, London: Sage.

Firat, F.A. (1994) 'Gender and consumption: transcending the feminine?' pp. 227–9 in A. Costa (ed.) *Gender Issues and Consumer Behaviour*, London: Sage.

Fiske, J. (1989) *Reading the Popular*, London: Unwin Hyman.

Flax, J. (1990) *Thinking Fragments: Psychoanalysis, Feminism and Postmodernism*, Berkeley: University of California Press.

Frankel, B. (1987) *The Post-Industrial Utopians: A Critical Assessment*, Cambridge: Polity.

Friedland, L. (1999) 'Covering the world', pp. 293–300 in F.J. Lechner and J. Boli (eds) *The Globalization Reader*, Oxford: Blackwell.

Fuller, S. (1998) 'From content to context: a social epistemology of the structure–agency craze', pp. 93–117 in A. Sica (ed.) *What is Social Theory? The Philosophical Debates*, Oxford: Blackwell.

Furedi, F. (1997) *Culture of Fear: Risk-Taking and the Morality of Low Expectation*, London: Cassell.

Furlong, A. and Cartmel, F. (1997) *Young People and Social Change: Individualization and Risk in Late Modernity*, Buckingham: Open University Press.

Gabriel, Y. and Lang, T. (1995) *The Unmanageable Consumer: Contemporary Consumption and Its Fragmentation*, London: Sage.

Gane, M. (1991) *Baudrillard: Critical and Fatal Social Theory*, London: Routledge.

Giddens, A. (1976) *New Rules of Sociological Method*, London: Hutchinson.

Giddens, A. (1990) *The Consequences of Modernity*, Cambridge: Polity.

Giddens, A. (1991) *Modernity and Self-Identity*, Cambridge: Polity.

Giddens, A. (1998) *The Third Way: The Renewal of Social Democracy*, Cambridge: Polity.

Giner, S. (1976) *Mass Society*, London: Martin Robertson.

Habermas, J. (1984) *The Theory of Communicative Action, Vol. 1: Reason and the Rationalization of Society*, Cambridge: Polity.

Habermas, J. (1987) *The Theory of Communicative Action, Vol. 2: The Critique of Functionalist Reason*, Cambridge: Polity.

Hage, J. and Powers, G.H. (1992) *Post-Industrial Lives: Roles and Relationships in the 21st Century*, London: Sage.

Hall, S. (1989) 'The meaning of New Times', pp. 117–34 in S. Hall and M. Jacques (eds) *New Times: The Changing Face of Politics in the 1990s*, London: Lawrence and Wishart.

Hannerz, U. (1990) 'Cosmopolitans and locals in world culture', *Theory, Culture and Society*, 7, 2–3, 237–51.

Hannerz, U. (1992) *Cultural Complexity*, New York: Columbia University Press.

Harvey, D. (1989) *The Condition of Postmodernity*, Oxford: Blackwell.

Hebdige, D. (1979) *Subculture: The Meaning of Style*, London: Methuen.

Held, D. (1980) *Introduction to Critical Theory*, Cambridge: Polity.

Hogan, T. (1996) 'Globalisation: experiences and explanations', pp. 275–90 in A. Kellehear (ed.) *Social Self, Global Culture*, Oxford: Oxford University Press.

Holbrook, M. (1997) 'Walking on the edge: a stereographic photo essay on the verge of consumer research', pp. 46–78 in S. Brown and D. Turley (eds) *Consumer Research: Postcards from the Edge*, London: Routledge.

Holland, R. (1977) *Self and Social Context*, London: Macmillan.

Hollinger, R. (1994) *Postmodernism and the Social Sciences*, London: Sage.

Horkheimer, M. and Adorno, T.W. (1972) *Dialectic of Enlightenment*, London: Allen Lane.

James, A. (1996) 'Cooking the books: global or local identities in contemporary British food cultures?', pp. 77–92 in D. Howes (ed.) *Cross-Cultural Consumption: Global Markets, Local Realities*, London: Routledge.

Jameson, F. (1984) 'Postmodernism, or, the cultural logic of late capitalism', *New Left Review*, 146, 53–92.

Jarvis, J. (1998) *Exploring the Modern*, Oxford: Blackwell.

Kellner, D. (1990) 'The postmodern turn: positions, problems, and prospects', pp. 255–86 in G. Ritzer (ed.) *Frontiers of Social Theory: The New Synthesis*, New York: Colombia University Press.

Kellner, D. (1992) 'Popular culture and the construction of postmodern identities', pp. 141–77 in S. Lash and J. Friedman (eds) *Modernity and Identity*, Oxford: Blackwell.

Kellner, D. (ed.) (1994) *Baudrillard: A Critical Reader*, Oxford: Blackwell.

Kellner, D. (1999) 'Theorizing/resisting McDonaldization: a multiperspectivist approach', pp. 186–206 in B. Smart (ed.) *Resisting McDonaldization*, London: Sage.

Kelly, P. (1999) 'Wild and tame zones: regulating the transitions of youth at risk', *Journal of Youth Studies*, 2, 2, 193–212.

Kivisto, P. (1998) *Key Ideas in Sociology*, London: Sage.

Kuisel, R. (1993) *Seducing the French: The Dilemma of Americanization*, London: University of California Press.

Kumar, K. (1978) *Prophecy and Progress: The Sociology of Industrial and Post-Industrial Society*, London: Allen Lane.

Kumar, K. (1995) *From Post-Industrial to Post-Modern Society*, Oxford: Blackwell.

Lash, S. (1990) *Sociology of Postmodernism*, London: Routledge.

Lash, S. and Urry, J. (1987) *The End of Organized Capitalism*, Cambridge: Polity.

Lash, S. and Urry, J. (1994) *Economies of Signs and Space*, London: Sage.

Lash, S. and Whimster, S. (1987) *Max Weber, Rationality and Modernity*, London: Allen and Unwin.

Lash, S. and Wynne, B. (1992) 'Introduction', pp. 1–8 in U. Beck (ed.) *Risk Society: Towards a New Modernity*, London: Sage.

Latouche, S. (1993) *In the Wake of the Affluent Society: An Exploration of Post-Development*, London: Zed Books.

Latouche, S. (1996) *The Westernization of the World*, Cambridge: Polity.

Layder, D. (1993) *Studying Society: Sociological Theories and Research Practices*, London: Collins.

Layder, D. (1998) *Sociological Practice: Linking Theory and Social Research*, London: Sage.

Lechner, F.J. and Boli, J. (1999) 'General introduction', pp. 1–3 in F.J. Lechner and J. Boli (eds) *The Globalization Reader*, Oxford: Blackwell.

Lee, M. (1993) *Consumer Culture Reborn*, London: Routledge.

Lipset, S.M. (1980) *The Third Century: America as a Post-Industrial Society*, Chicago: University of Chicago Press.

Luhmann, N. (1993) *Risk: A Sociological Theory*, Berlin: Walter de Gruyter.

Lupton, D. (1999) *Risk*, London: Routledge.

Lyon, D. (1994) *Postmodernity*, Buckingham: Open University Press.

Lyotard, J.-F. (1984) *The Postmodern Condition: A Report on Knowledge*, Minneapolis: Minnesota University Press.

Mac An Ghaill, M. (ed.) (1996) *Understanding Masculinities: Social Relations and Cultural Arenas*, Buckingham: Open University Press.

McCracken, G. (1990) *Culture and Consumption*, Bloomington, IN: Indiana University Press.

MacDonald, D. (1957) 'A theory of mass culture', pp. 59–73 in B. Rosenberg and D. White (eds) *Mass Culture*, Glencoe, IL: Free Press.

McDowell, L. and Pringle, R. (eds) (1992) *Defining Women: Social Institutions and Gender Divisions*, Cambridge: Polity; Buckingham: Open University Press.

McGrew, A. (1992) 'A global society?', pp. 61–116 in S. Hall, D. Held and A. McGrew (eds) *Modernity and Its Futures*, Cambridge: Polity; Buckingham: Open University Press.

McGuigan, J. (1999) *Modernity and Postmodern Culture*, Buckingham: Open University Press.

MacKenzie, I. (1999) 'Social criticism', pp. 25–46 in F. Ashe, A. Finlayson, M. Lloyd, I. MacKenzie, J. Martin and S. O'Neil (eds) *Contemporary Social and Political Theory: An Introduction*, Buckingham: Open University Press.

Macnaghten, P. and Urry, J. (1998) *Contested Natures*, London: Sage.

McRobbie, A. (1994) *Postmodernism and Popular Culture*, London: Routledge.

Mandel, E. (1978) *Late Capitalism*, London: Verso.

Mannheim, K. (1929) *Ideology and Utopia*, New York: Harcourt, Brace and World.

Mannheim, K. (1935) *Man and Society in an Age of Reconstruction*, New York: Harcourt, Brace and World.

Marcuse, H. (1964) *One-Dimensional Man*, Boston: Beacon Press.

Marling, S. (1993) *American Affair: The Americanisation of Britain*, London: Boxtree.

Marsden, T., Flynn, A. and Harrison, M. (2000) *Consuming Interests: The Social Provision of Foods*, London: UCL Press.

Marx, K. (1990) *Capital: A Critique of Political Economy* (2nd edn), Vol. 1, Harmondsworth: Penguin.

Marx, K. (2000) 'The fetishism of the commodity and its secret', pp. 10–18 in M. Lee (ed.) *The Consumer Society Reader*, Oxford: Blackwell.

Mayle, P. (1992) *A Year in Provence*, London: Penguin.

Miles, S. (1997) 'Fashion by Georg Simmel', pp. 240–1 in C. Ballard, J. Gubbay and C. Middleton (eds) *The Student's Companion to Sociology*, Oxford: Blackwell.

Miles, S. (1998a) *Consumerism as a Way of Life*, London: Sage.

Miles, S. (1998b) 'McDonaldization and the global sports store: constructing consumer meanings in a rationalized society', pp. 53–66 in M. Alfino, J.S. Caputo and R. Wynard (eds) *McDonaldization Revisited: Critical Essays on Consumer Culture*, London: Praeger.

Miles, S. (2000) *Youth Lifestyles in a Changing World*, Buckingham: Open University Press.

Miles, S., Cliff, D. and Burr, V. (1998) '"Fitting in and sticking out": consumption, consumer meanings and the construction of young people's identities', *Journal of Youth Studies*, 1, 1, 81–96.

Mills, C. Wright (1959) *The Sociological Imagination*, Oxford: Oxford University Press.

Mommsen, W.J. (1989) *The Political and Social Theory of Max Weber: Collected Essays*, Cambridge: Polity.

Mort, F. (1996) *Cultures of Consumption: Masculinities and Social Space in Late Twentieth-Century Britain*, London: Routledge.

Murray, R. (1989) 'Fordism and Post-Fordism', pp. 38–53 in S. Hall and M. Jacques (eds) *New Times: The Changing Face of Politics in the 1990s*, London: Lawrence and Wishart.

Nava, M. (1991) 'Consumerism reconsidered: buying and power', *Cultural Studies*, 5, 157–73.

Nixon, S. (1996) *Hard Looks: Masculinities, Spectatorship and Contemporary Consumption*, London: UCL Press.

Ohmae, K. (1990) *The Borderless World*, London: Collins.

Piore, M. and Sabel, C. (1984) *The Second Industrial Divide: Possibilities for Prosperity*, London: Basic Books.

Ray, L. and Reed, M. (1994) *Organizing Modernity: New Weberian Perspectives on Work, Organization and Society*, London: Routledge.

Ritzer, G. (1992) *Contemporary Sociological Theory*, London: McGraw-Hill.

Ritzer, G. (1993) *The McDonaldization of Society*, London: Pine Forge.

Ritzer, G. (1995) *Expressing America: A Critique of the Global Credit Card Society*, London: Pine Forge.

Ritzer, G. (1998) *The McDonaldization Thesis*, London: Sage.

Ritzer, G. (1999) *Enchanting a Disenchanted World*, London: Pine Forge.

Roberts, K. (1995) *Youth and Employment in Modern Britain*, Oxford: Oxford University Press.

Robertson, R. (1992) *Globalization*, London: Sage.

Robins, K. (1997) 'What in the world's going on?', pp. 12–47 in P. du Gay (ed.) *Production of Culture/Cultures of Production*, Buckingham: Open University Press; London: Sage.

Rose, N. (1996) 'Refiguring the territory of government', *Economy and Society*, 25, 327–56.

Rose, M. (1991) *The Post-Modern and the Post-Industrial*, Cambridge: Cambridge University Press.

Rosenau, P.M. (1992) *Post-Modernism and the Social Sciences: Insights, Inroads and Intrusions*, Princeton: Princeton University Press.

Sassen, S. (1991) *The Global City*, Princeton: Princeton University Press.

Saunders, P. (1981) *Social Theory and the Urban Question*, London: Hutchinson.

Saunders, P. (1984) 'Beyond housing classes: the sociological significance of private property rights in means of consumption', *International Journal of Urban and Regional Research*, 8: 202–25.

Sayer, D. (1991) *Capitalism and Modernity: An Excursus on Marx and Weber*, London: Routledge.

Scaff, L. (1989) *Fleeing the Iron Cage: Culture, Politics and Modernity in the Thought of Max Weber*, London: University of California Press.

Scott, S., Jackson, S. and Backett-Milburn, K. (1998) 'Swings and roundabouts: risk anxiety and the everyday worlds of children', *Sociology*, 32, 4, 689–705.

Short, J. and Kim, Y.H. (1999) *Globalization and the City*, Harlow: Addison Wesley Longman.

Simmel, G. (1950) 'The metropolis and mental life', pp. 324–39 in K. Wolff (ed.) *The Sociology of Georg Simmel*, London: Collier-Macmillan.

Simmel, G. (1957) 'Fashion', *American Journal of Sociology*, 62, 541–8.

Simmel, G. (1990) *The Philosophy of Money*, ed. D. Frisby, London: Routledge.

Simmel, G. (1971) *On Individuality and Social Forms*, Chicago: University of Chicago Press.

Slater, D. (1997) *Consumer Culture and Modernity*, Cambridge: Polity.

Smart, B. (1992) *Modern Conditions; Postmodern Controversies*, London: Routledge.

Smart, B. (ed.) (1999a) *Resisting McDonaldization*, London: Sage.

Smart, B. (1999b) 'Resisting McDonaldization: theory, process and critique', pp. 1–21 in B. Smart (ed.) *Resisting McDonaldization*, London: Sage.

Spybey, T. (1996) *Globalization and World Society*, Cambridge: Polity.

Stones, R. (1996) *Sociological Reasoning: Towards a Past-Modern Sociology*, Basingstoke: Macmillan.

Storey, J. (1993) *An Introductory Guide to Cultural Theory and Popular Culture*, Hemel Hempstead: Harvester Wheatsheaf.

Storey, J. (1999) *Consumption and Everyday Life*, London: Arnold.

Street, A. (1999) '"Across the universe": the limits of global popular culture', pp. 55–89 in T. Skelton and T. Allen (eds) *Culture and Global Change*, London: Routledge.

Strinati, D. (1995) *An Introduction to Theories of Popular Culture*, London: Routledge.

Swingewood, A. (1977) *The Myth of Mass Culture*, London: Macmillan.

Swingewood, A. (1984) *A Short History of Sociological Thought*, Basingstoke: Macmillan.

Taylor-Gooby, P. (1999) 'Opportunity's knocks', *The Guardian*, 28 September: 17.

Tetzlaff, D. (1986) 'MTV and the politics of postmodern pop', *Journal of Communication Inquiry*, 10, 1, 63–80.

Thomas, H. and Walsh, D. (1998) 'Modernity/Postmodernity', pp. 363–90 in C. Jenks (ed.) *Core Sociological Dichotomies*, London: Sage.

Thomson, R. and Scott, S. (1991) *Learning About Sex*, London: Tufnell Press.

Tomlinson, J. (1991) *Cultural Imperialism*, London: Pinter.

Tomlinson, J. (1999a) *Globalization and Culture*, Cambridge: Polity.

Tomlinson, A. (1999b) 'Globalized culture: the triumph of the West', pp. 22–9 in T. Skelton and T. Allen (eds) *Culture and Global Change*, London: Routledge.

Touraine, A. (1974) *The Post-Industrial Society*, London: Wildwood House.

Turner, B. (1992) *Max Weber: From History to Modernity*, London: Routledge.

Urry, J. (1990) *The Tourist Gaze*, London: Sage.

Urry, J. (1998) 'Contemporary transformations of time and space', pp. 1–17 in P. Scott (ed.) *The Globalization of Higher Education*, Buckingham: SRHE/Open University Press.

Veblen, T. (1899) *The Theory of the Leisure Class*, London: Constable.

Wagner, P. (1994) *A Sociology of Modernity: Liberty and Discipline*, London: Routledge.

Wallerstein, I. (1993) 'The world-system after the cold war', *Journal of Peace Research*, 30, 1, 1–6.

Wallerstein, I. (2000) 'From sociology to historical social science: prospects and obstacles', *British Journal of Sociology*, 51, 1, 25–35.

Warde, A. (1992) 'Notes on the relationship between production and consumption', pp. 15–31 in R. Burrows and C. Marsh (eds) *Consumption and Class: Divisions and Change*, Basingstoke: Macmillan.

Warde, A. (1998) 'Afterword: the future of the sociology of consumption', pp. 302–12 in S. Edgell, K. Hethertington and A. Warde (eds) *Consumption Matters*, Oxford: Blackwell.

Waters, M. (1995) *Globalization*, London: Routledge.

Waters, M. (1996) *Daniel Bell*, London: Routledge.

Watts, M.J. and Goodman, D. (1997) 'Agrarian questions: global appetite, local metabolism: nature, culture, and industry in fin-de-siècle agro-food systems', pp. 1–34 in D. Goodman and M.J. Watts (eds) *Globalising Food: Agrarian Questions and Global Restructuring*, London: Routledge.

Weber, M. (1992) *The Protestant Ethic and the Spirit of Capitalism*, London: Routledge.

Wildavsky, A. (1988) *Searching for Safety*, Oxford: Transition Books.

Willis, P. (1977) *Learning to Labour: How Working-Class Kids Get Working-Class Jobs*, London: Saxon House.

Willis, S. (1990) 'Work(ing) out', *Cultural Studies*, 4, 1, 1–18.

Wiseman, J. (1995) 'Globalization is not Godzilla', *Frontline*, 26, 5–6.

Wynne, D. and O'Connor, J. (1998) 'Consumption and the postmodern city', *Urban Studies*, 35, 5–6, 841–64.

Zukin, S. (1990) 'Socio-spatial prototypes of a new organization of consumption: the role of real cultural capital', *Sociology*, 24, 1, 37–56.

INDEX